IMAGES
of America

SOUTHAMPTON

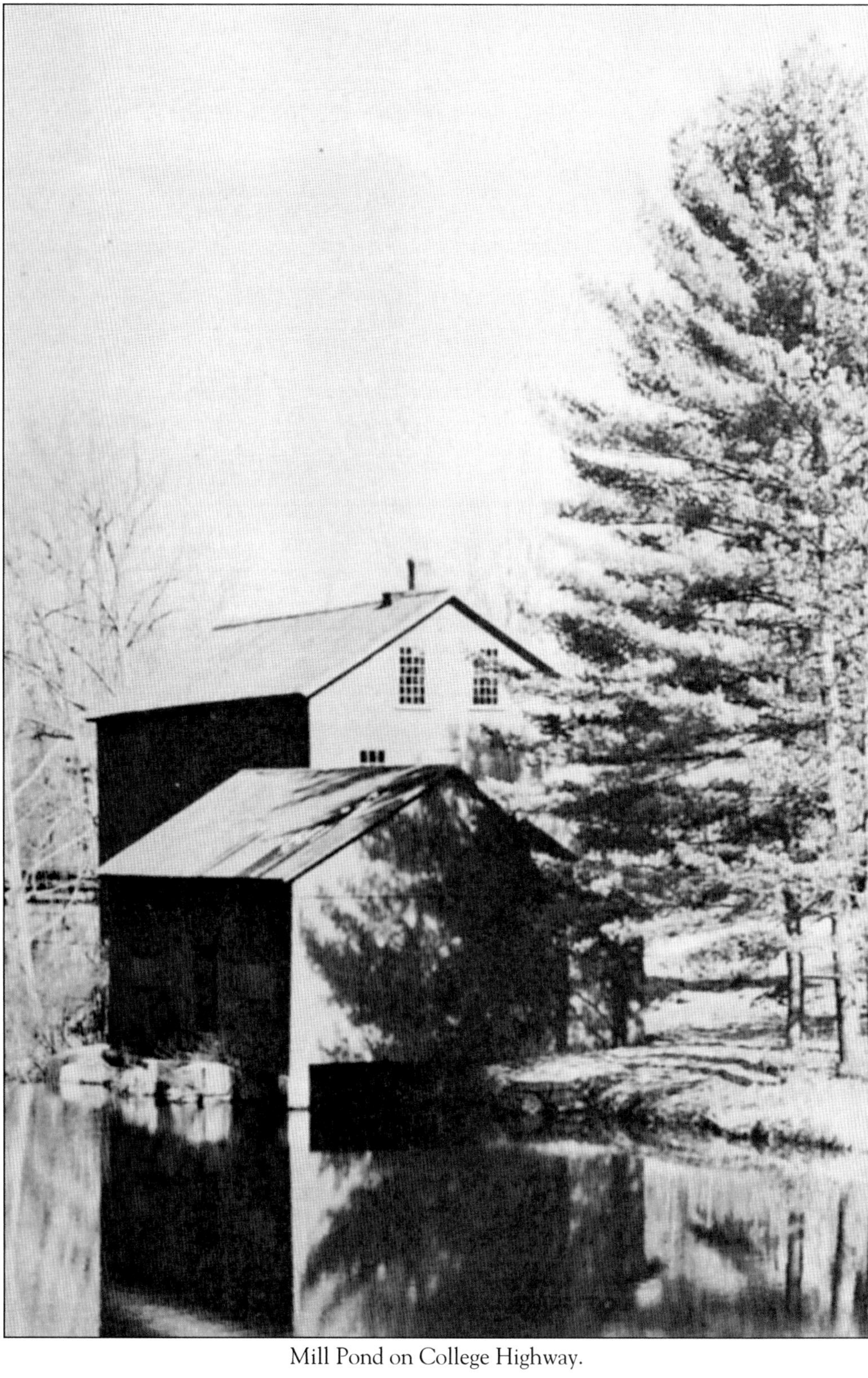

Mill Pond on College Highway.

IMAGES
of America

SOUTHAMPTON

Ted and Maxine Hendrick

ARCADIA
PUBLISHING

Copyright © 1998 by Ted and Maxine Hendrick
ISBN 978-0-7385-9003-5

Published by Arcadia Publishing
Charleston, South Carolina

Printed in the United States of America

Library of Congress Catalog Card Number: 98-86897

For all general information contact Arcadia Publishing at:
Telephone 843-853-2070
Fax 843-853-0044
E-mail sales@arcadiapublishing.com
For customer service and orders:
Toll-Free 1-888-313-2665

Visit us on the Internet at www.arcadiapublishing.com

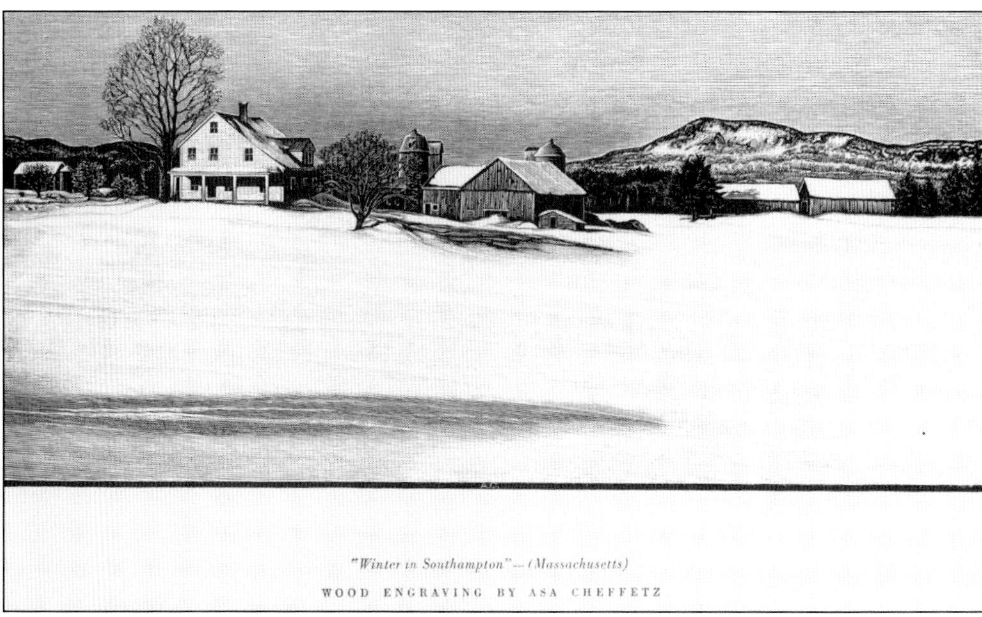

Winter in Southampton, a woodcut by Asa Cheffetz, who was a nationally known Springfield engraver. He received an award from the National Academy for this print in 1949. Appearing in reverse is the Fowles Farm at 11 Gunn Road with Mount Tom in the distance.

Contents

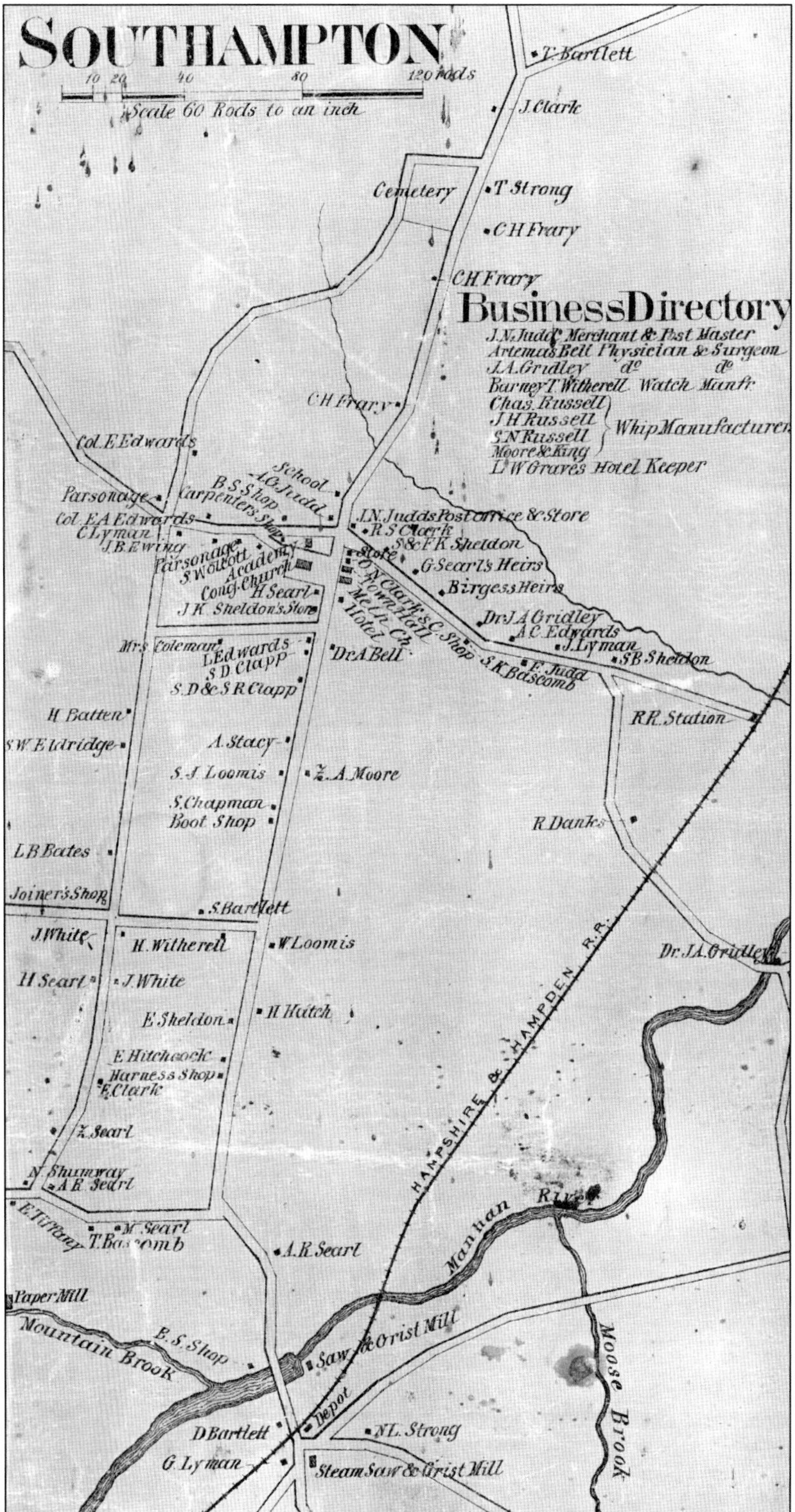

Inset from the 1860 Walling Map.

INTRODUCTION

The adventurous spirit that brought the Pilgrims to Plymouth did not disappear as the coastal area was settled. Instead, the search for good available land continued as more of the new arrivals hoped for a piece of property to call their own. In 1654 negotiations with the Nonotuck Indian tribe resulted in the purchase of a large tract of land, and a settlement was started in the Northampton meadows. Within ten years the towns of Hadley and Hatfield were begun, and in 1674 a sawmill was built on the Manhan River near what is now the center of Easthampton.

Author Clifton Johnson wrote in his book *Historic Hampshire in the Connecticut Valley*, "What is now Southampton was an unbroken wilderness in 1730." In that year a plan was made to settle 30 families under the condition that each would build a house of at least one room within two years. A sawmill was constructed on the Manhan River in the area of the present millpond, and a gristmill, also a necessity for the coming community, was established on the same site. Between 1733 and 1738, 28 permanent settlers arrived in the area they called New Hampton. In 1752 the town was declared a district and was renamed Southampton.

We have attempted here to show the reader how the 28 families who made the original move to the new settlement stayed on and prospered in different ways as they cleared their lands, built their houses, and raised their families. In the early years, the Manhan River and other streams provided numerous sites for water-powered mills. They all added to the economy of the growing town, and over the years other adventurous souls arrived, joining with those already here. As times changed and neighboring cities offered employment opportunities, many residents chose to find work out of town. During this era several longtime farms were purchased by newcomers, many of Polish extraction and all eager to work the land, thus contributing greatly to the town's growth and well-being.

We hope you will agree with us. Southampton has been, and remains, a wonderful town, all of it . . . farms and streams, hills and valleys, highways and byways. Enjoy it.

ACKNOWLEDGMENTS

Since 1963 the Southampton Historical Society has been actively collecting, copying, and cataloging all maps, documents, books, and especially photographs which would reveal any historical information of interest to the town. The images in this book represent only a fraction of the photographs stored in the museum files. Selecting those that best portray the town's history and growth was not an easy task.

The backbone of the collection is the work of the Howes Brothers of Ashfield. They canvassed the entire town in the spring of 1900, and we are fortunate to have 189 of their pictures. You will note that many of their scenes are credited throughout the book. Fred Judd was our local photographer and many of his images survived, although his glass-plate negatives were lost many years ago. Out-of-town professionals who labeled their prints include Homestead View of Springfield; the Northern Survey Co. of Albany, N.Y.; Buchholz & Hendrick of Springfield; Charles Keene from Easthampton; Richardson, also from Easthampton; and Walter Corbin of Florence.

Many snapshots by Ethel Tiffany, Bob Madsen, Hugh Scott, and others were borrowed from family photograph albums. The *Daily Hampshire Gazette* is always a source of good, old photographs, and the Jones Library of Amherst allowed us to copy from their collection of prints by Clifton Johnson of Hadley.

Our special thanks go to Helena (Trecia) Alves, whose technical assistance and endless hours at the computer made it possible to meet our publisher's deadline.

One

Early Settlement

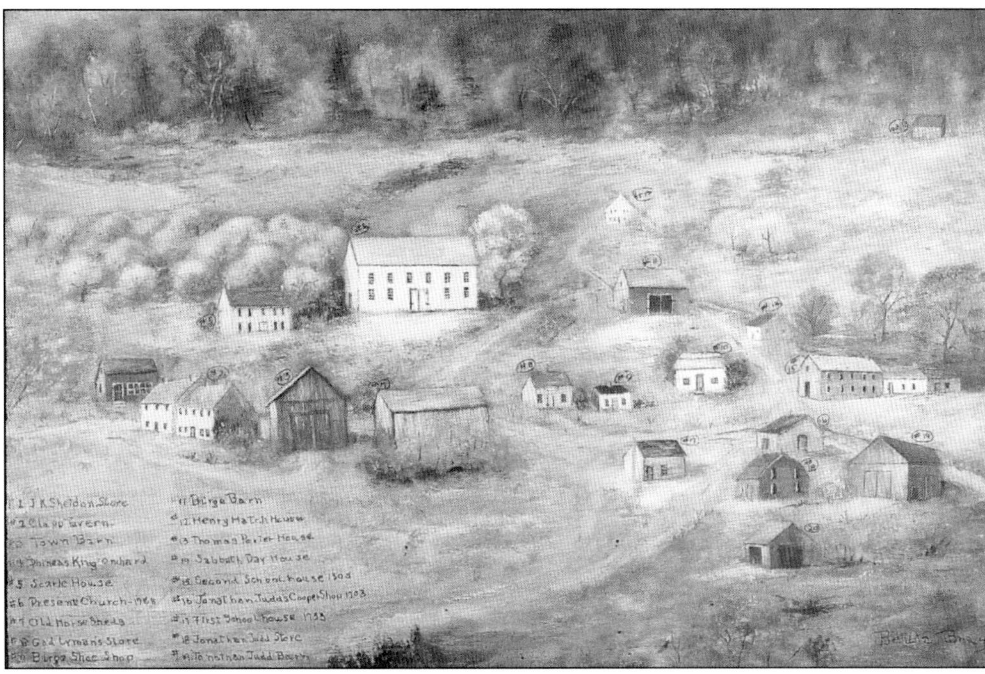

Southampton in 1800. This painting on board was executed by Beula Bray Randall. Note that the meetinghouse has not yet been turned. The first schoolhouse was located in the triangle of what is now East Street and the College Highway, and the Rev. Jonathan Judd House can be seen on Meetinghouse Hill, now Maple Street.

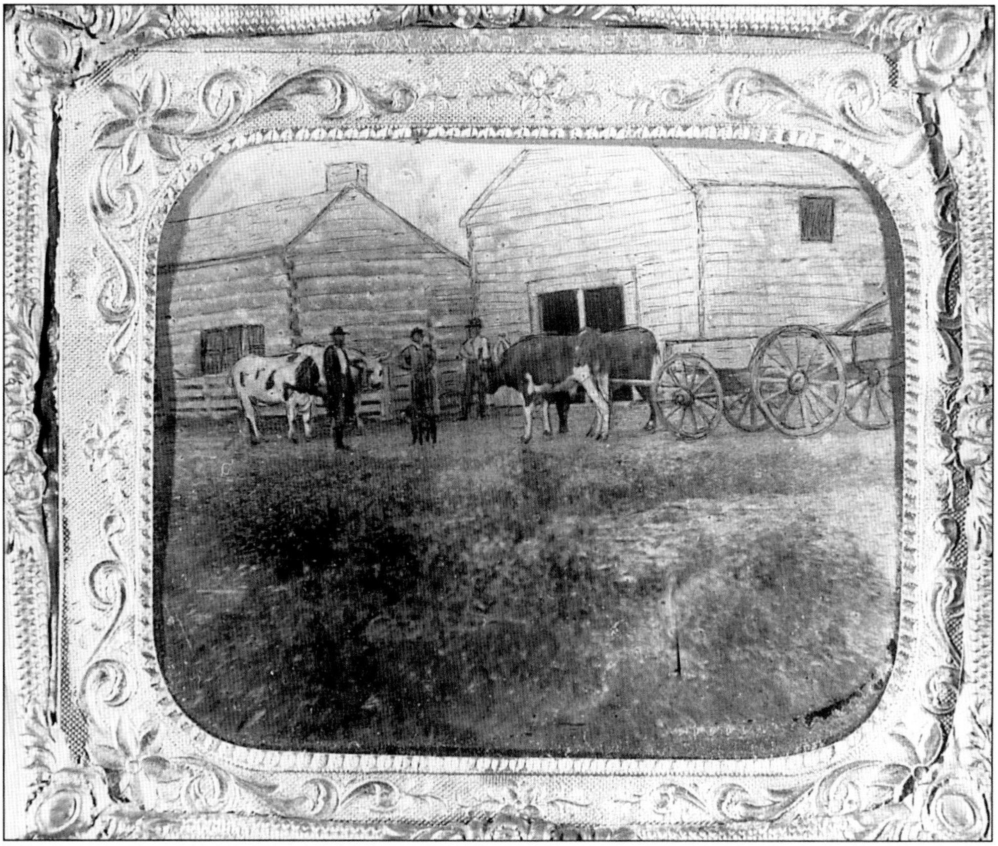

Coleman Farm, 38 College Highway. Historian Sam Wright wrote, "When Eleazar and Mehitable Coleman came to Southampton in 1761, they settled in a log cabin north of the present house." The structure featured in this copy of a *c.* 1860 daguerreotype—discovered in the attic of the old house still on the property (see p. 24)—fits Mr. Wright's description. We believe it to be the ancient Coleman cabin.

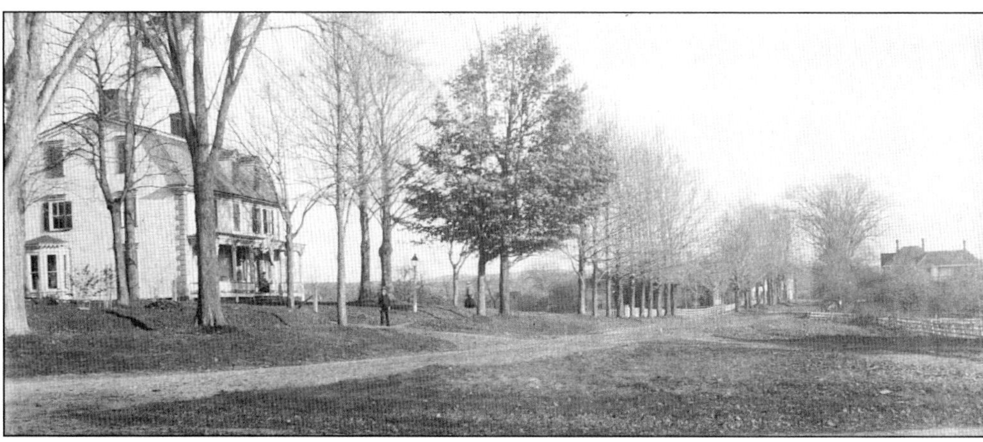

Woodbridge Hall, 7 East Street. This structure was built by Dr. Sylvester Woodbridge, the town's first doctor, who arrived in 1776. Dr. Woodbridge enjoyed an extensive practice for 50 years. His original cottage was enlarged in 1784, and the handsome residence remains looking out over the town's center. (Judd photograph, *c.* 1890.)

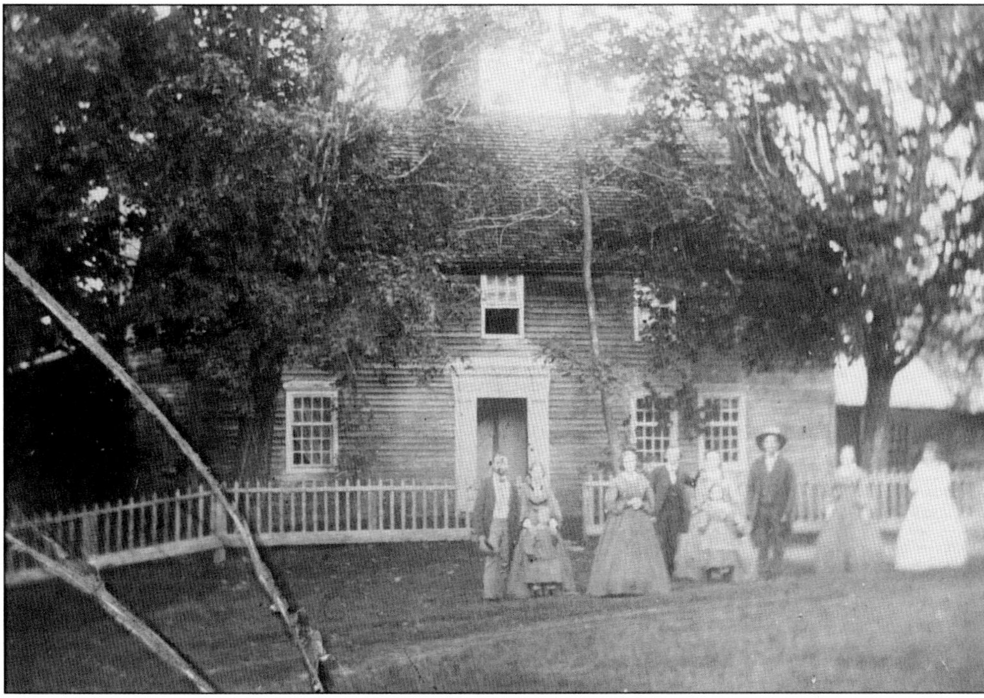

Thomas Porter House, 35 High Street. Mr. Porter settled here in a two-room house in 1732. In 1753 Deacon Samuel Edwards bought the property and built this large two-story home. The family continued to live here until 1888. This photograph was taken c. 1880 and the house was torn down in 1927.

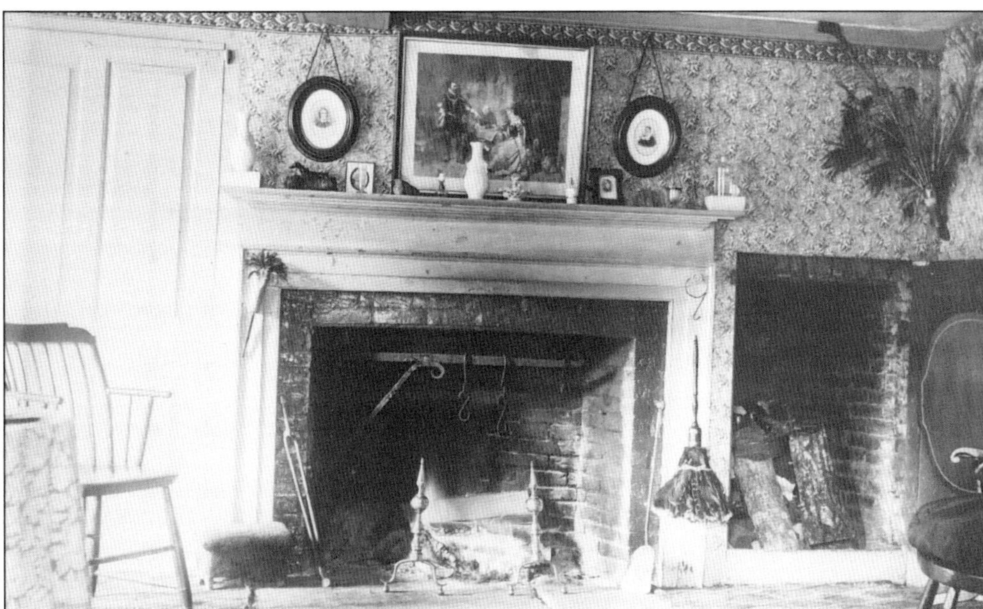

Parlor of the Porter-Edwards House (exterior shown at the top of the page). It is presumed that the picture dates back to the era of the Edwards family.

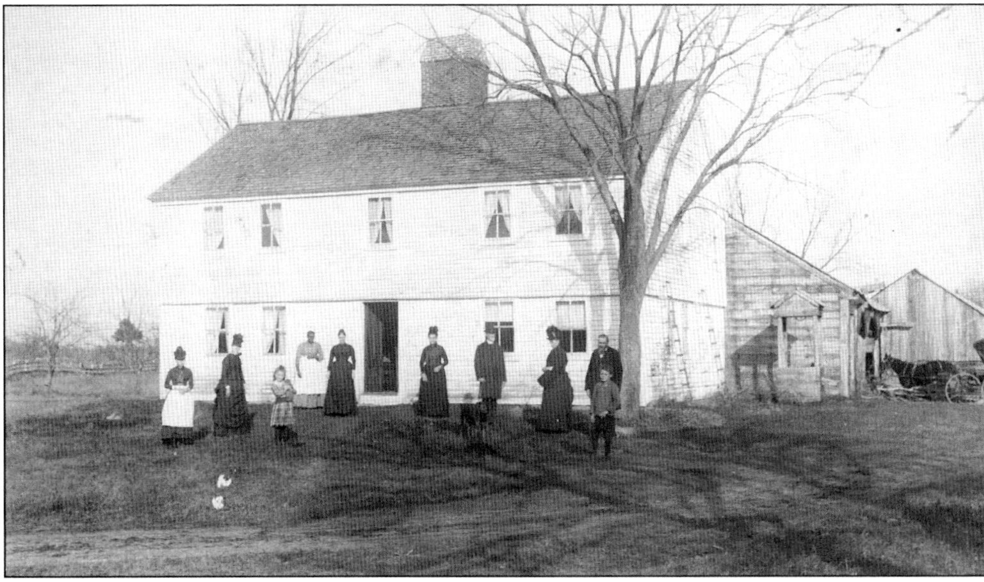

Ebenezer Kingsley Home, 181 College Highway. Among the first settlers, Mr. Kingsley surely had a smaller house for the first few years. Jonathan Judd's diary notes on May 27, 1752, "Kingsley's house raised today," with reference to this larger house. After several owners, the home passed to the Rathbun family in the late 1800s and to the Conant family in 1928. (Judd photograph, *c.* 1890.)

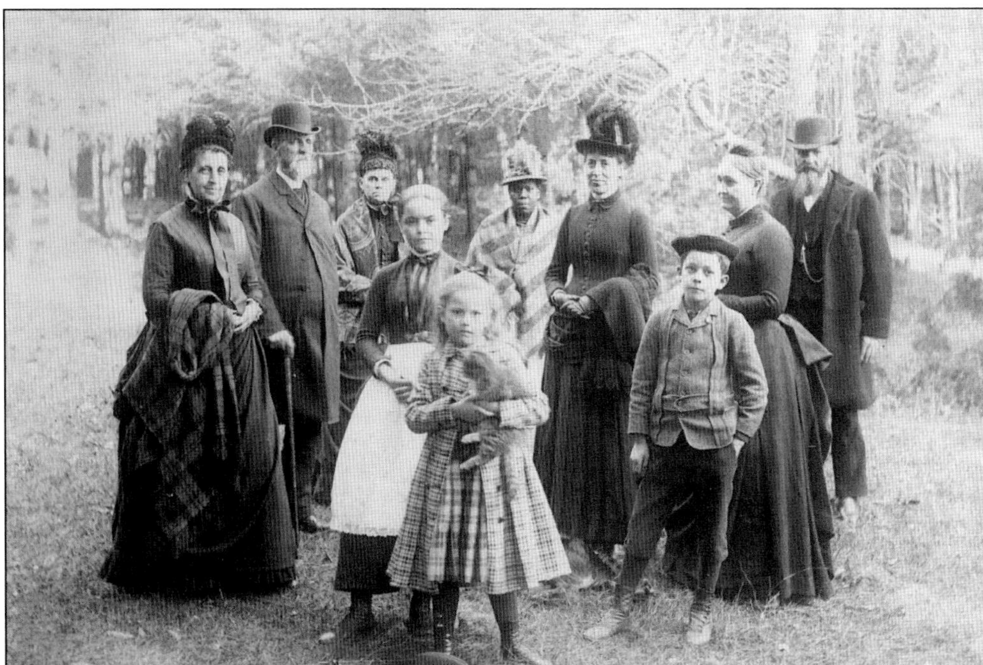

Rathbun family gathering, 181 College Highway. The older girl in this *c.* 1890 family group is Mary Elizabeth Rathbun. Mary later married Frederick Judd, the local photographer who took this and several other pictures used here.

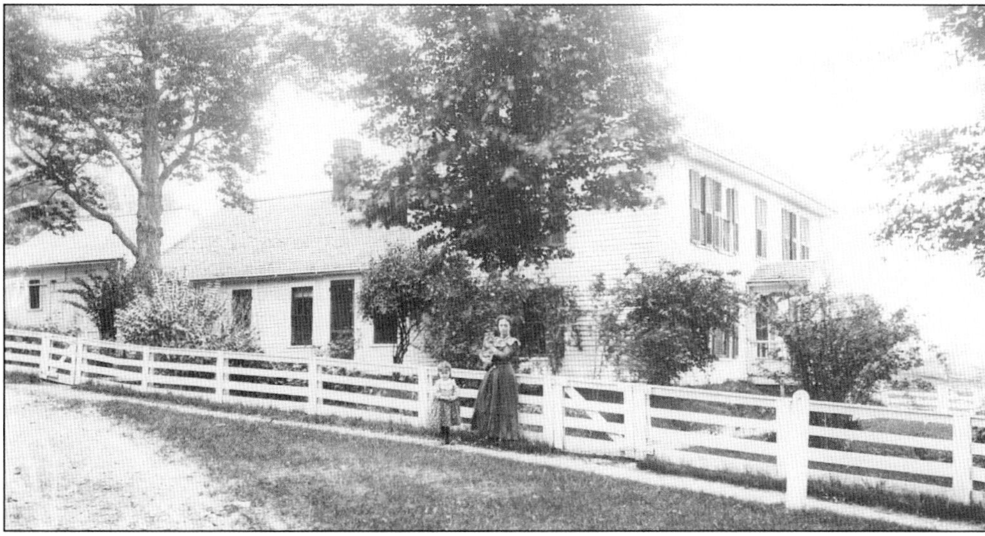

Rev. Jonathan Judd House, 12 Maple Street. Reverend Judd was called to serve as minister of the new settlement in 1743 before the separation of church and state. The townspeople assisted with the construction, and a palisade was later built for the safety of the residents during the French and Indian War. (Howes Brothers photograph, 1900.)

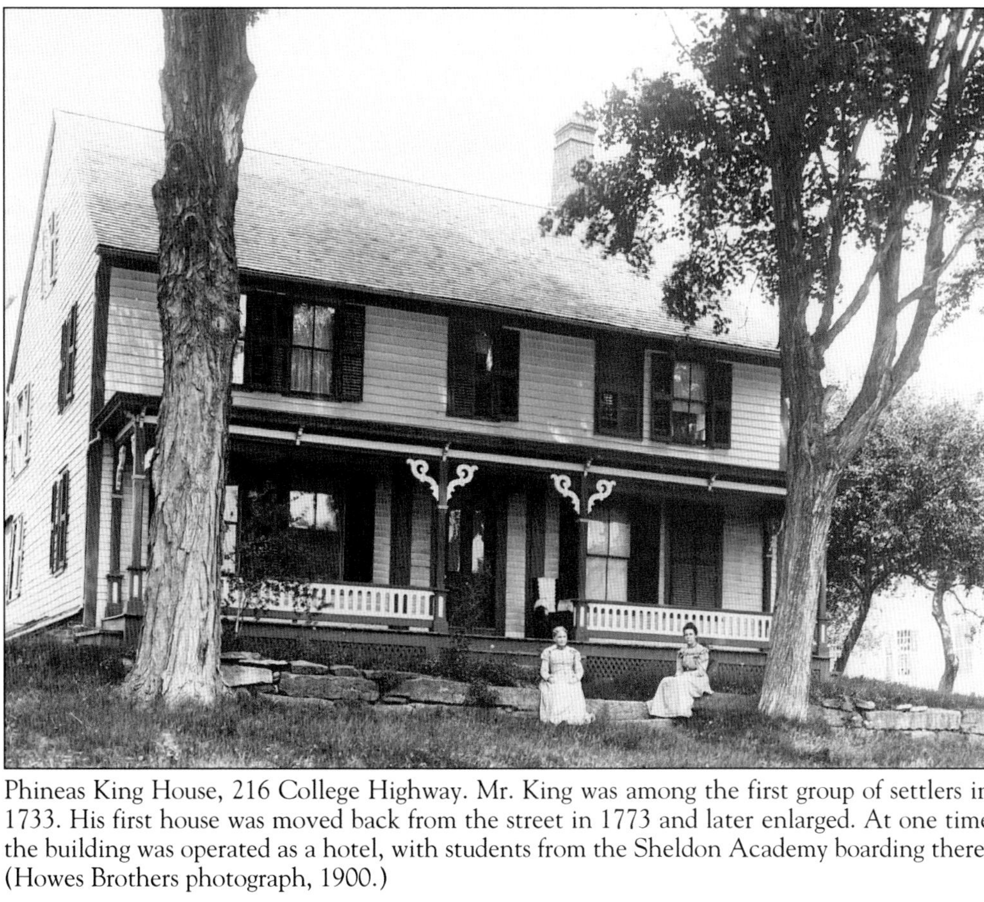

Phineas King House, 216 College Highway. Mr. King was among the first group of settlers in 1733. His first house was moved back from the street in 1773 and later enlarged. At one time the building was operated as a hotel, with students from the Sheldon Academy boarding there. (Howes Brothers photograph, 1900.)

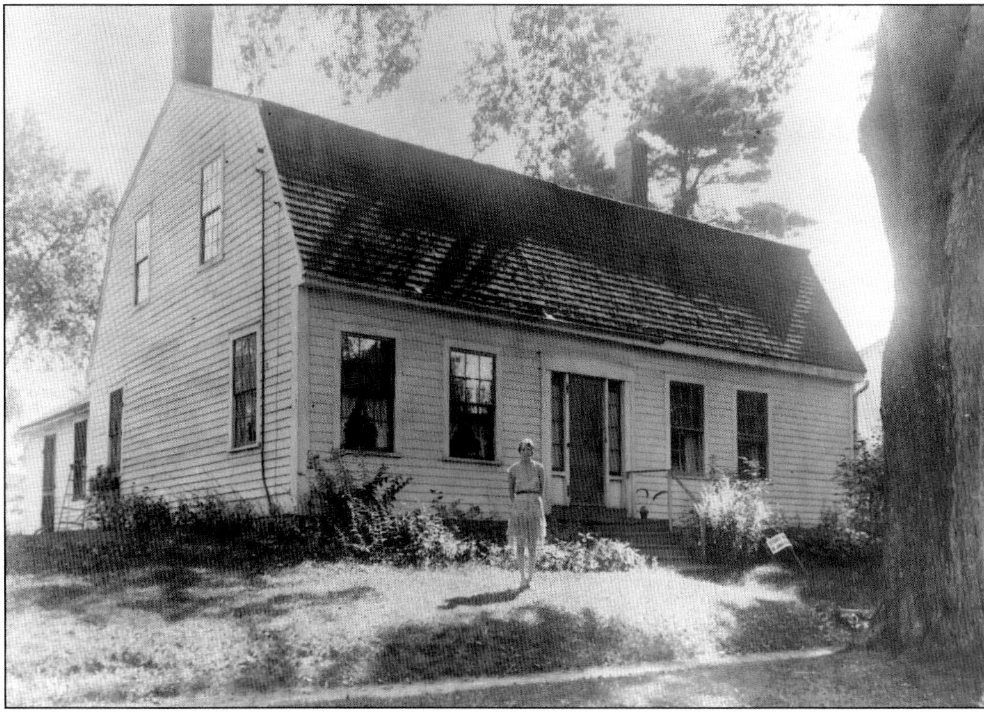

Jonathan Judd Jr.'s store, 5 East Street. Erected in 1800 as a store and dwelling, this building housed Mr. Judd's business. A bachelor, Judd frequently traveled to Hartford and Boston. Like his father, he kept diaries, and they provide insight into his busy life. This photograph was taken *c.* 1930.

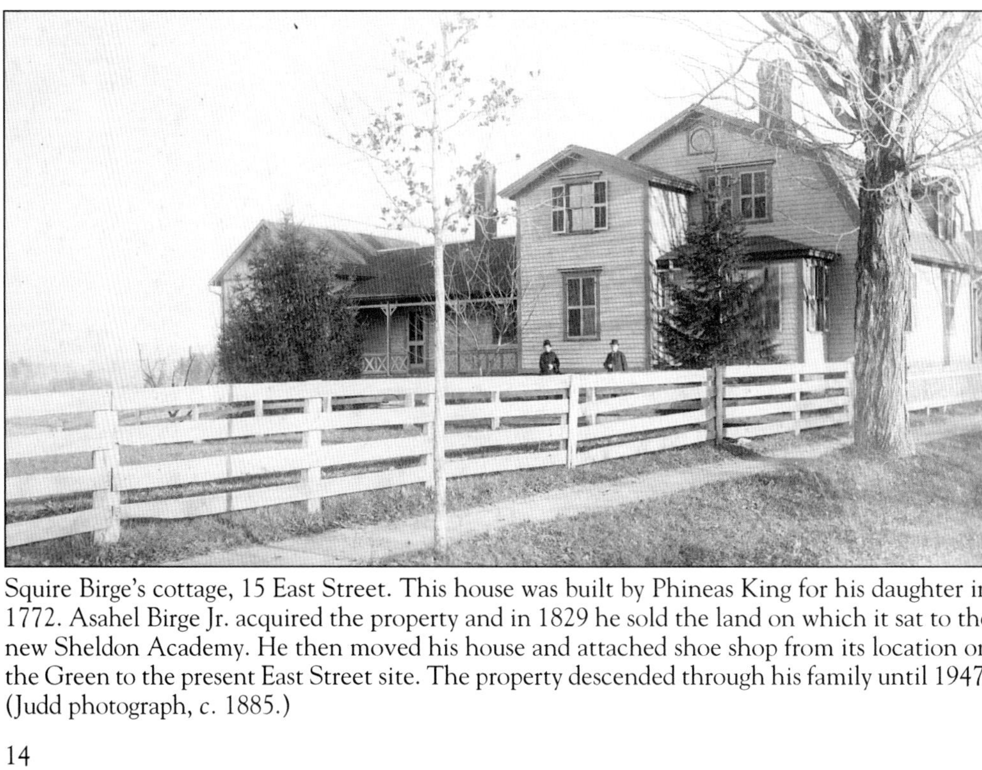

Squire Birge's cottage, 15 East Street. This house was built by Phineas King for his daughter in 1772. Asahel Birge Jr. acquired the property and in 1829 he sold the land on which it sat to the new Sheldon Academy. He then moved his house and attached shoe shop from its location on the Green to the present East Street site. The property descended through his family until 1947. (Judd photograph, *c.* 1885.)

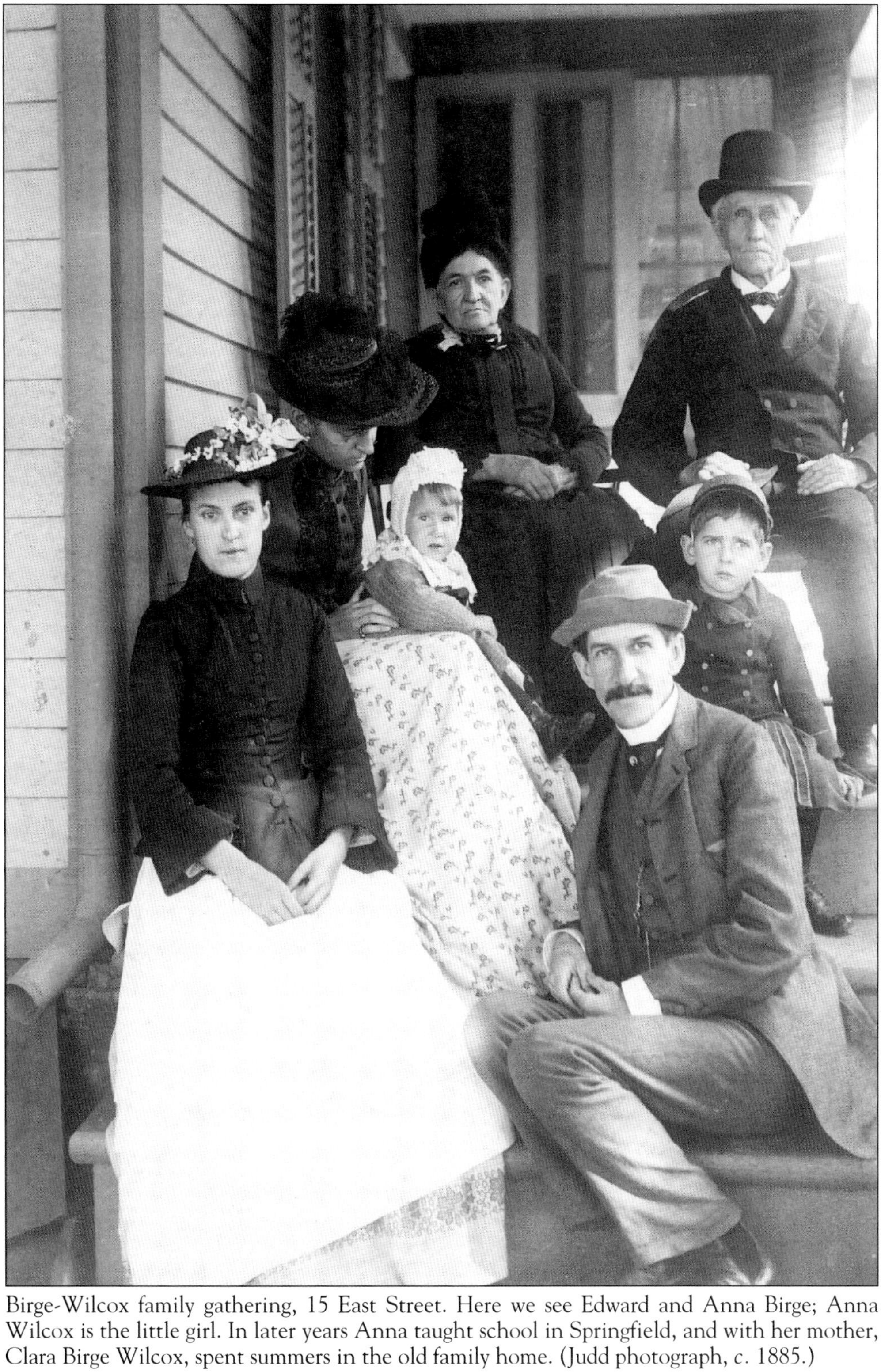

Birge-Wilcox family gathering, 15 East Street. Here we see Edward and Anna Birge; Anna Wilcox is the little girl. In later years Anna taught school in Springfield, and with her mother, Clara Birge Wilcox, spent summers in the old family home. (Judd photograph, c. 1885.)

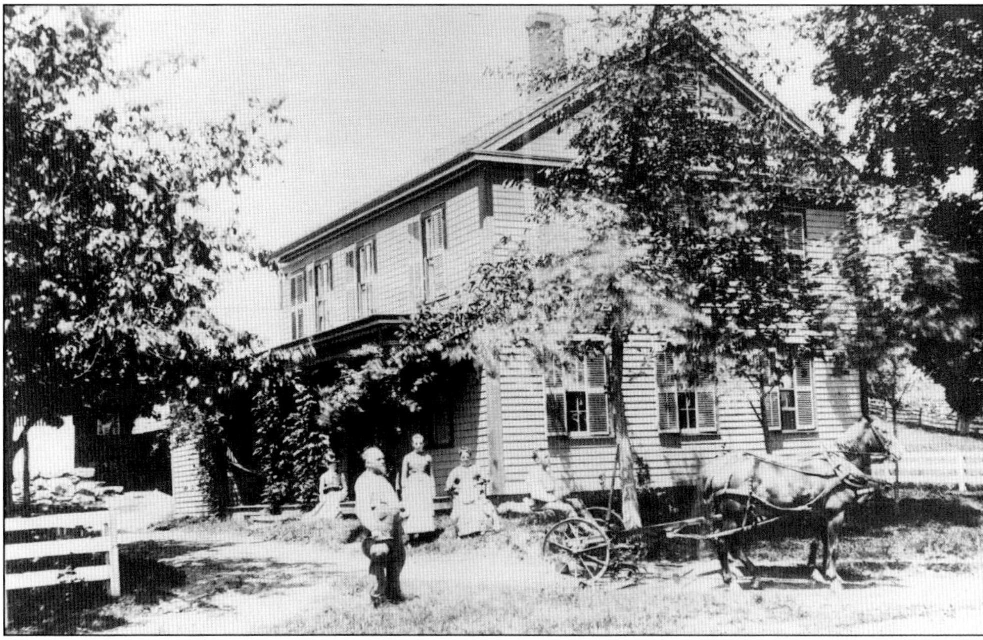

Moses Searle House, 74 High Street. Mr. Searle erected his house soon after he acquired the land in 1830. It passed to his son Hymenas, and then after a series of owners the property was sold to Edward R. Swasey, who built his new large home high on the hill and back from the street (see p. 62). The old house was then rented or occupied by family members until it was sold in 1946. This photograph was taken *c.* 1890.

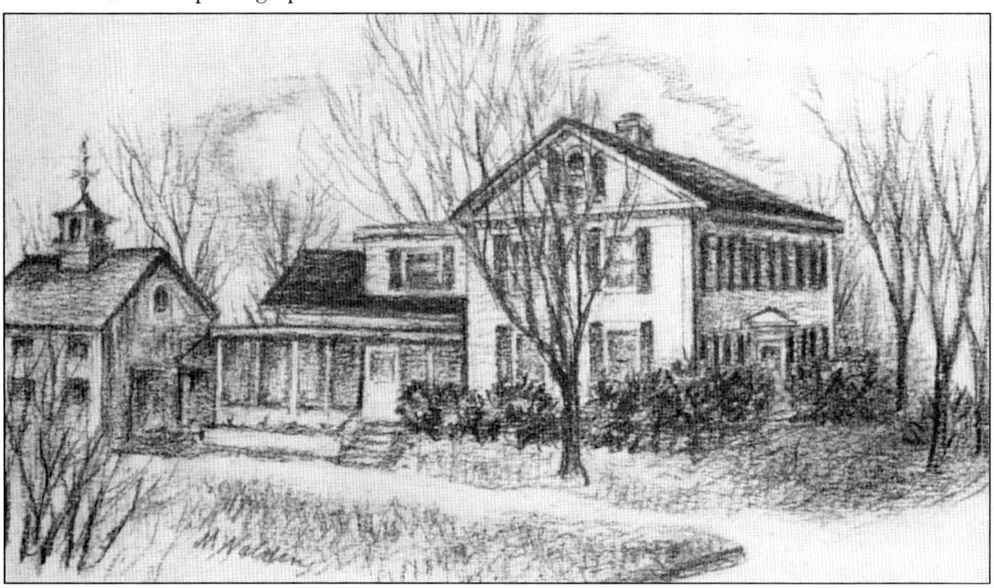

Steven Clapp House, 19 Fomer Road. This house was built about 1872, soon after Mr. Clapp acquired the land. There was already a history of a variety of mills operating on Red Brook, which flows through the rear of the property. According to Evert's *History of the Connecticut Valley*, a sawmill, a shingle mill, and a woolen mill had been located on this site. The Lyon family purchased the property in 1874 and occupied it for the next 72 years. This drawing was made by Margaret Walden.

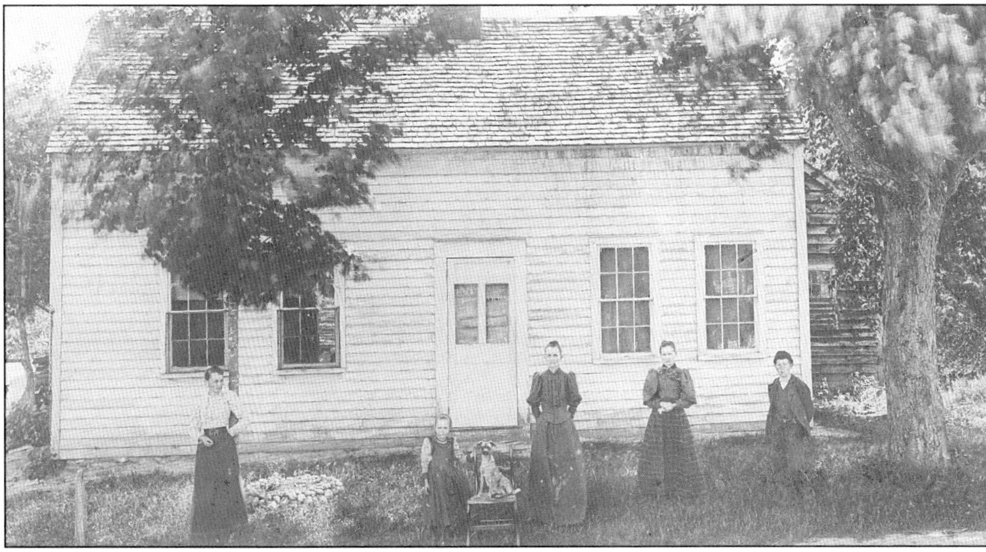

The Wreath Shop, 13 Fomer Road. Tradition has it that this house was constructed in 1782, and was acquired by Gaius Lyman in 1892. Maria Lyman (Mrs. Edward) conducted a business in greens in the house for over 40 years, beginning in the early 1900s. She probably did not live here, but resided next door (on another piece of Lyman property).

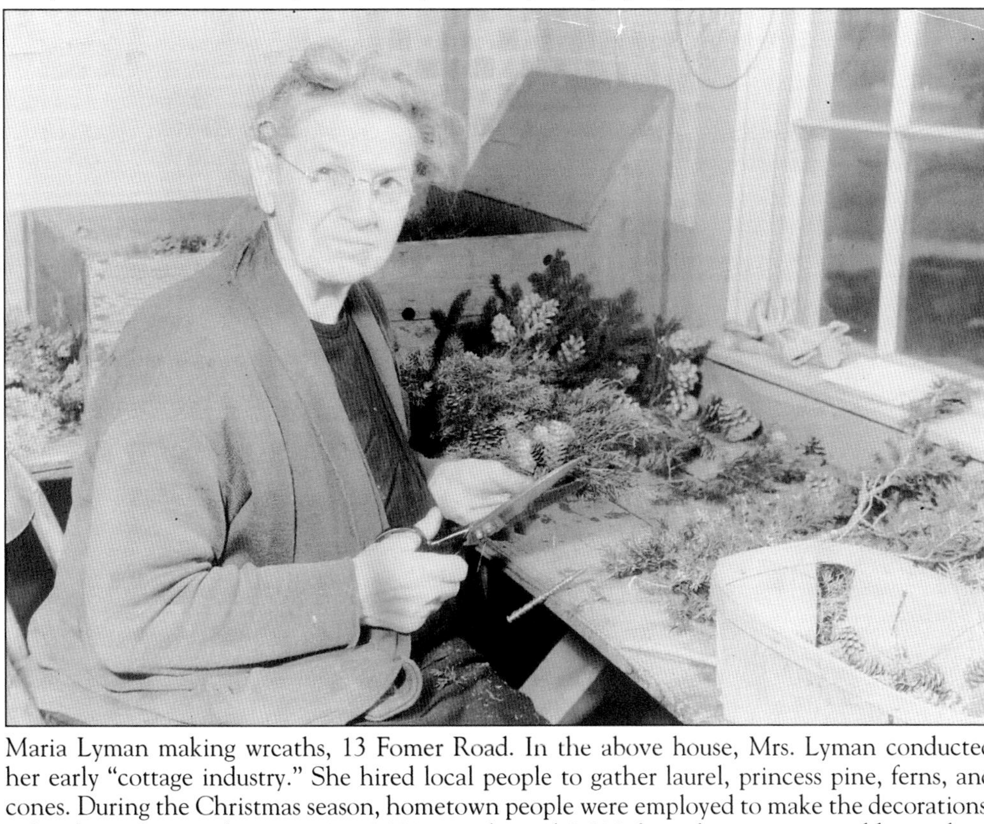

Maria Lyman making wreaths, 13 Fomer Road. In the above house, Mrs. Lyman conducted her early "cottage industry." She hired local people to gather laurel, princess pine, ferns, and cones. During the Christmas season, hometown people were employed to make the decorations. It has been written that in 1904, 6,800 wreaths and 9,000 feet of roping were sold, mostly to wholesalers in Boston and the Faneuil Hall Marketplace.

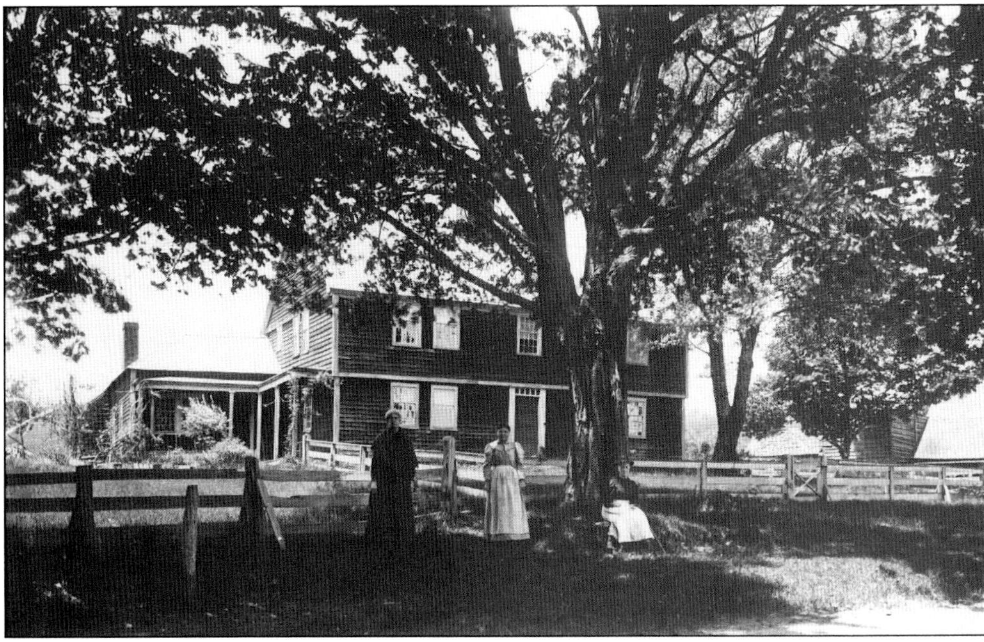

Eleazer Hannum House, 43 Pomeroy Meadow Road. Today this fine home stands as one of our best examples of early architecture. The center chimney remains. The second-story overhang and the lean-to at the back create the saltbox profile. The three ladies in this picture are daughters of the Bascomb family, owners of record in 1900. Leon Fowles purchased the property in 1909, and the family remained here until 1964, when the house was restored by Charles and Shirley Fisher. (Howes Brothers photograph, 1900.)

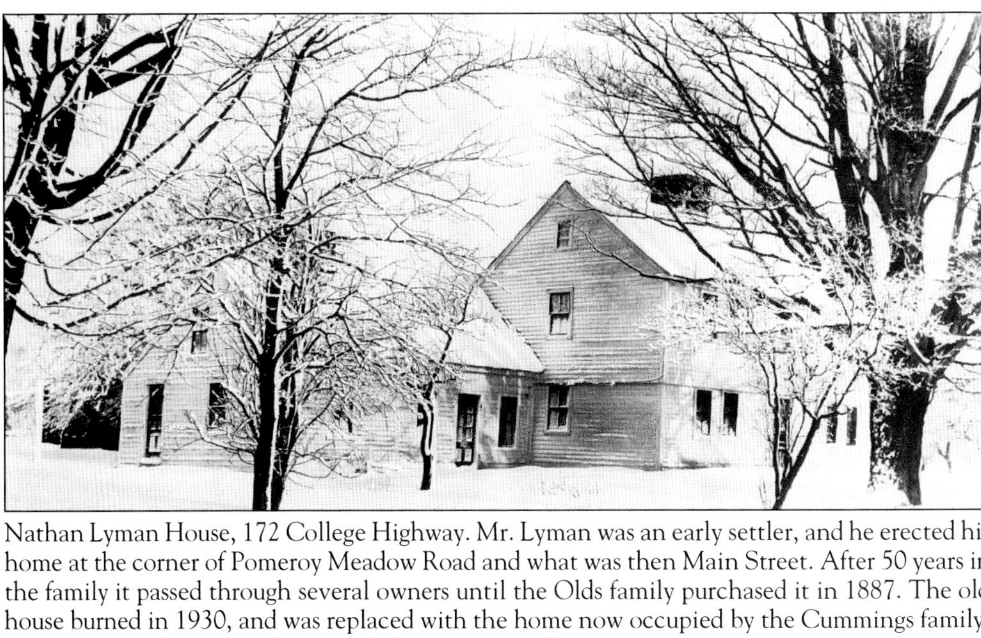

Nathan Lyman House, 172 College Highway. Mr. Lyman was an early settler, and he erected his home at the corner of Pomeroy Meadow Road and what was then Main Street. After 50 years in the family it passed through several owners until the Olds family purchased it in 1887. The old house burned in 1930, and was replaced with the home now occupied by the Cummings family, adjacent to their antiques business. This image is c. 1910.

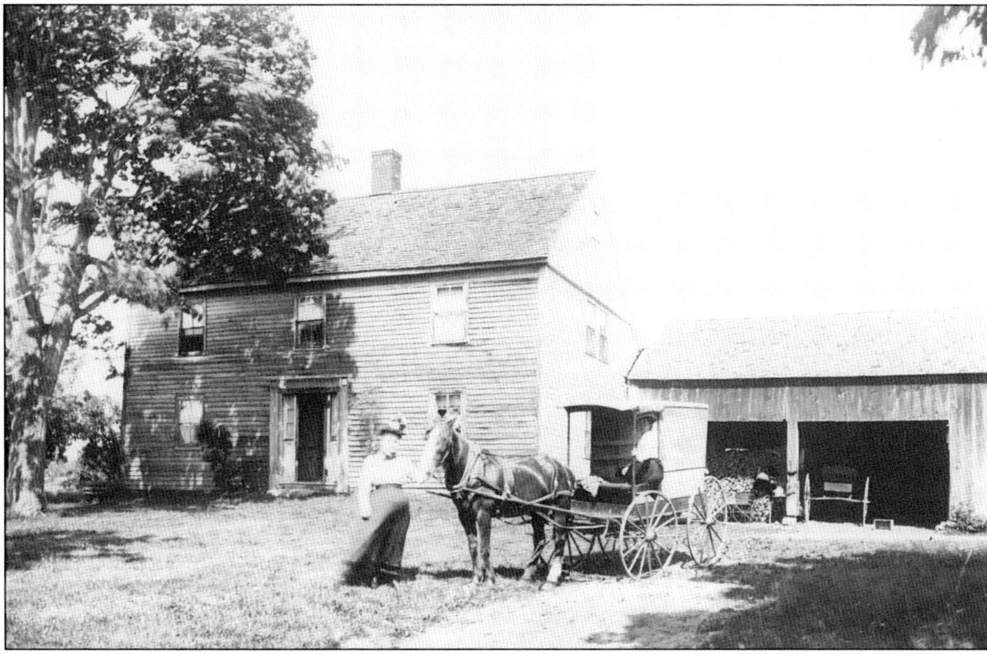

Calvin Torrey Home, 80 College Highway. We believe that Mr. Torrey built his large home in the late 1700s. It is well known that he and William Baldwin were, in 1786, the builders of the second meetinghouse. Very little is recorded of his later years, but we do know that his descendants still live in Southampton. The house deteriorated and was salvaged for rebuilding in 1960. (Howes Brothers photograph, 1900.)

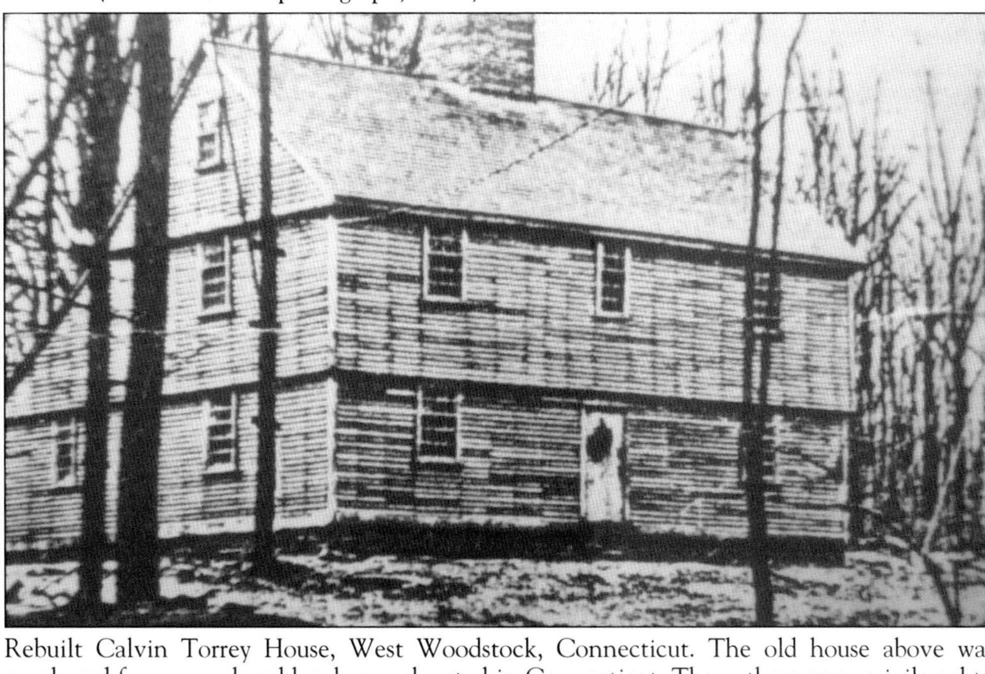

Rebuilt Calvin Torrey House, West Woodstock, Connecticut. The old house above was purchased for removal and has been relocated in Connecticut. The authors were privileged to have a tour of the rebuilt house, and can report that the owners are delighted with their "new" home. Southampton's loss was West Woodstock's gain!

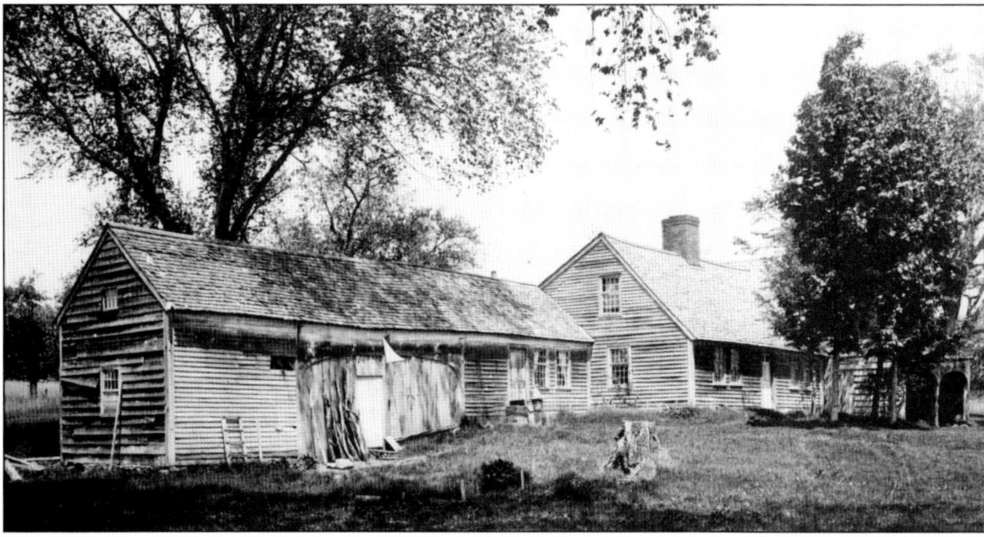

Ancient Pomeroy House, 145 Pomeroy Meadow Road. Early records indicate that this house was built in the meadows by Caleb Pomeroy several years prior to the settlement of the town in the 1730s. At least five generations of Pomeroys occupied this property until 1910, when it was purchased by the Zoudlick family. After their parents' death, Margaret and her brother Wencel lived on in the old house. Margaret was a well-liked schoolteacher, first at the old North School, then at the Sheldon School, and finally at the new Center School. (Keene photograph, *c.* 1898.)

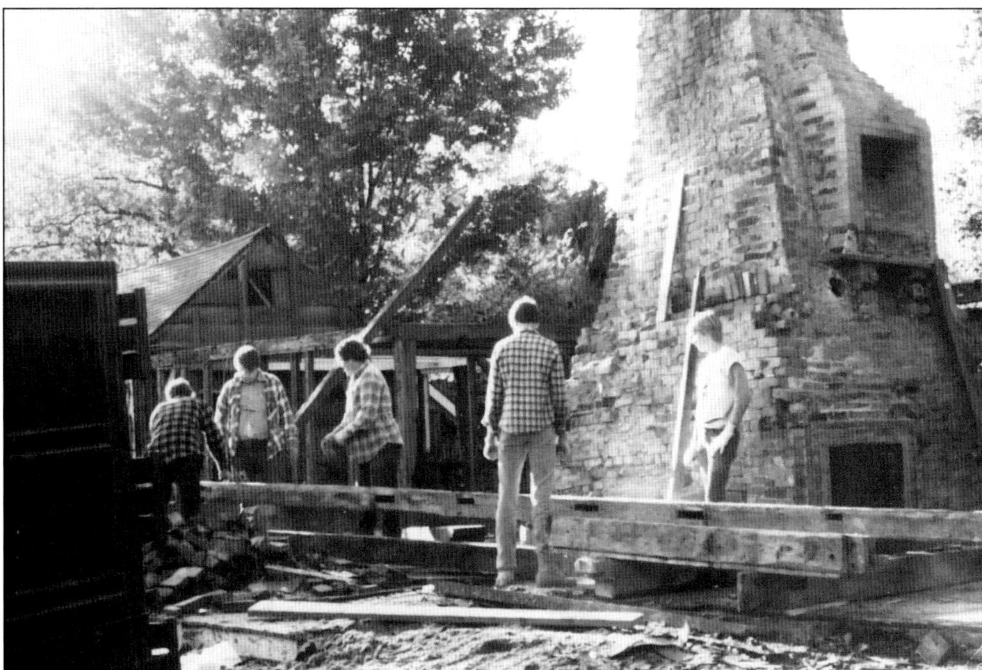

Removal of Pomeroy-Zoudlick House, 145 Pomeroy Meadow Road. The town lost its oldest house in 1983 when this ancient structure, dating back to the earliest settlers, was torn down and sold for rebuilding in Connecticut. It had survived for approximately three hundred years.

Great white oak tree, 146 Pomeroy Meadow Road. This magnificent tree towered above the spring house. The spring was the water supply for the old Pomeroy house across the street. (Keene photograph, *c.* 1898.)

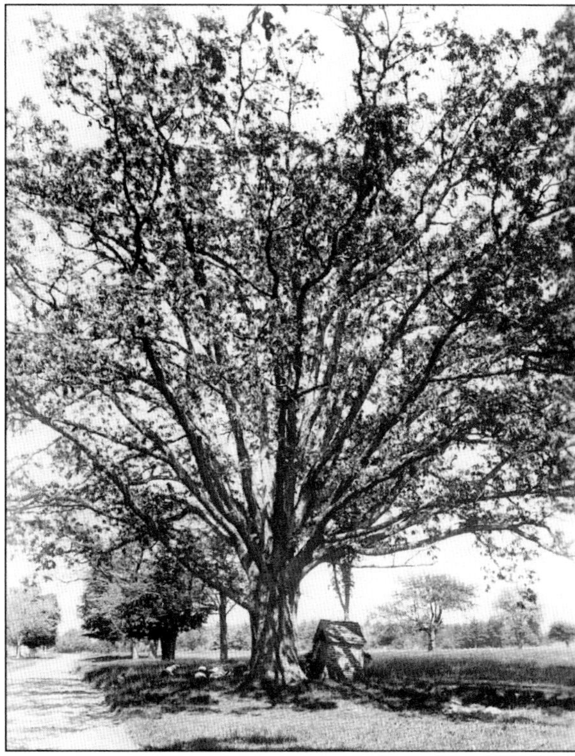

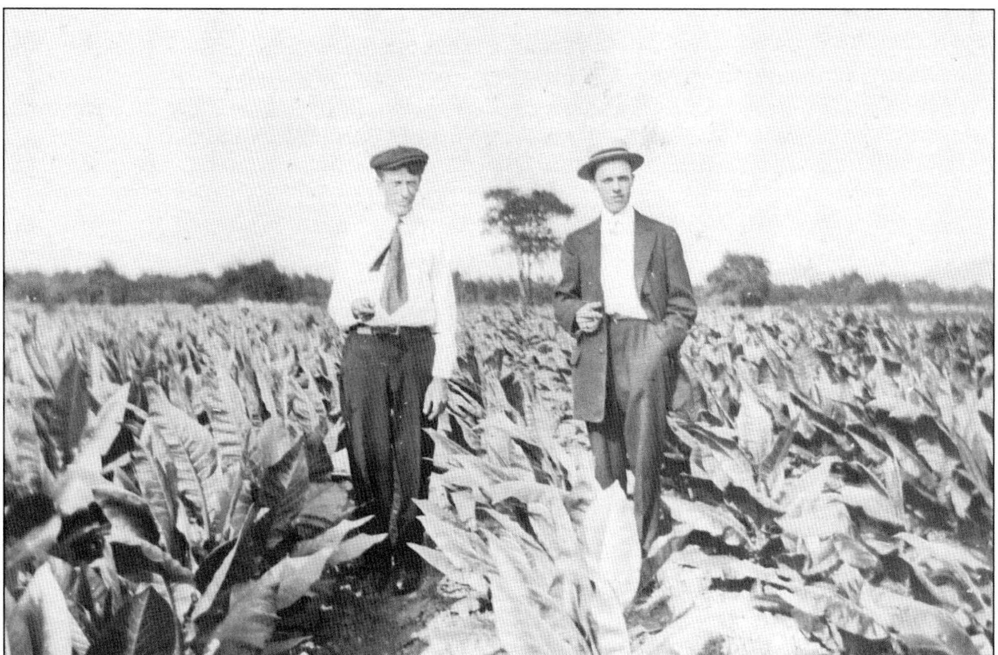

Field of tobacco, 146 Pomeroy Meadow Road. Wencel Zoudlick and an unidentified gentleman survey the crop. Wencel was an artist, and most of his paintings were of local scenes. Many were donated to the historical society's Clark Chapman House. This real-photo postcard was made *c.* 1912.

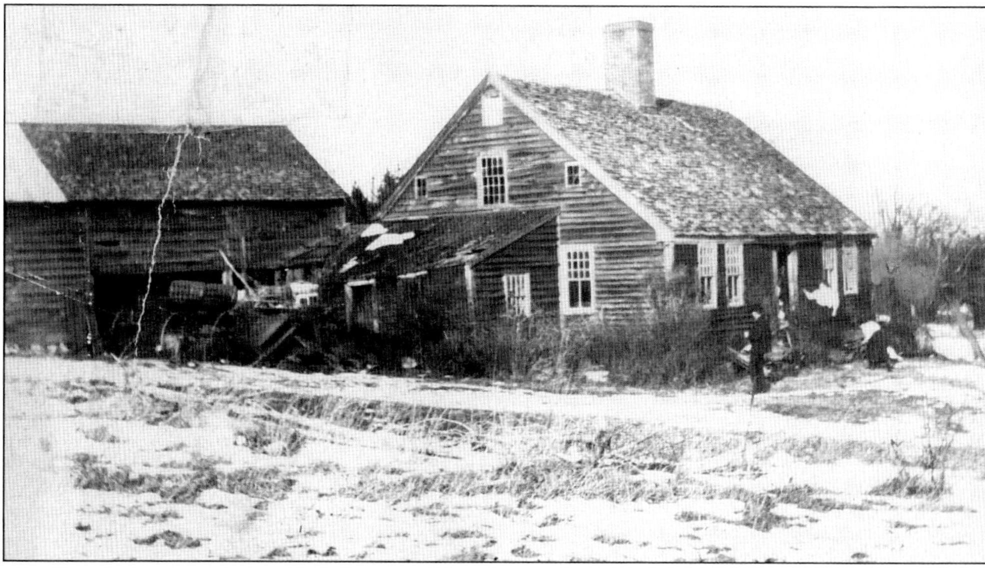

Oliver Clark Jr. House, 52 Cold Spring Road. This classic, old Cape was built in 1793 by Mr. Clark. His grandfather, Elisha Clark, was one of the original settlers, and had built his house on the high ground across the road. Elisha was killed by Nonotuck Indians in his barn in 1747, during a time of general Native American unrest in the area. The fifth-grade students from Norris School stop for a rest by the old cellar hole as they wind up their annual hike on Mount Pomeroy. The Myrick-Manley family bought the property in 1908 and it remained in the family until purchased for restoration in 1967. (Myrick family postcard, 1908.)

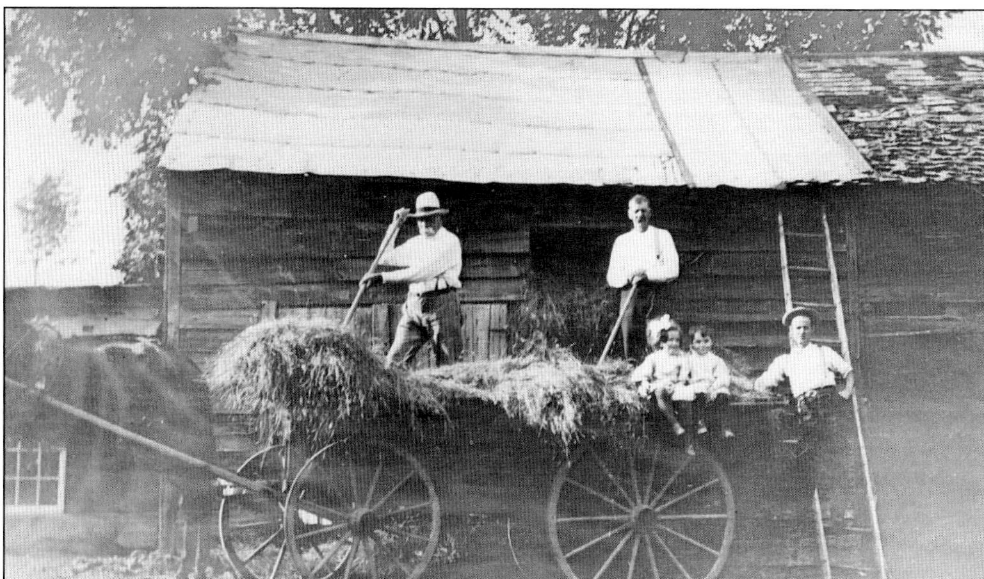

Summer on the farm, 52 Cold Spring Road. Above is the barn on the Oliver Clark property. Getting a ride in the hay wagon with his sister is Harold Myrick, who today lives on East Street in Southampton. (Myrick family photograph, *c.* 1909.)

Two

Farmers Arrive

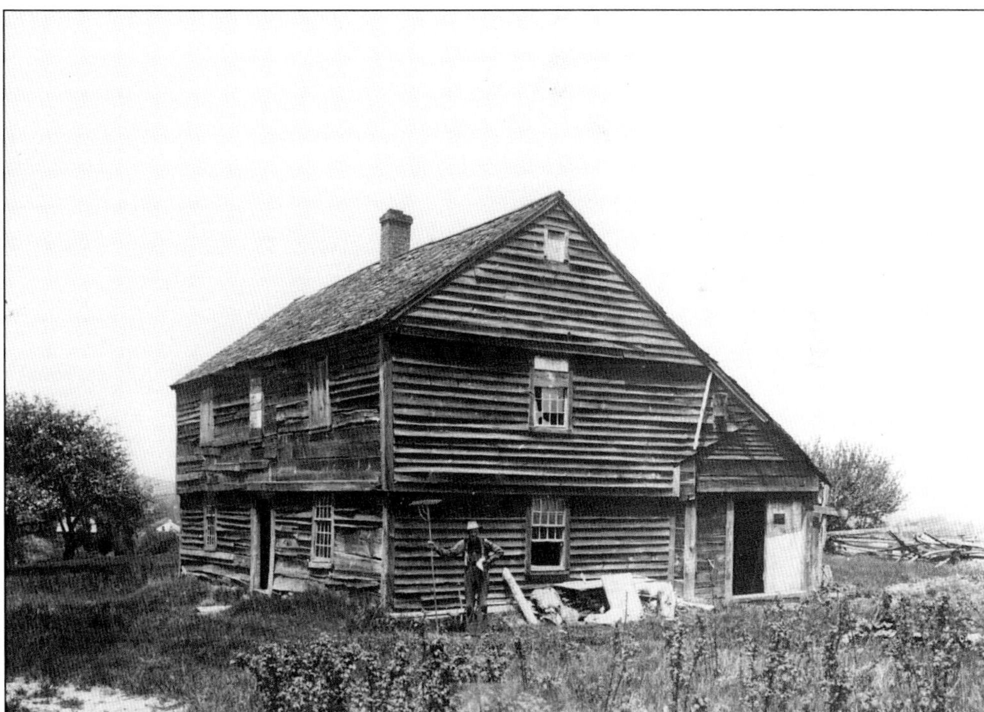

Ancient Frary House, 69 Gunn Road. Records show that four Frary families built their houses on this road. We know that Obadiah lived farther down the street, and in 1828 Jessie Frary owned the sawmill on the Manhan River at Frary Bridge. Situated at the top of the hill, this derelict was falling down by the turn of the century. (Keene photograph, c. 1890.)

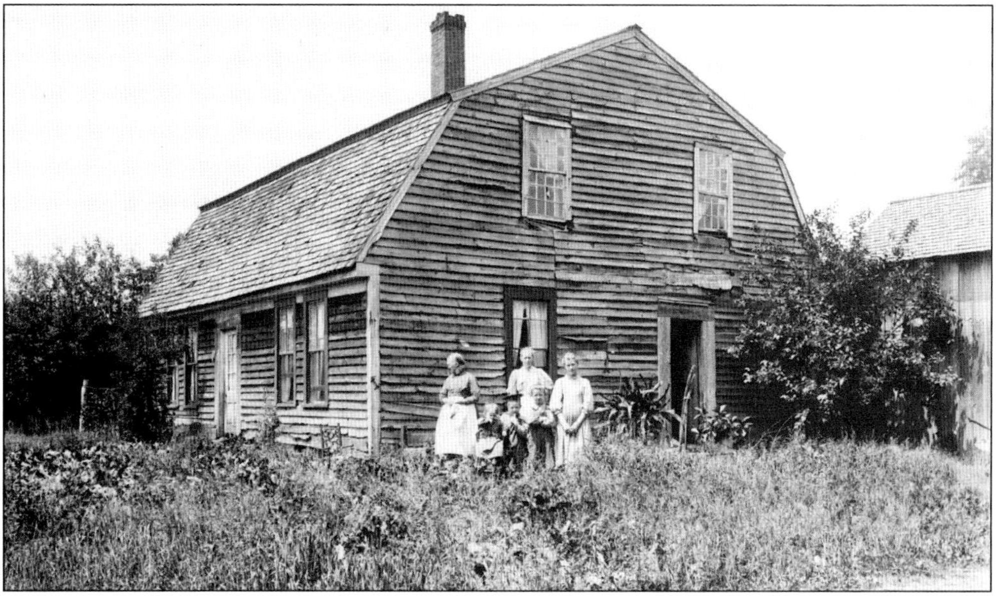

Zeno Coleman Farmhouse, 38 College Highway. Built in 1805, this house was located next to the original log cabin on the property (see p. 10). Ownership passed through seven generations bearing the Coleman name until 1979. (Keene photograph, 1898.)

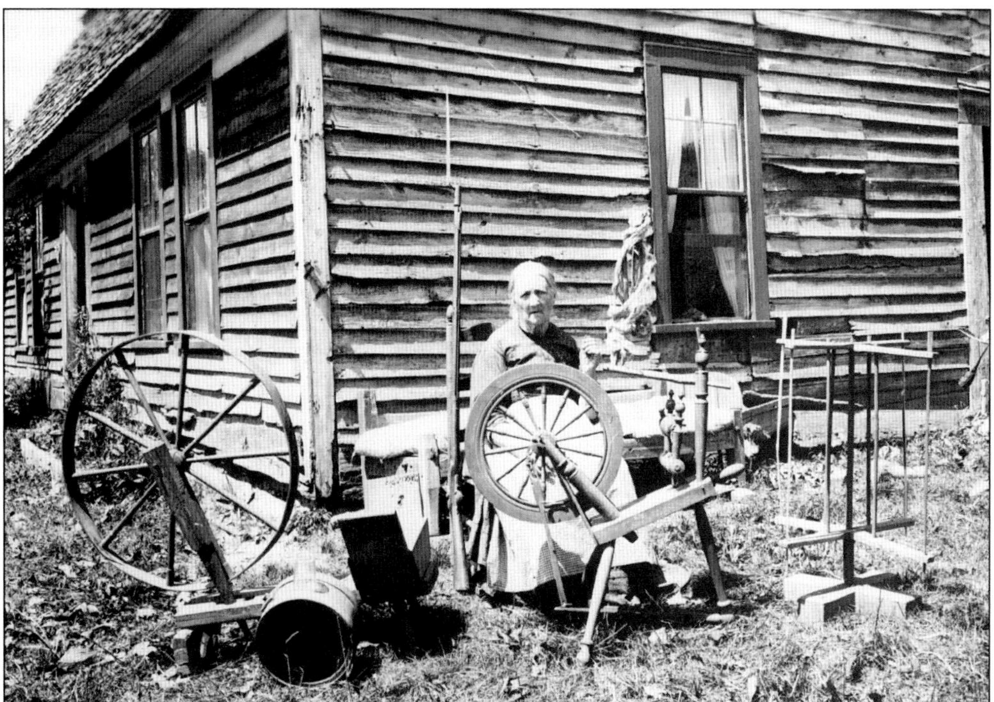

Grandma Coleman, 38 College Highway. An elderly Coleman ancestor poses in her yard with family heirlooms. (Keene photograph, 1898.)

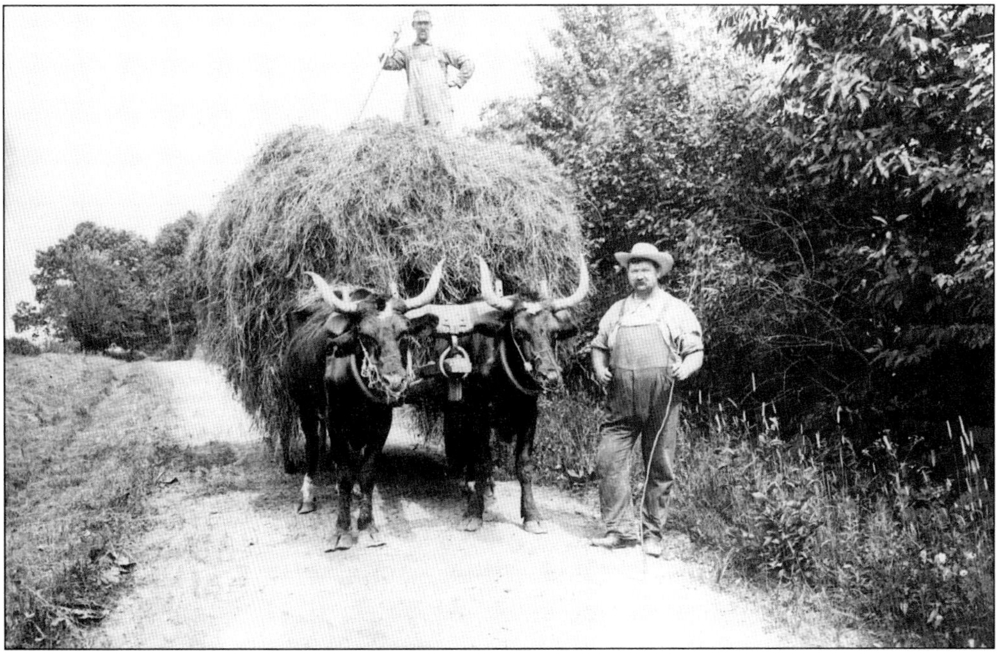

Old-time farming scene on the College Highway. This ox-drawn hay wagon is on the College Highway with Dwight and Sylvester in the picture. The Colemans were well known for farming the old-fashioned way. (Keene photograph, 1898.)

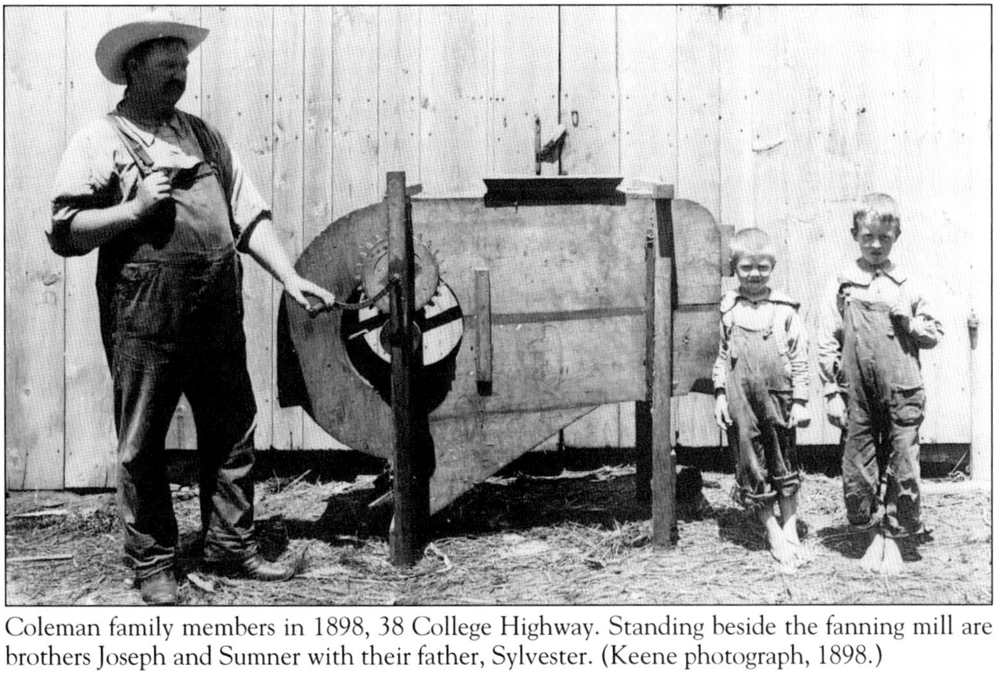

Coleman family members in 1898, 38 College Highway. Standing beside the fanning mill are brothers Joseph and Sumner with their father, Sylvester. (Keene photograph, 1898.)

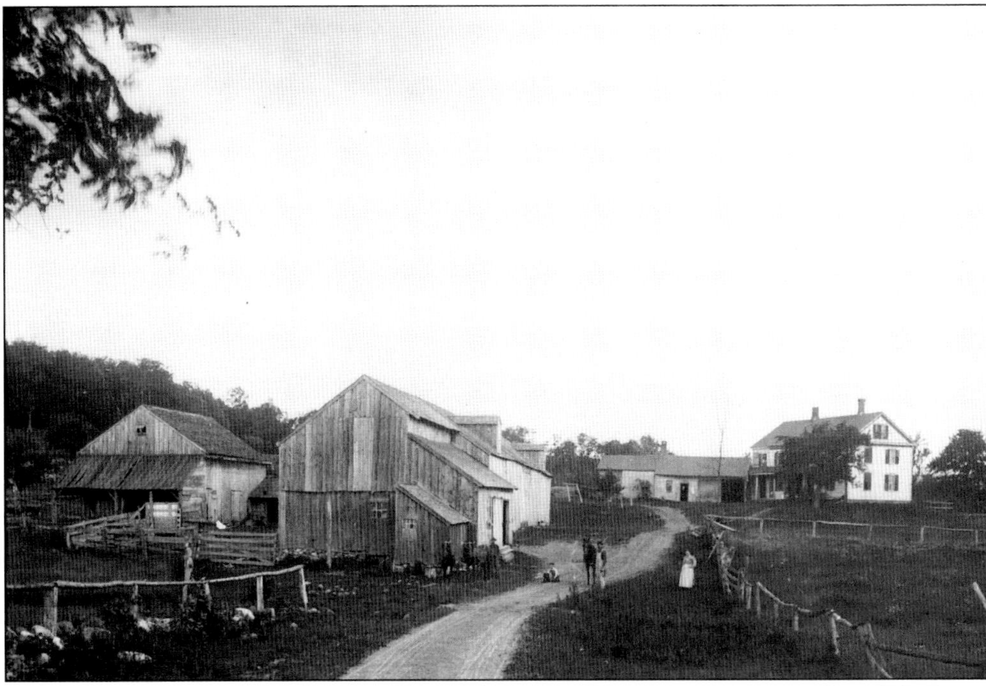

Barnes-Douglas-Miller Farm, 10 Douglas Road. In 1810 Farrington Barnes purchased the house and barn, including 20 acres on the west side of the College Highway (bounded on the south by the Westfield line). The property has passed through several generations and is still occupied by the same family today. (Howes Brothers photograph, 1900.)

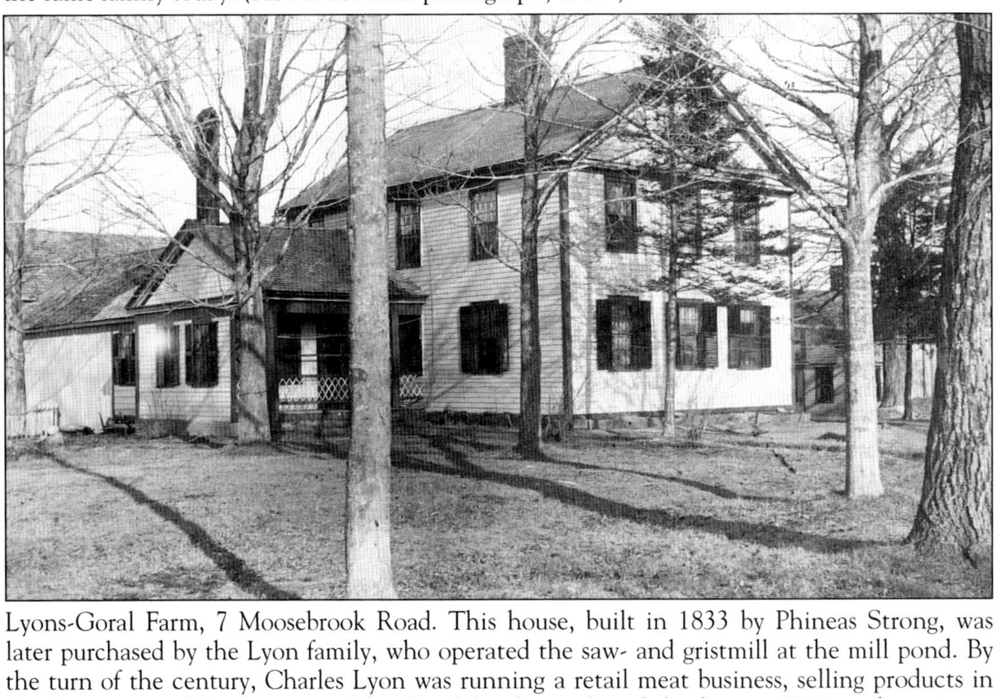

Lyons-Goral Farm, 7 Moosebrook Road. This house, built in 1833 by Phineas Strong, was later purchased by the Lyon family, who operated the saw- and gristmill at the mill pond. By the turn of the century, Charles Lyon was running a retail meat business, selling products in Southampton and Easthampton. The Goral family purchased the farm in 1919, and continues to farm here. (Judd photograph, *c.* 1890.)

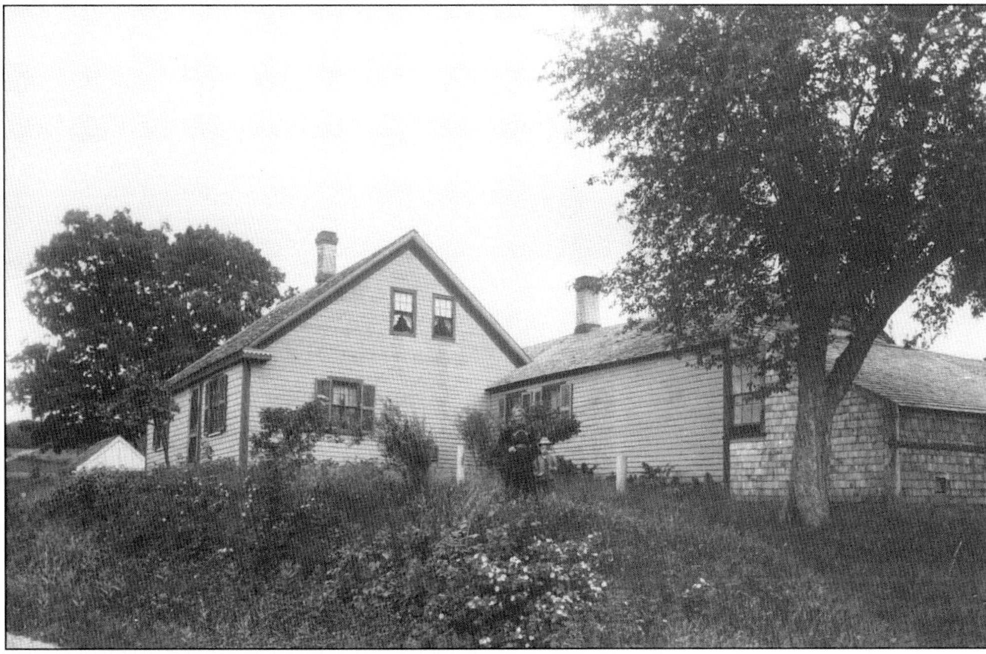

Breyer Farm, 37 Middle Road. The Breyer family was told when it purchased this obviously very old piece of property in 1916 that it had been an inn on a road to West Holyoke. Historians can find no record of that being so. It is an interesting building in a pastoral setting, and is still owned by the Breyer family. (Howes Brothers photograph, 1900.)

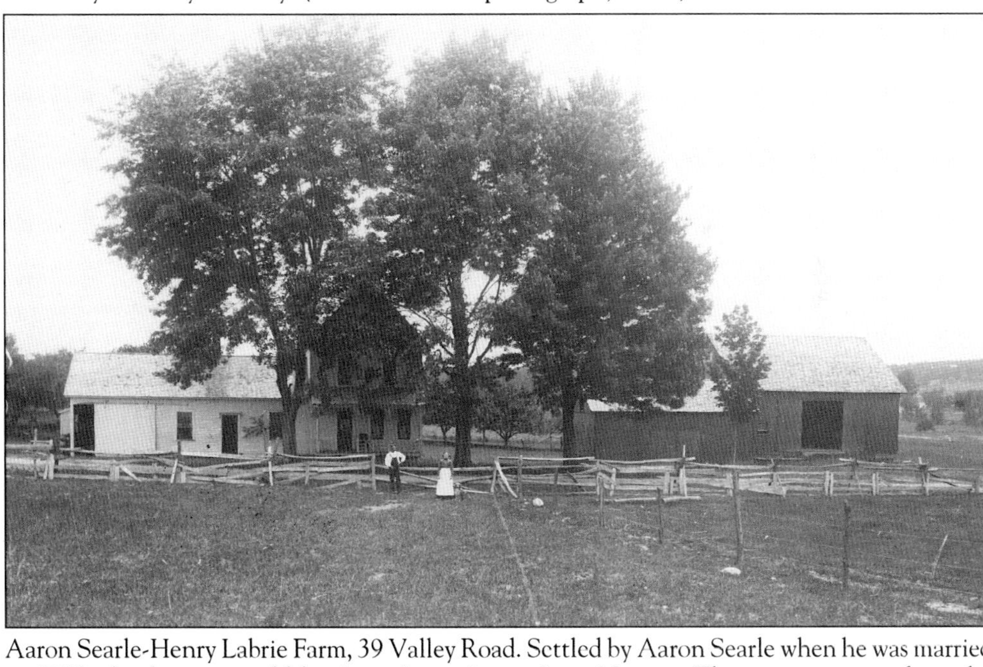

Aaron Searle-Henry Labrie Farm, 39 Valley Road. Settled by Aaron Searle when he was married in 1752, the farm was sold by Aaron's son Ira to Isaac Norton. The property went from the Norton family through several owners, namely Spooner, Lanoue, Buckley, Wiesel, Kangisser, Bourbou, and Bickel. Finally, in 1932, it was purchased by Mr. Labrie and has remained a large, prosperous, family-owned dairy farm. (Howes Brothers photograph, 1900.)

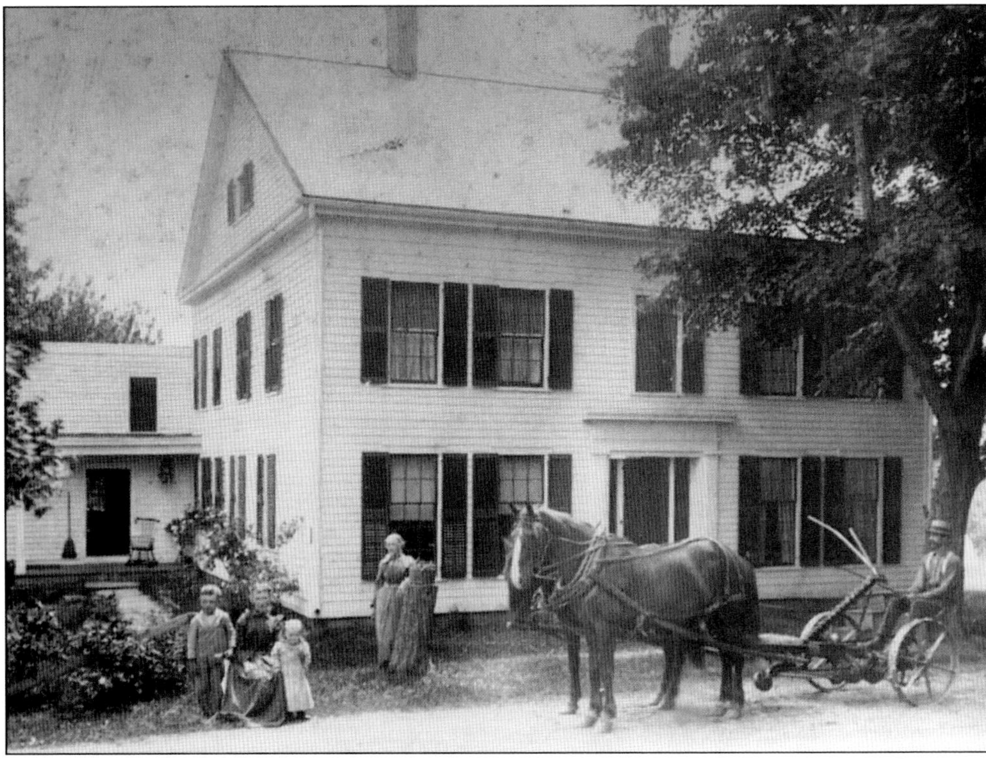

Clark-Lyman Farmhouse, 339 College Highway. Deacon John Clark came out from Northampton and settled here in 1733. The property passed on to the Lyman family by marriage, and in 1855 Samuel Lyman removed the old house, replacing it with this larger building. Ownership continued in the same family until the land was converted to a golf course in 1930. (Howes Brothers photograph, 1900.)

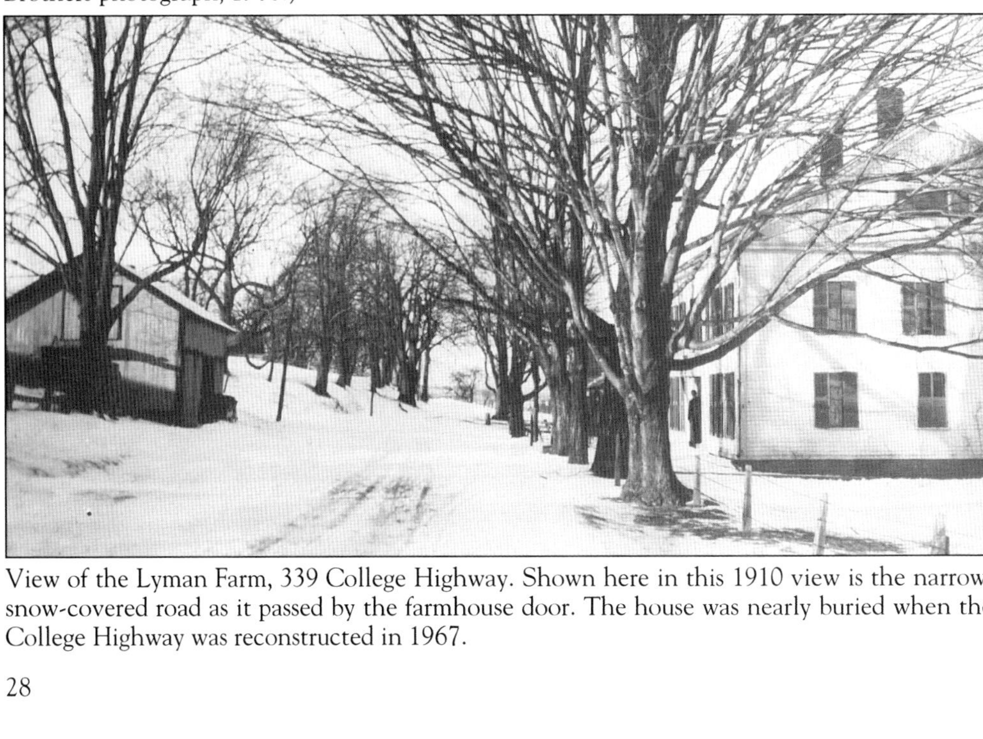

View of the Lyman Farm, 339 College Highway. Shown here in this 1910 view is the narrow, snow-covered road as it passed by the farmhouse door. The house was nearly buried when the College Highway was reconstructed in 1967.

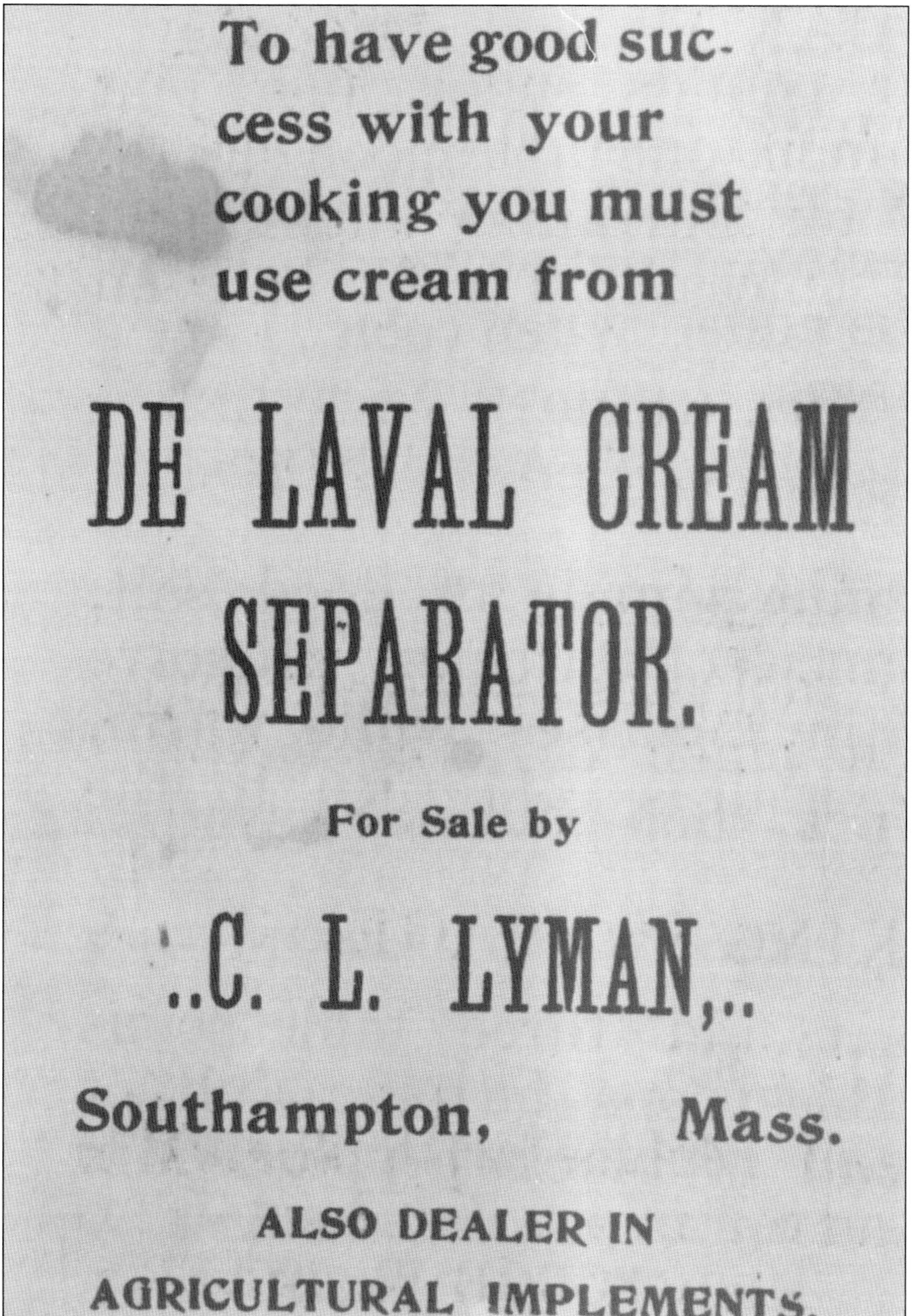

C.L. Lyman commercial. Charles L. Lyman, in addition to being a farmer, was a dealer in farm implements and advertised in the *Southampton Ladies Aid Cookbook* in 1900.

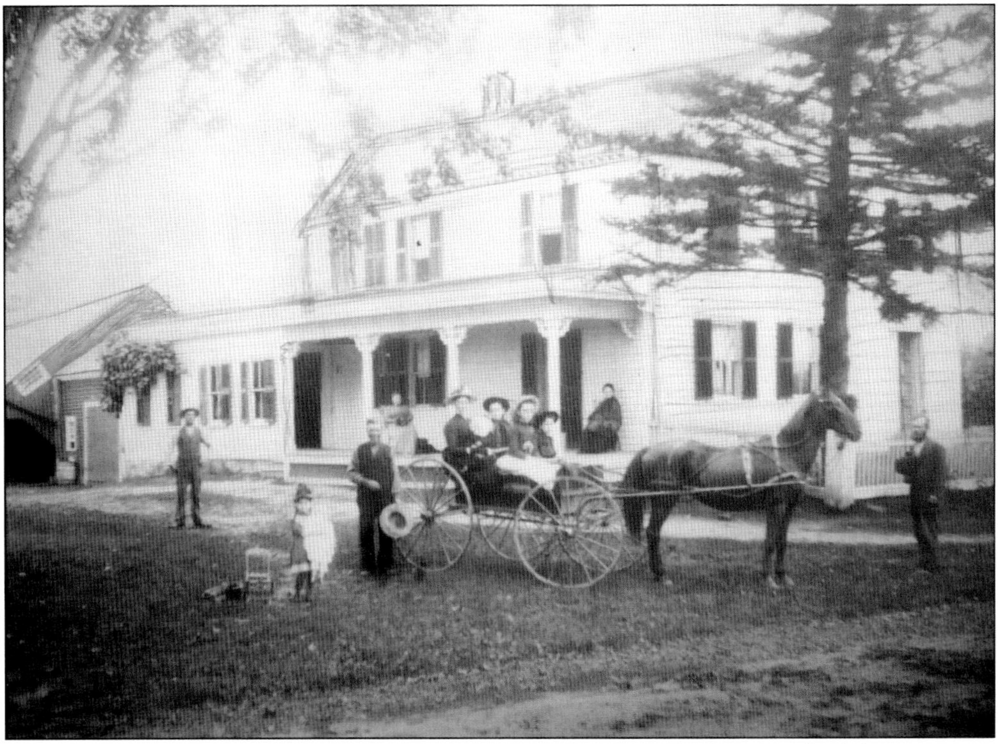

Wolf Hill Farm, 52 Russellville Road. Seven generations of Searles have worked this extensive farm since it was settled by Zophar in 1764. The first house, located below Wolf Hill in Alder Meadow, burned in 1831, and Cornelius Edward (of the third generation) built the present farmhouse. The fifth generation planted several acres of apple orchards and conducted a mail-order business in superior Northern Spies. The fruit trees are now gone, but the dairy business continues to be operated by the seventh generation.

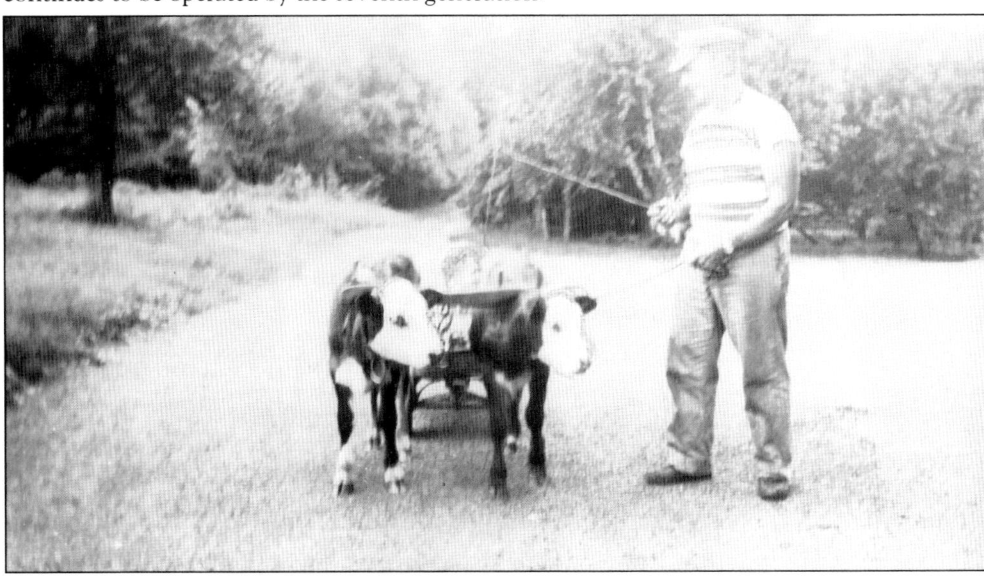

Training a pair of young steers on Searle Farm. Edward Cornelius Searle breaks in his future ox team in approximately 1948.

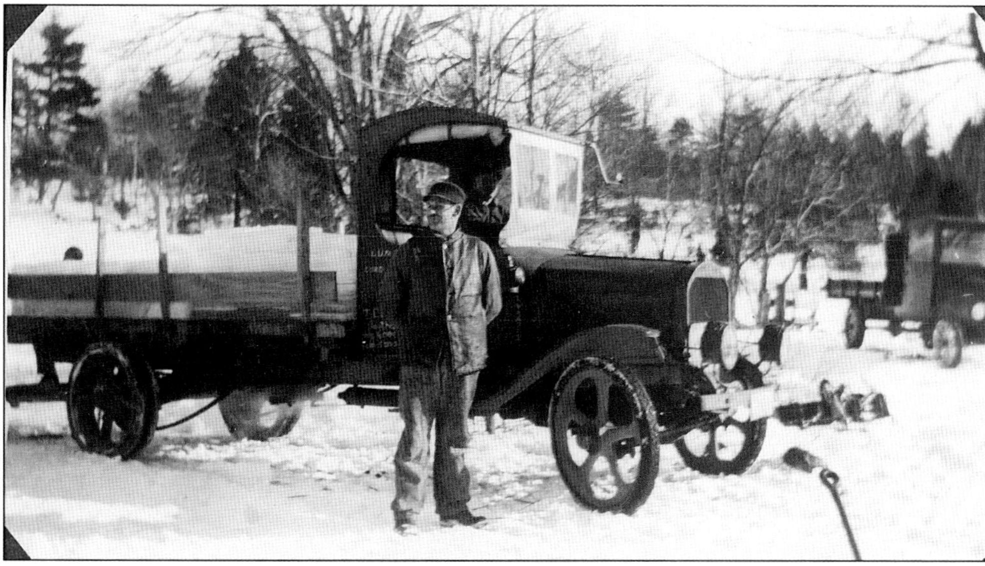

Ice-cutting on Searles Pond at Wolf Hill Farm in 1930. Neighbors gather for their annual ritual, cutting ice on the pond in Alder Meadow.

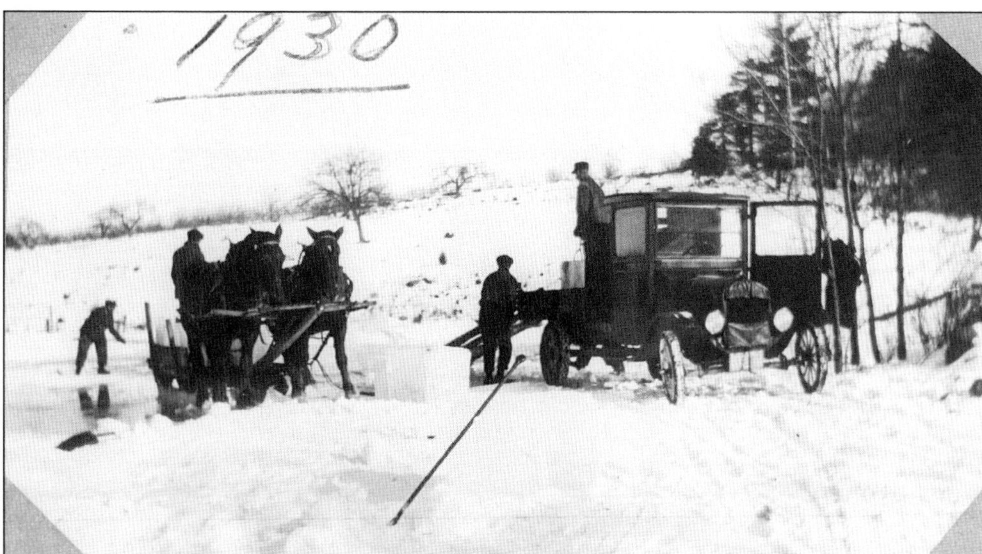

Harvesting ice on Searle's Wolf Hill Farm in 1930. Note the thickness of the ice cake. It seems obvious that our winters are now not what they used to be.

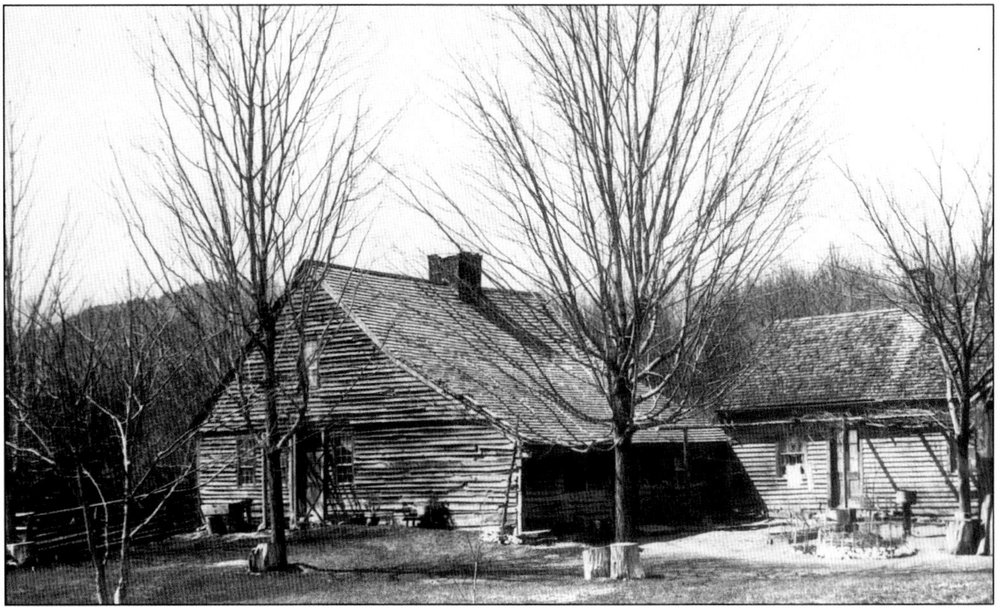

Southworth-Crowell House, Fomer Road. This saltbox-style house is a classic example of early architecture and was built in 1786. As with many older houses, it did not survive and burned in 1899. (Corbin print, c. 1885.)

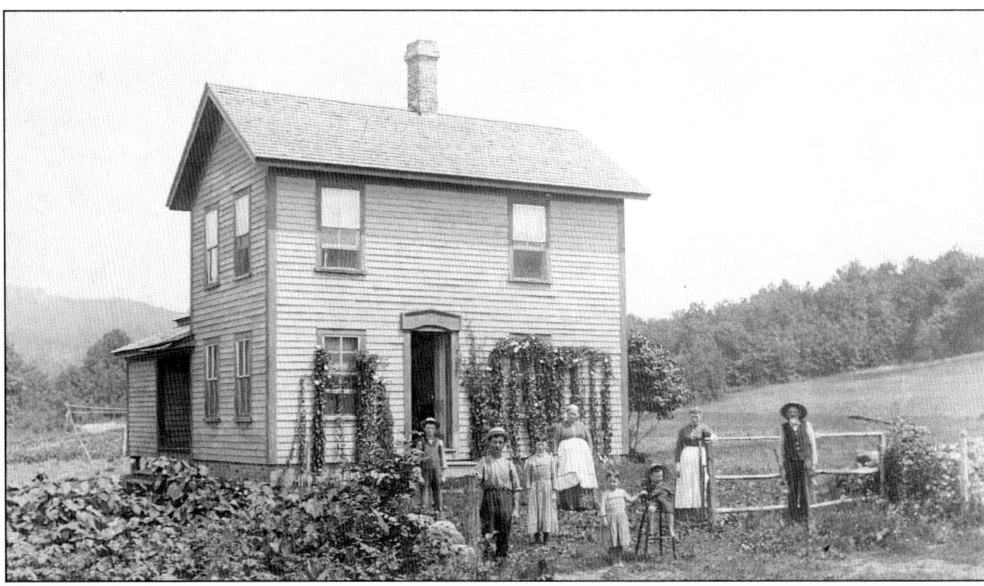

James Duggan Jr. Home, 70 Maple Street. Historian Sam Wright recorded in 1899 that Mr. Duggan had a large family and lived on upper Maple Street on the west side of Little Mountain. (Judd photograph, c. 1890.)

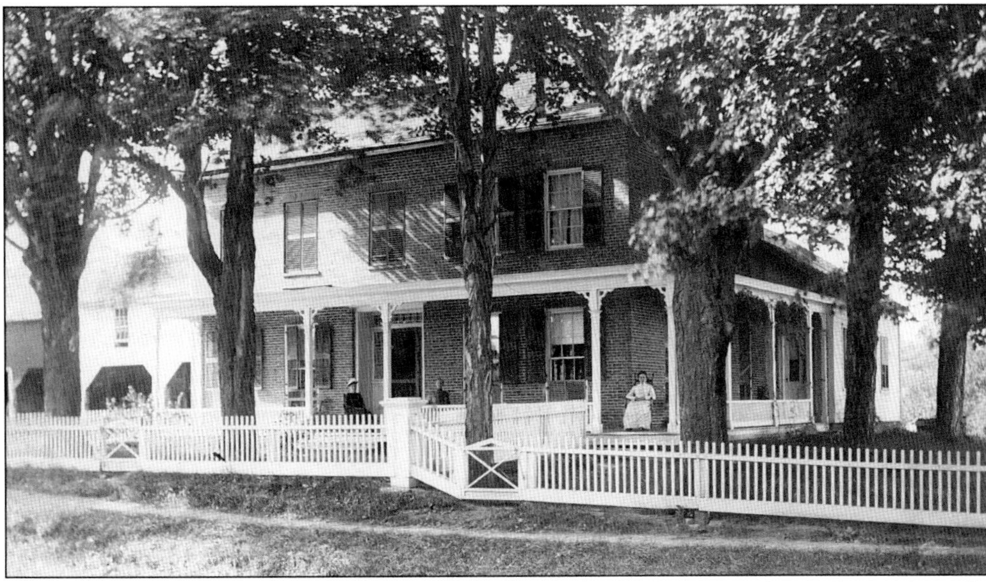

Timothy Clark Tavern, 106 Clark Street. Captain Clark built his tavern here after 1747, and it passed on through the family until the building burned in 1838. The next owner, Seth Bartlett, built this brick house, and in 1875 Isaac Parsons bought the farm and worked it until 1930. (Judd photograph, *c.* 1895.)

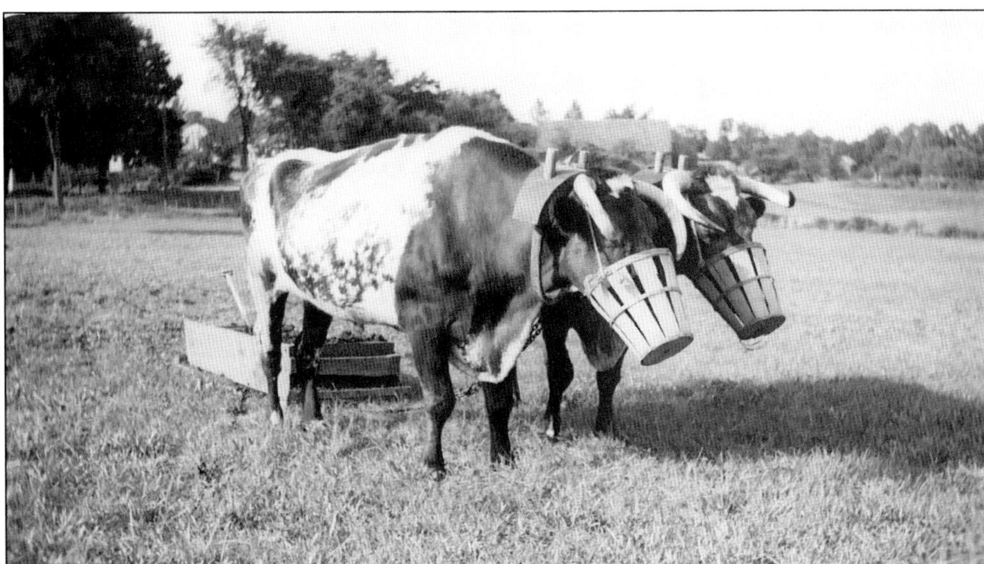

Lunch break for Ed Clark's oxen, Clark Street. This farm activity was taking place at what is now Conant Park. It appears that the oxen are dragging a manure sled in this 1941 snapshot.

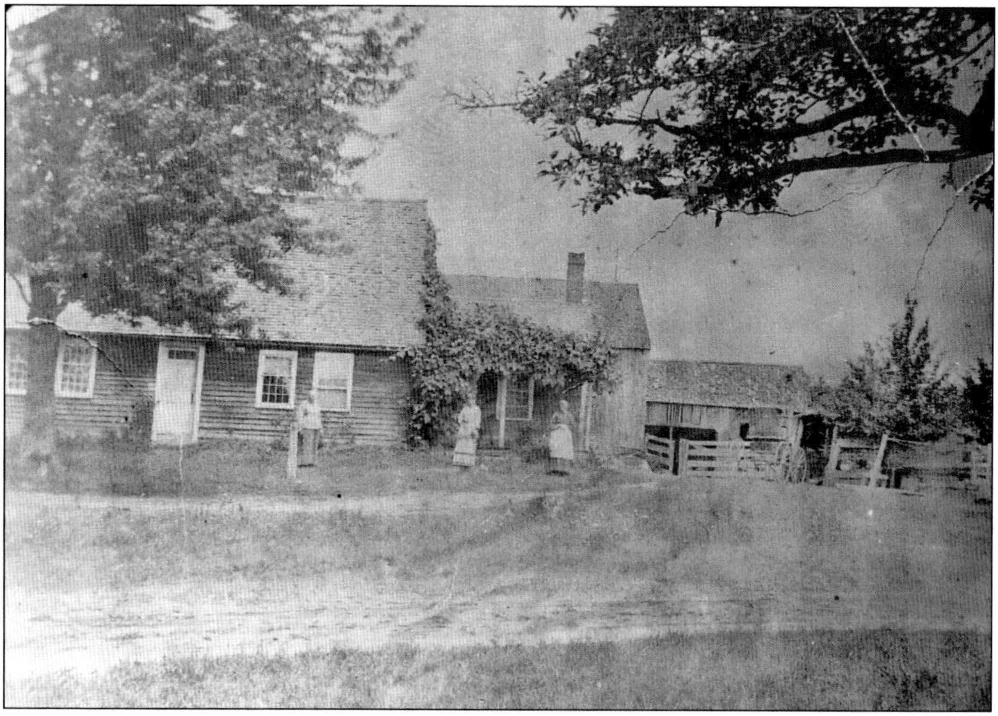

Early farmhouse, 158 College Highway. Can you believe this picturesque house, shown here c. 1890, stood in the exact location of the present Trading Post Corner building? It was occupied by the Rowleys, Thorpes, and possibly many others. About 1894 a newer house was built on this site and it was occupied by the Banas family until the 1950s.

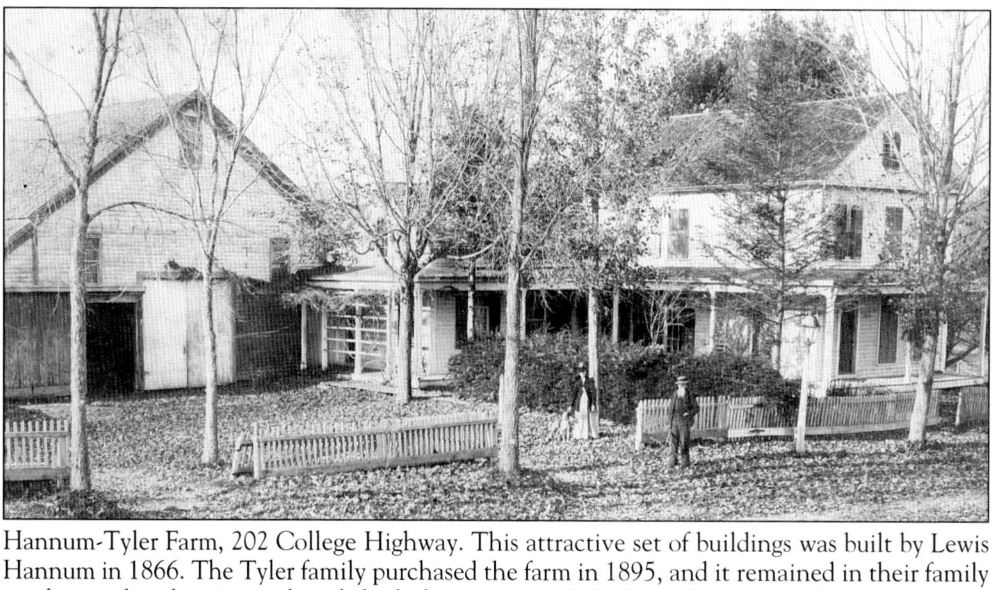

Hannum-Tyler Farm, 202 College Highway. This attractive set of buildings was built by Lewis Hannum in 1866. The Tyler family purchased the farm in 1895, and it remained in their family until recently, when it was demolished after an automobile drove through the kitchen at a high rate of speed. The occupant of the car survived but the house did not. The photograph was taken in 1895.

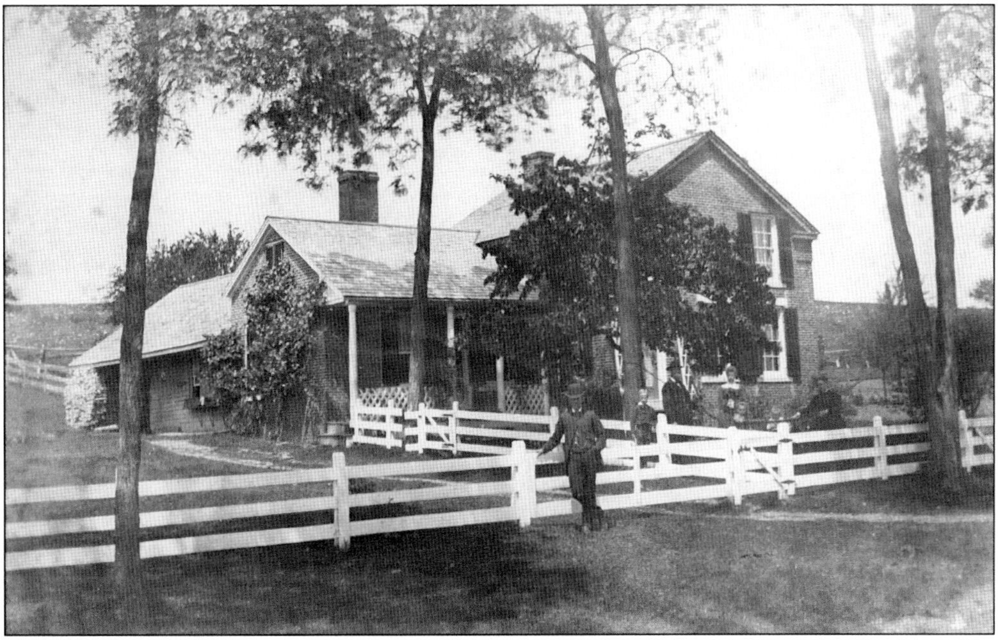

Pomeroy-Kingsley Farmhouse, 145 Glendale Road. Historians believe that this brick cottage was built by Samuel Pomeroy in 1846, and it passed to the Joseph Kingsley family prior to 1880. Mr. Kingsley found several Native American artifacts while plowing his fields, and they were given to the historical society, where they are now on display. (Richardson photograph, 1895.)

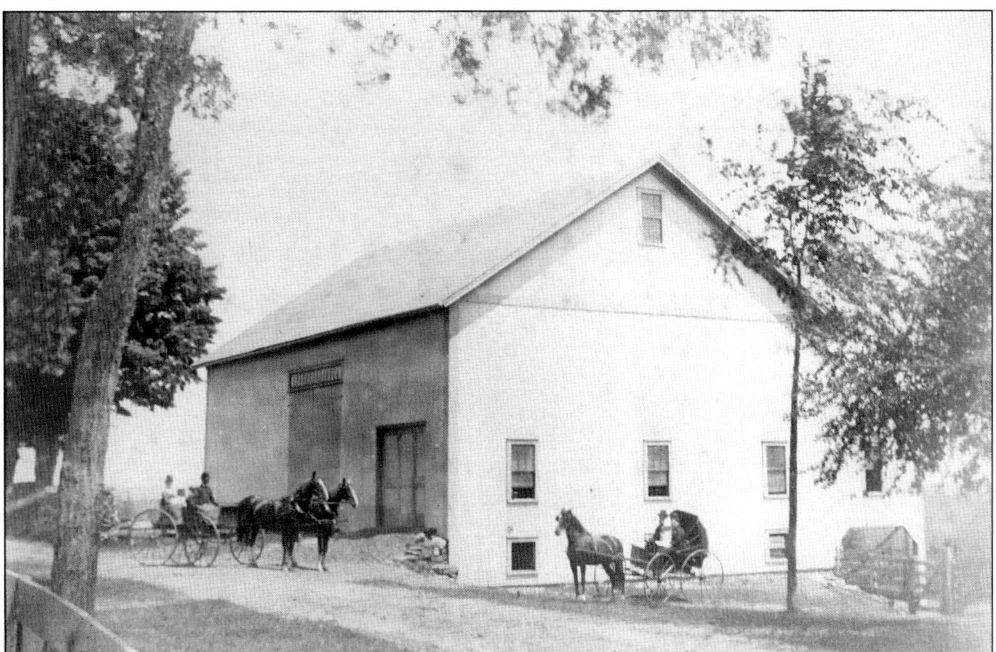

Kingsley Farm Barn, 145 Glendale Road. This fine barn was built in 1890 and burned in recent years. Three identical barns were built on the street and the two to the north still stand. (Richardson photograph, 1895.)

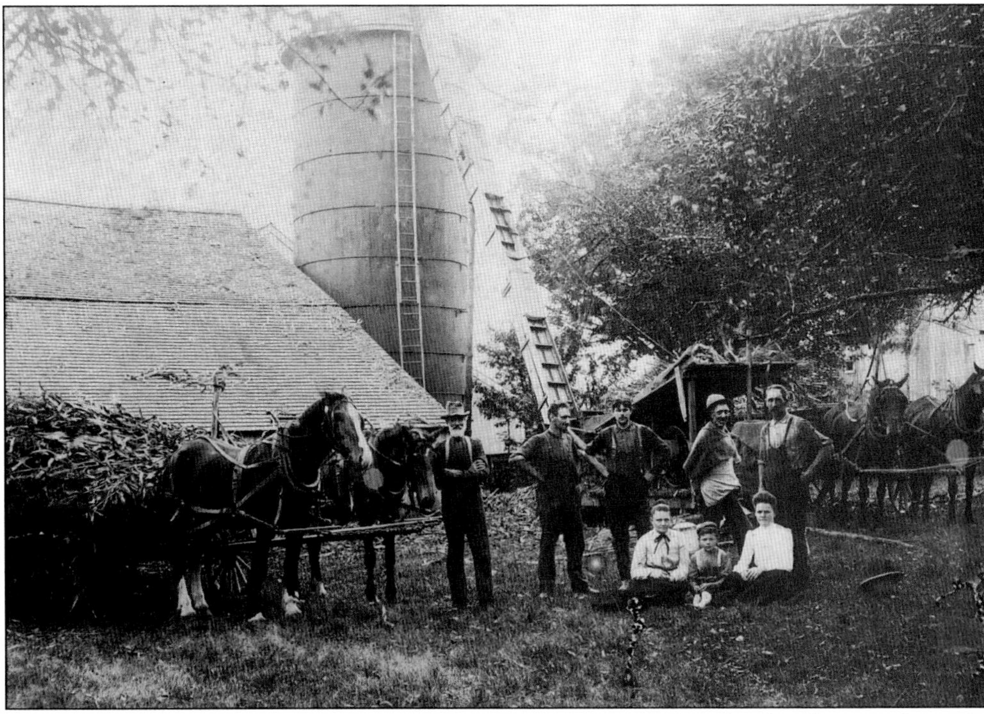

Filling the silo, 40 Miller Avenue. Depicted are the Pease and Miller families watching the men-folk at work at the Miller farm, getting the summer's crop up and into the silo. (Pease photograph, 1920.)

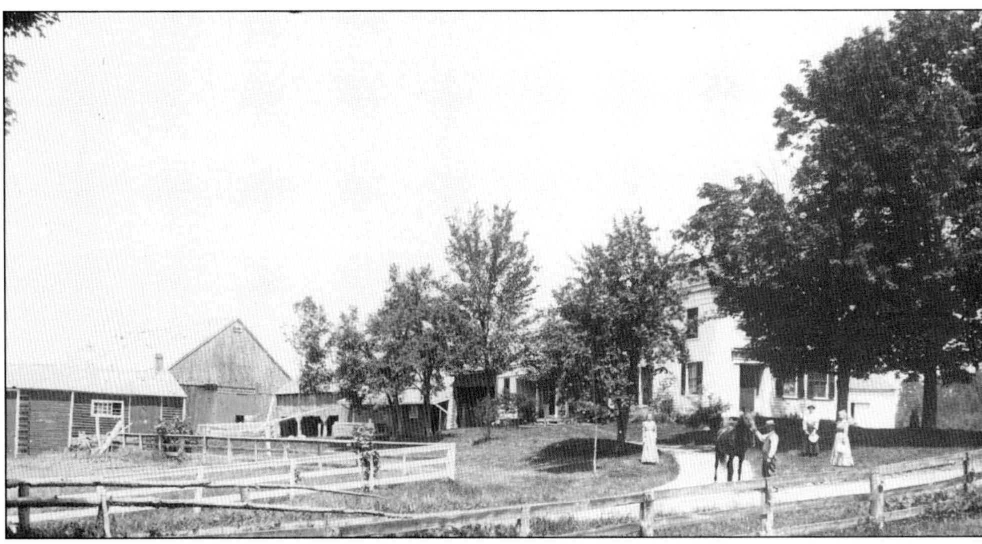

Nimocks-Bashista Farm, 53 Pleasant Street. Mr. Nimocks purchased this property with buildings in 1842, and probably built the present house at that time. Since 1939 the farm has been operated by the Edward Bashista family. A replacement barn was built in 1953 after the old structure was struck by lightning. In earlier days the official name of the street was Bedlam, but it was renamed Pleasant Street at a 1946 town meeting. (Howes Brothers photograph, 1900.)

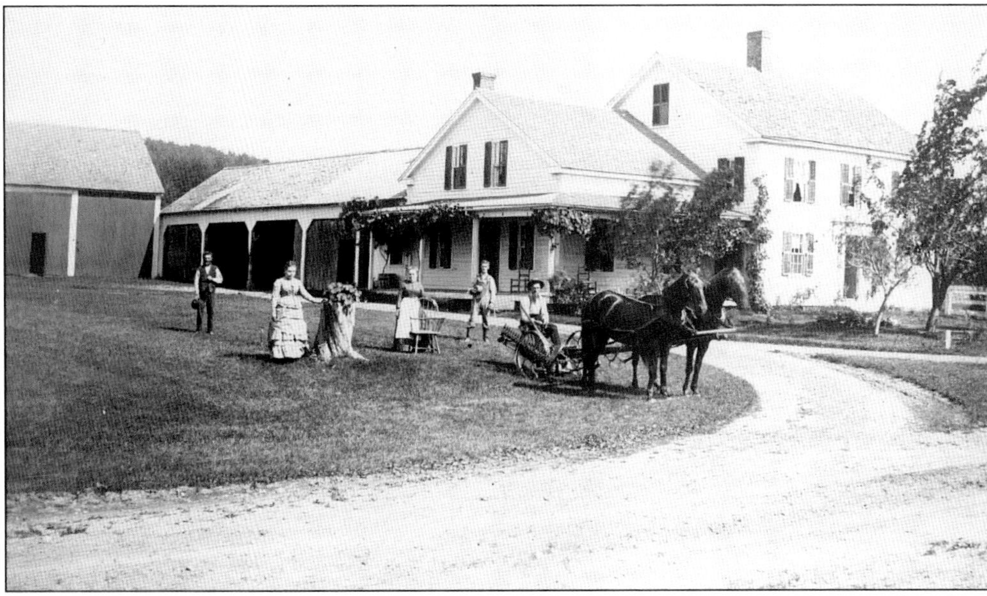

Clapp-Hannum Farm, 59 Pomeroy Meadow Road. Early records show that Chester Clapp built this house in 1854. It was later occupied by the Hannums, and this c. 1900 family picture shows them at home. In 1930 the farm was purchased by the Konopka family, and it is now considered one of the most scenic areas in town.

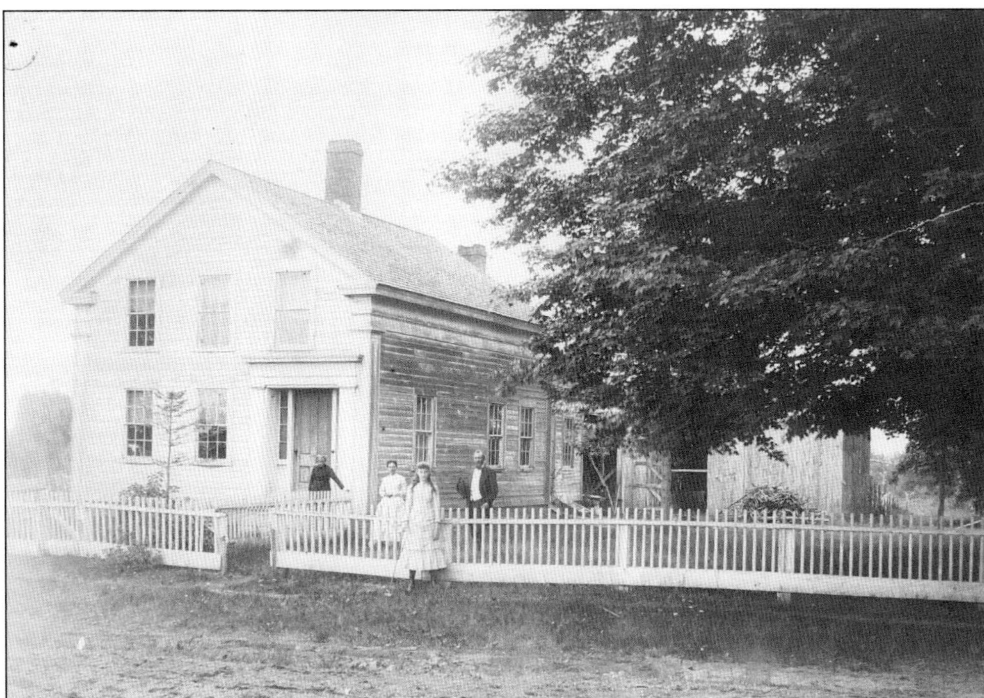

Aretus Pomeroy Place, 190 Pomeroy Meadow Road. This home, built by Mr. Pomeroy in 1856, is listed in the 1987 Historic Resource Survey as "certainly one of Southampton's most stylish houses from the Homestead Period." In the 1950s the fields were sold for development; the structure is now surrounded by newer housing. The photograph was taken c. 1900.

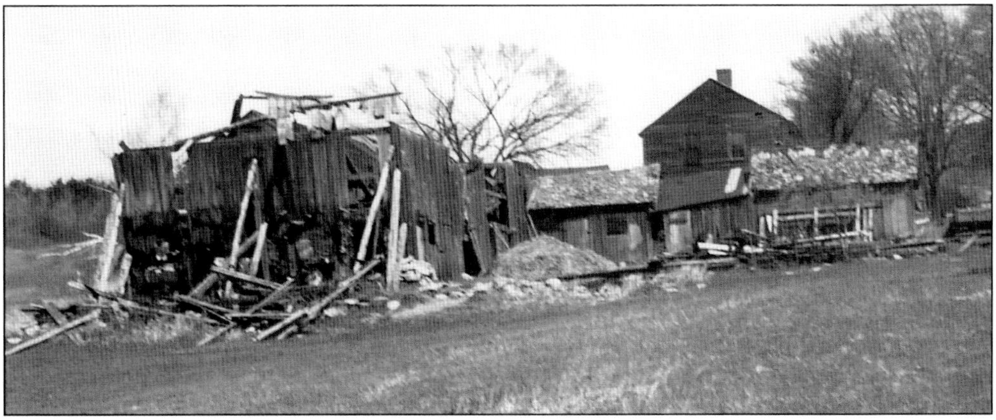

Obadiah Frary Farm, 59 Gunn Road. Mr. Frary married in Deerfield in 1750 and settled in Southampton soon after. According to Sardis Chapman's genealogy records, he was a clockmaker by trade; he also had a stake in the Frary mill. He raised six children in this house. One son, Obadiah, was killed in August 1777 during a skirmish with General Burgoyne's troops. (Keene photograph, 1950.)

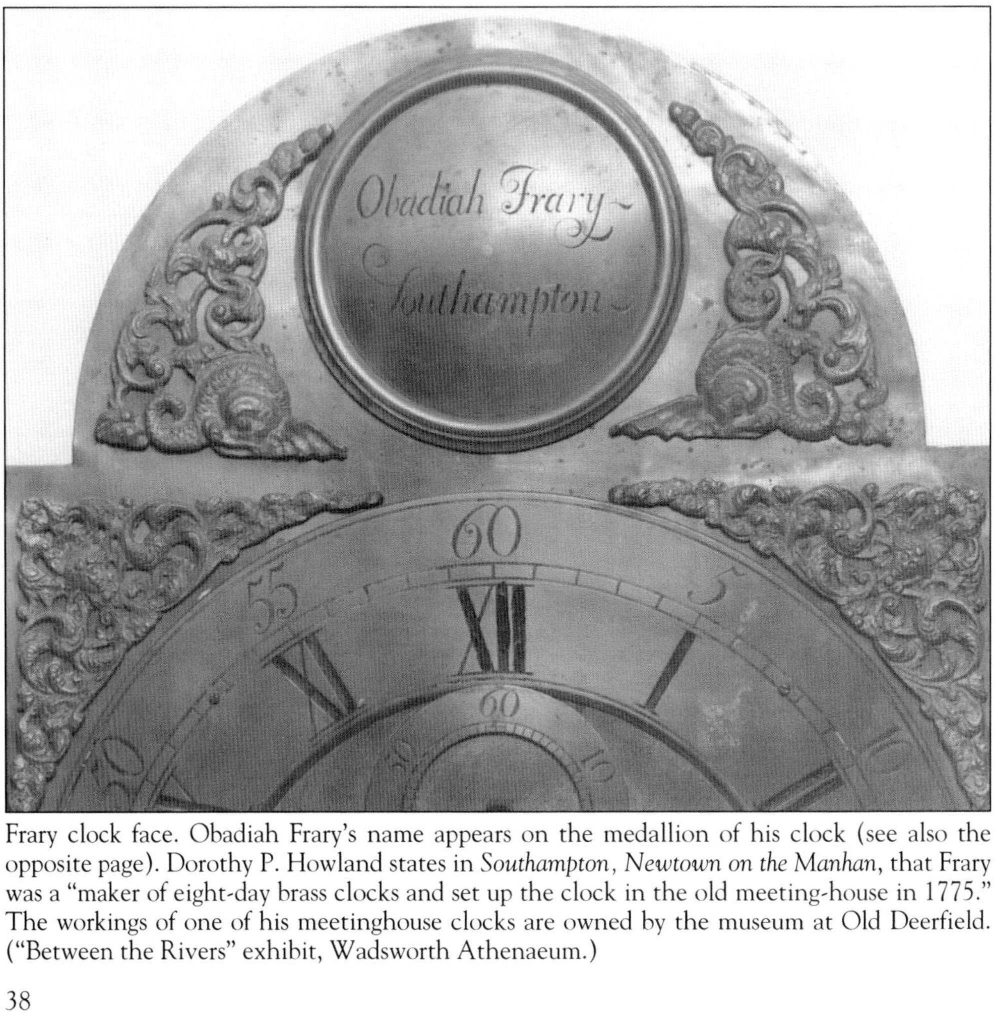

Frary clock face. Obadiah Frary's name appears on the medallion of his clock (see also the opposite page). Dorothy P. Howland states in *Southampton, Newtown on the Manhan*, that Frary was a "maker of eight-day brass clocks and set up the clock in the old meeting-house in 1775." The workings of one of his meetinghouse clocks are owned by the museum at Old Deerfield. ("Between the Rivers" exhibit, Wadsworth Athenaeum.)

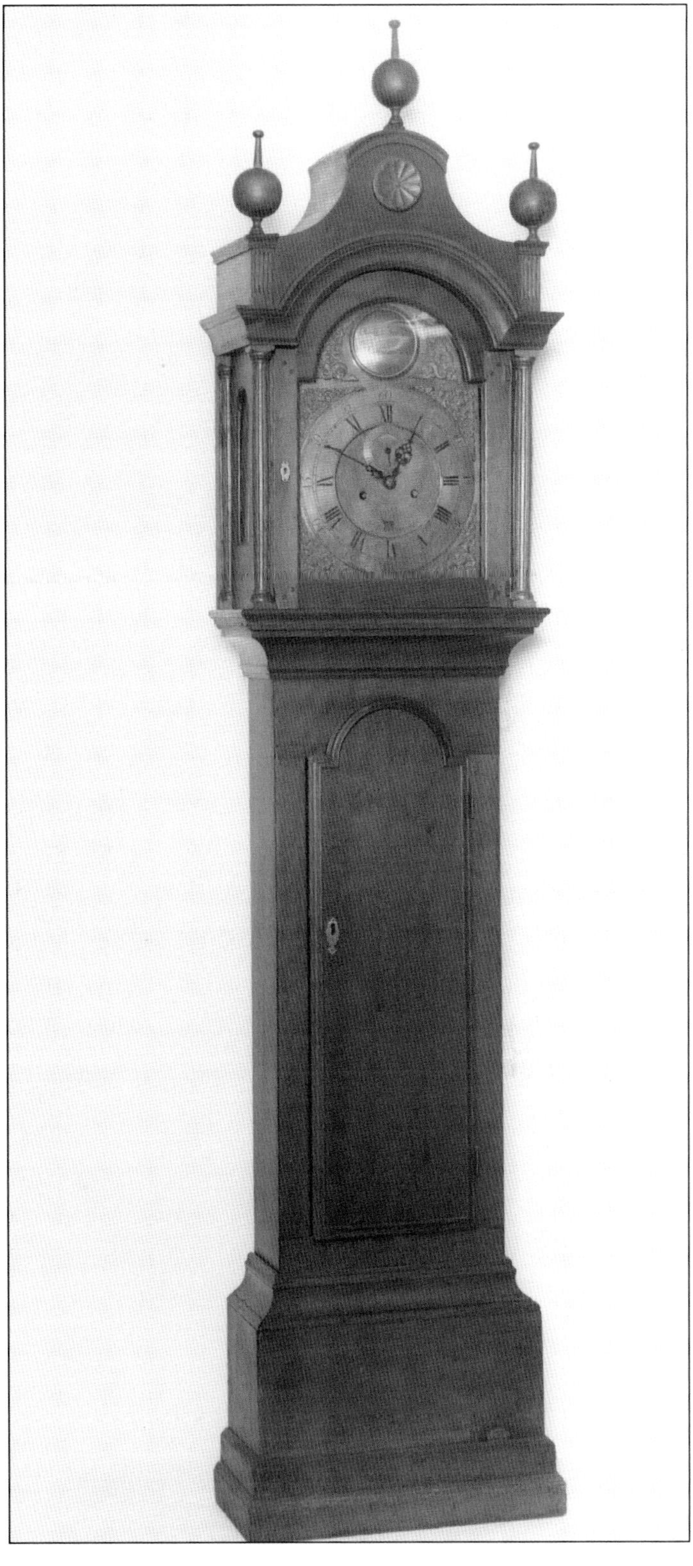

Tall clock by Frary. The works of this handsome clock were made by Obadiah Frary, and, as was the custom, the case was made elsewhere, likely by a local cabinetmaker. Very few of Frary's clocks are known to exist. ("Between the Rivers" exhibit, Wadsworth Athenaeum.)

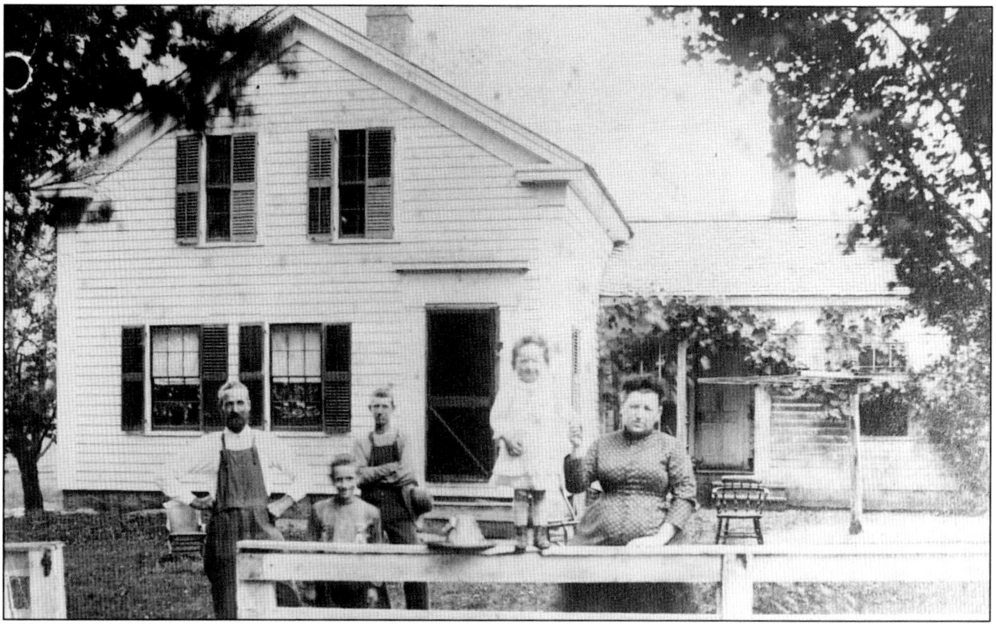

Pease Family Farm, 153 East Street. This 1885 picture shows the Pease family. The farmer is Ashahel, and the boy by the fence is Forrest, father of Raymond Pease. Earlier the farm had been owned by the Spooner family; it has been worked by the Peases for the last 110 years. (Pease photograph.)

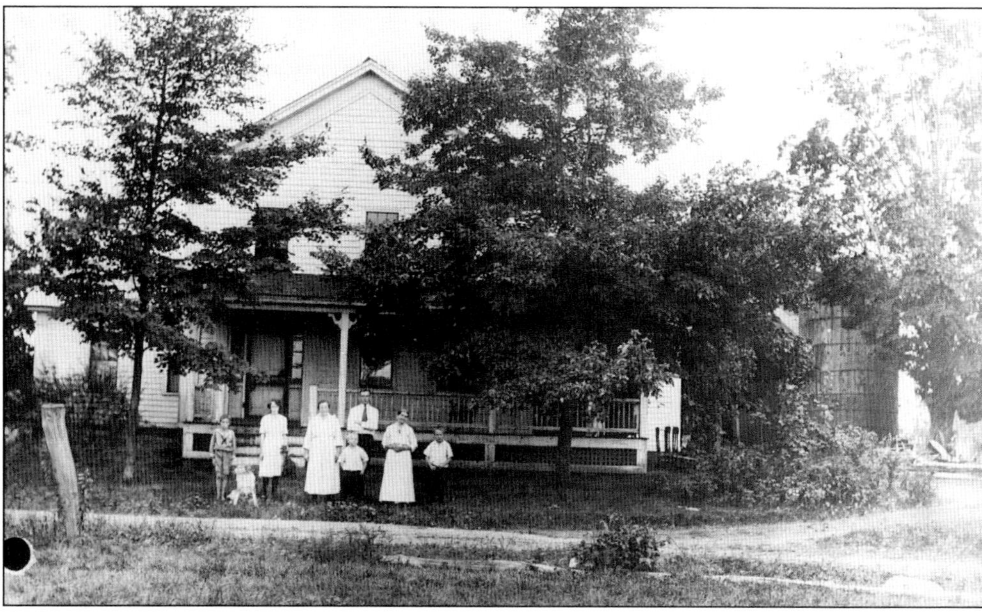

Bashista Family Farm, 160 East Street. In 1920 Jacob Bashista purchased the well-known Spooner Farm. Mr. Bashista stayed on the farm, raising his family here, until passing it on to his son Walter. The farm has been worked by the Bashistas for the last 78 years. In later years the family specialized in apple production, and it was in one of those hillside orchards that Senator Ted Kennedy's plane crashed in 1964. (Pease photograph.)

Three

WEST PART AREA

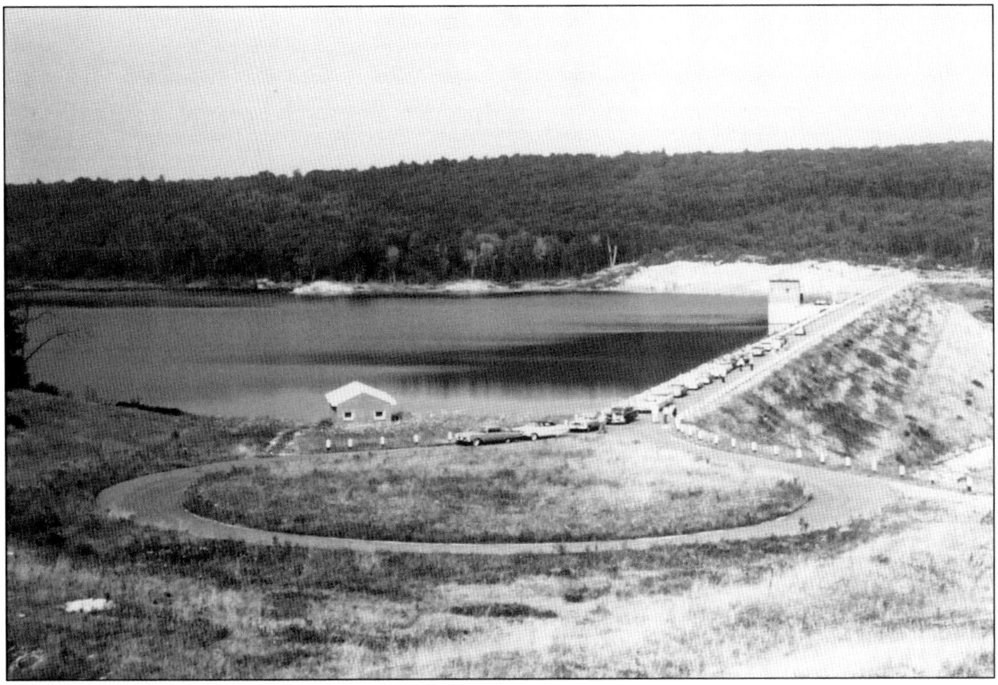

Tighe-Carmody Dam and Reservoir, Manhan Road. In 1898 the Beacon Hill Legislature approved a request by Holyoke to take water from the Manhan River in the West Part of Southampton. After acquiring a few farms and several wood lots, the state built the Foamer Reservoir. In 1912 Holyoke needed even more water, so, after several more farms were taken along with a few hundred more acres, the White Reservoir was constructed. Then in 1953 a repeat of the action of 1912 resulted in the Tighe-Carmody being built. A 400-acre reservoir that buried the original Foamer water supply was created. A prosperous farming community, the West Part, then ceased to exist. Only the cemetery and one dwelling house remain. This photograph was taken on Old Home Day in 1961.

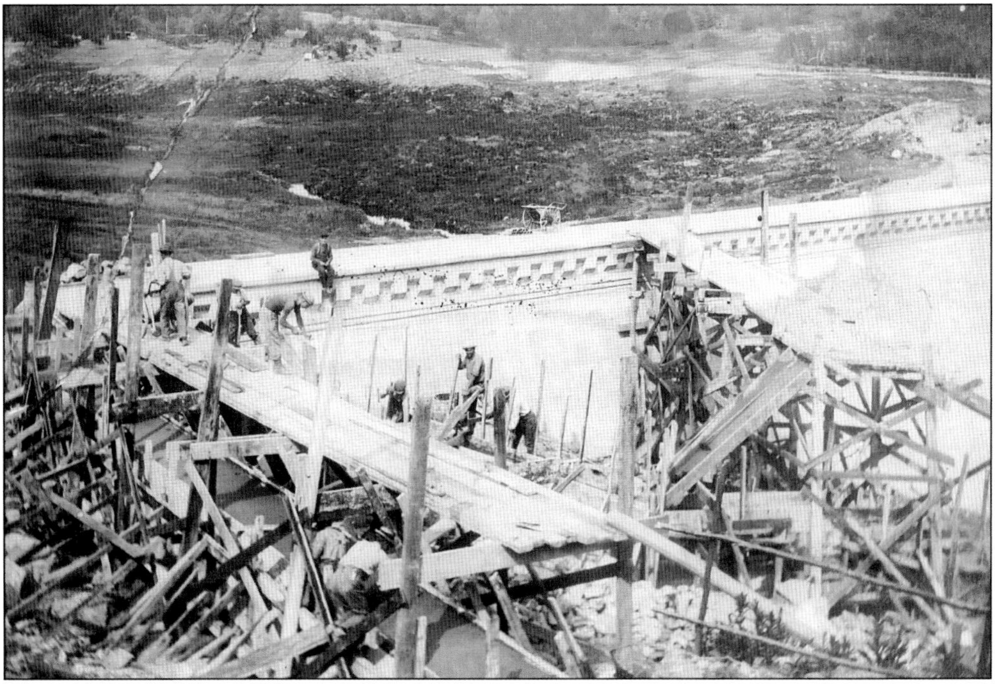

White Reservoir construction, Fomer Road. When this 1912 photograph was taken, dam construction was well underway. Historian Sam Wright's farm appears in the distant background.

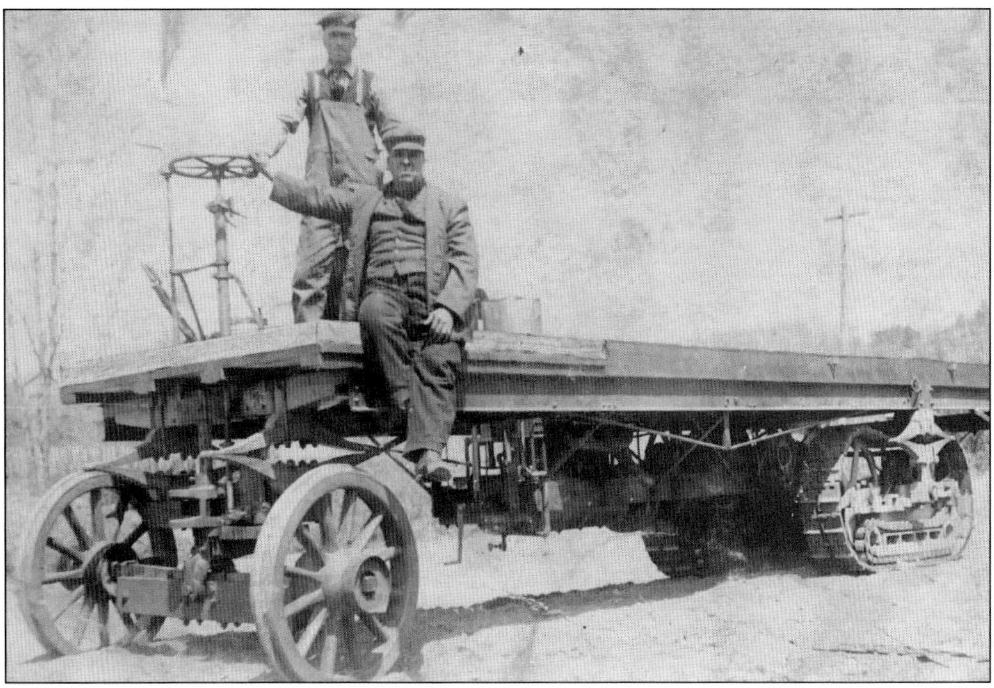

Vehicle of unknown origin, Russellville. Edward C. Searle Sr., who contributed this photograph, likely saw the vehicle during the construction of the pipeline to Holyoke. (Searle photograph.)

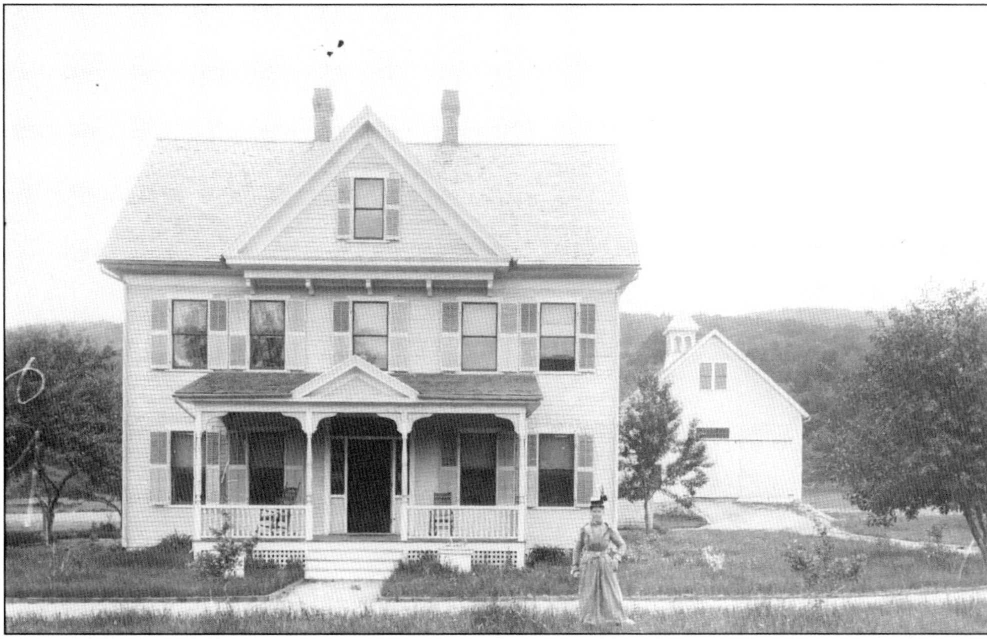

The Holyoke House, Manhan Road. The city built this fine residence for the caretaker's use when the Foamer Reservoir was built. Richard Powers served in that capacity, and his widow, shown here, stayed on after his death. Fire resulting from a lightning strike burned the house after 1939. (Howes Brothers photograph, 1900.)

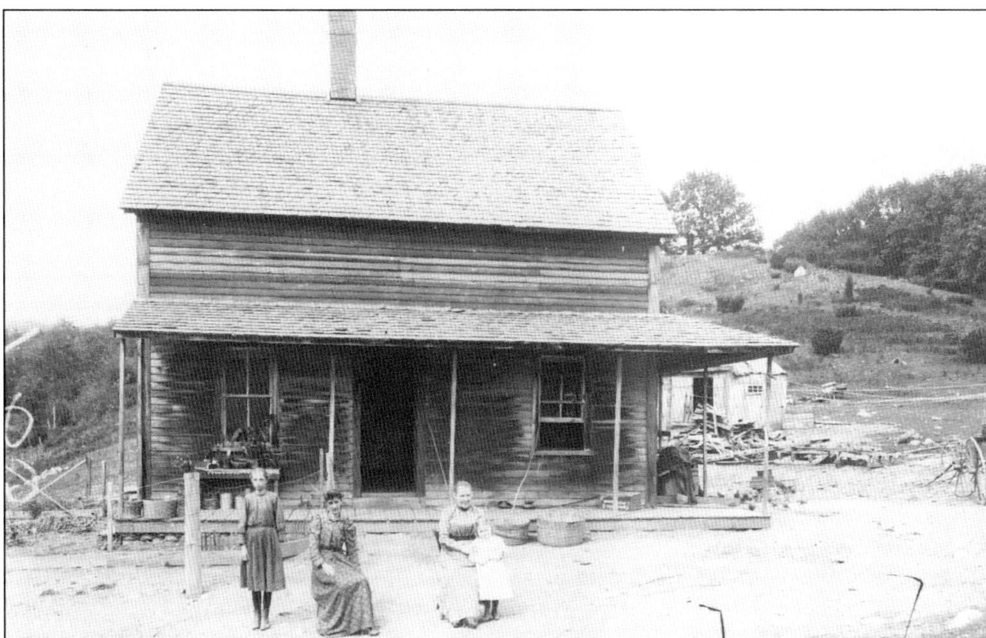

Niels Mink Home, Manhan Road. This property across the road from the Holyoke House was purchased by the City of Holyoke in 1901. Sam Wright's *History of Homesteads* refers to this location as "No. 25." Obviously not all farmers in the West Part were prosperous. (Howes Brothers photograph, 1900.)

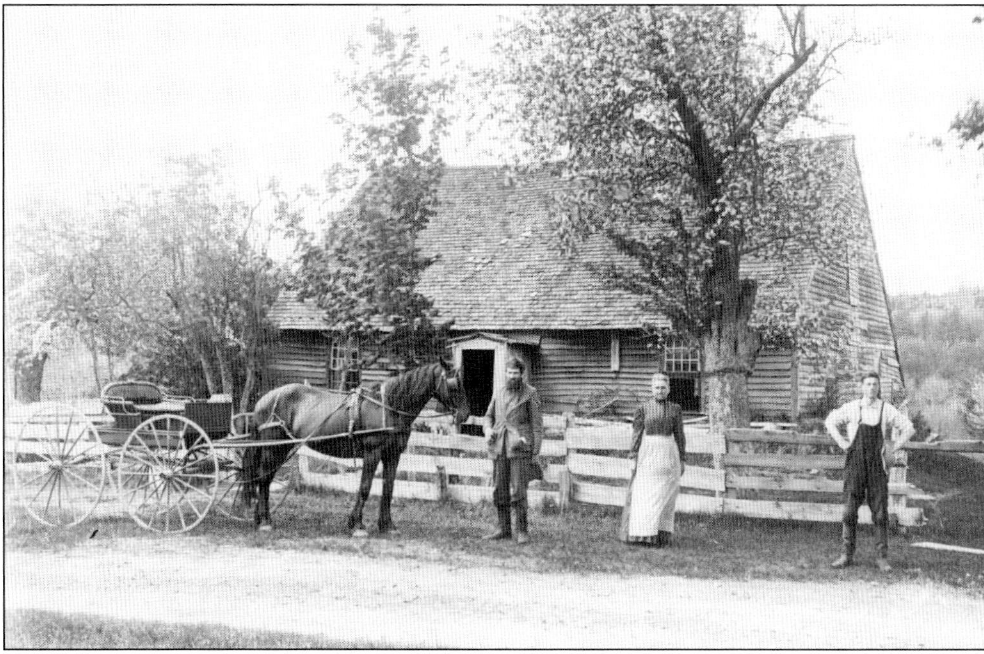

Sam Wright's farmhouse, Fomer Road. Samuel L.T. Wright, West Part farmer turned full-time historian, commenced his *History of Homesteads* in 1881. It was to become a consuming interest. Copies of his unpublished manuscripts are available at the Edwards Library. Shown here is Sam with his wife, Nellie, and their son William. (Howes Brothers photograph, 1900.)

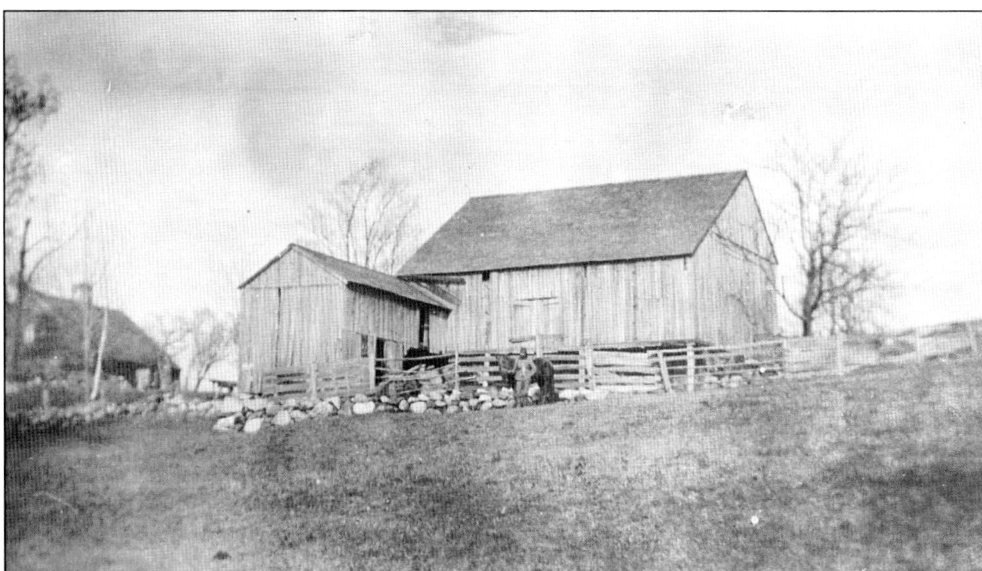

The Wright Barn, Fomer Road. Sam's farm, more picturesque than profitable, was adjacent to the Westhampton town boundary. It met its demise at the age of 130, when the White Reservoir dam was constructed. (Corbin print, c. 1895.)

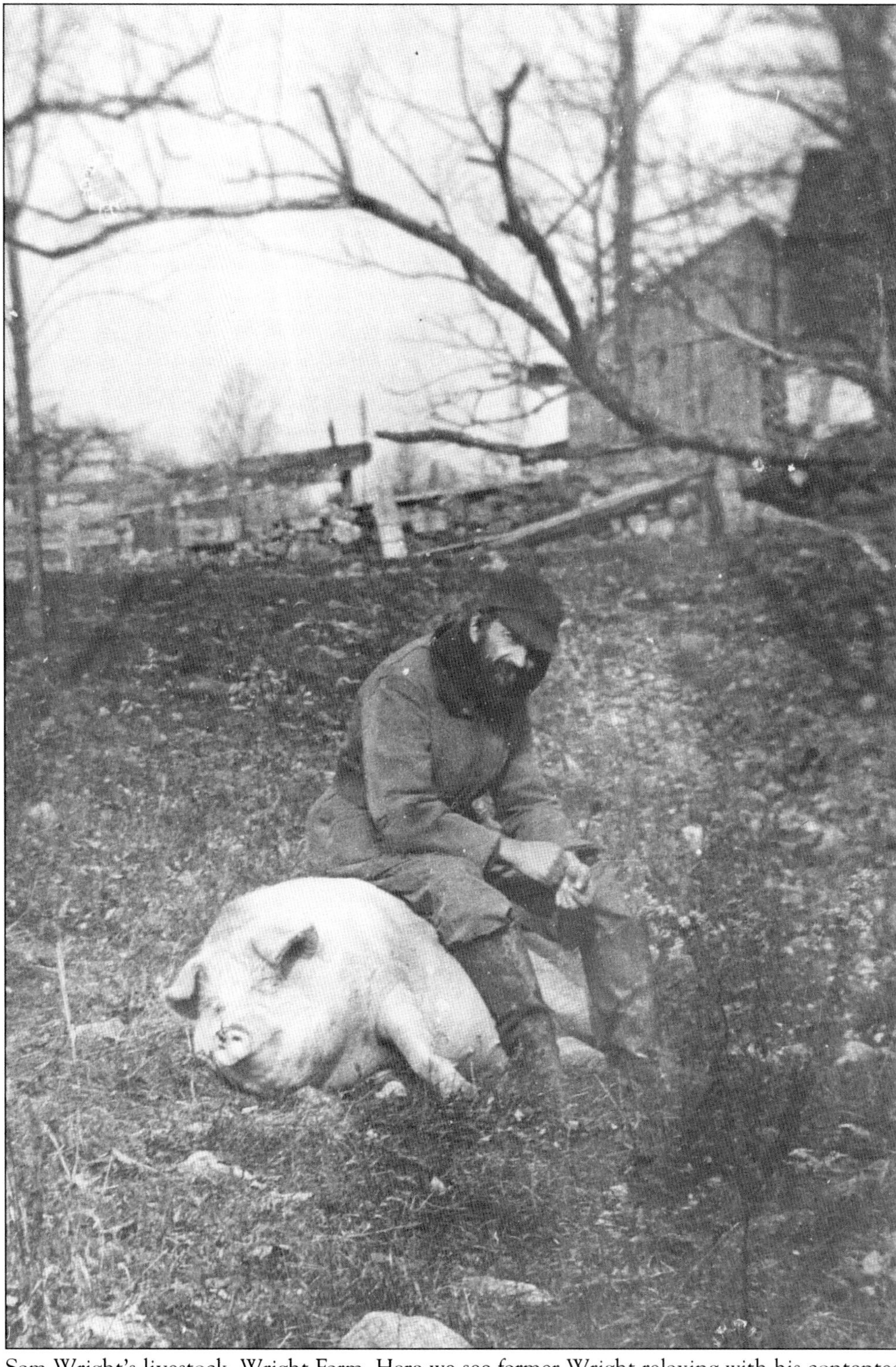

Sam Wright's livestock, Wright Farm. Here we see farmer Wright relaxing with his contented sow. (Corbin print, *c*. 1895.)

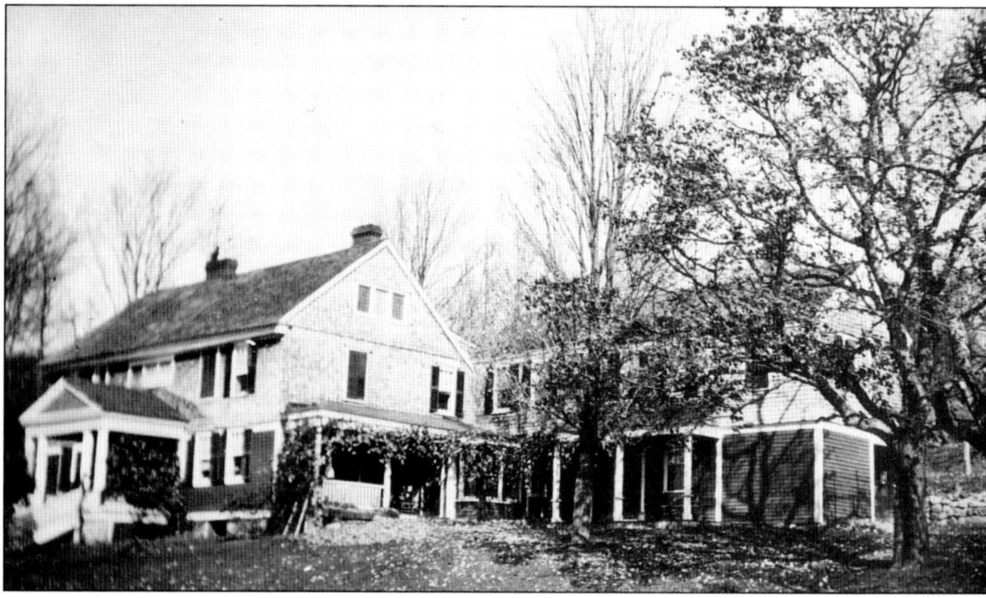

Israel Searle Farmstead, off Fomer Road. This farm's original owner was one of the five sons of Zophar Searle to be provided with a farm. It was passed to his son Wharton, and then to the next generation for a total of 118 years in one family. It was torn down by order of the City of Holyoke in 1931. This is identified by Sam Wright as "No. 30." (Corbin print, *c.* 1895.)

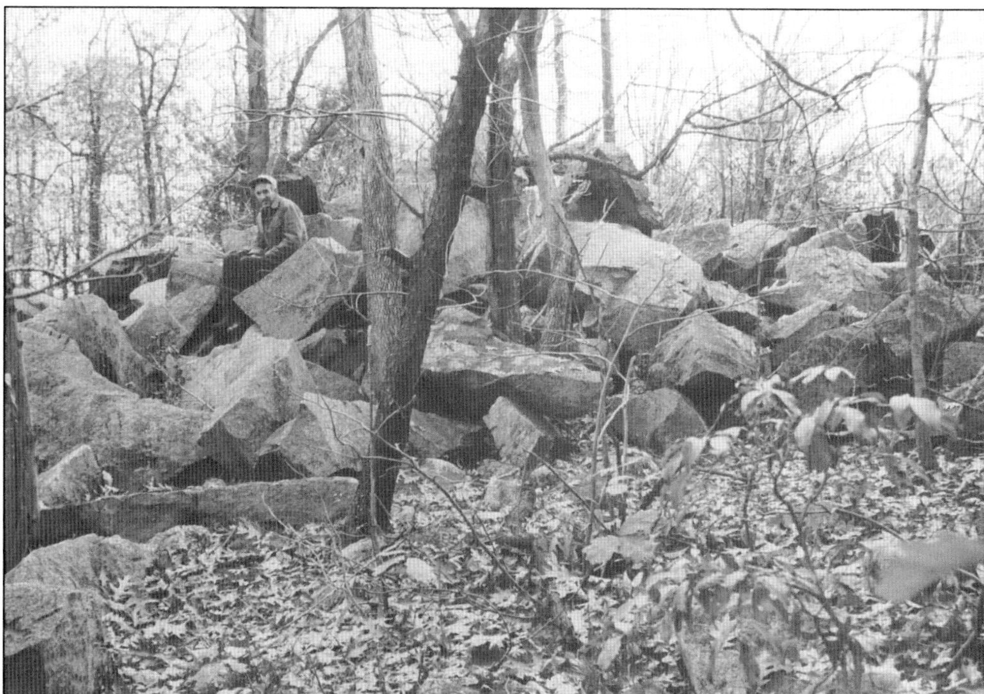

Searle's Granite Quarry off Fomer Road. This old quarry was located above the Searle farmhouse. Sam Wright wrote that it supplied a great deal of granite for the Canal Railroad, so called because it followed the route of the failed canal. (Hendrick photograph, 1960.)

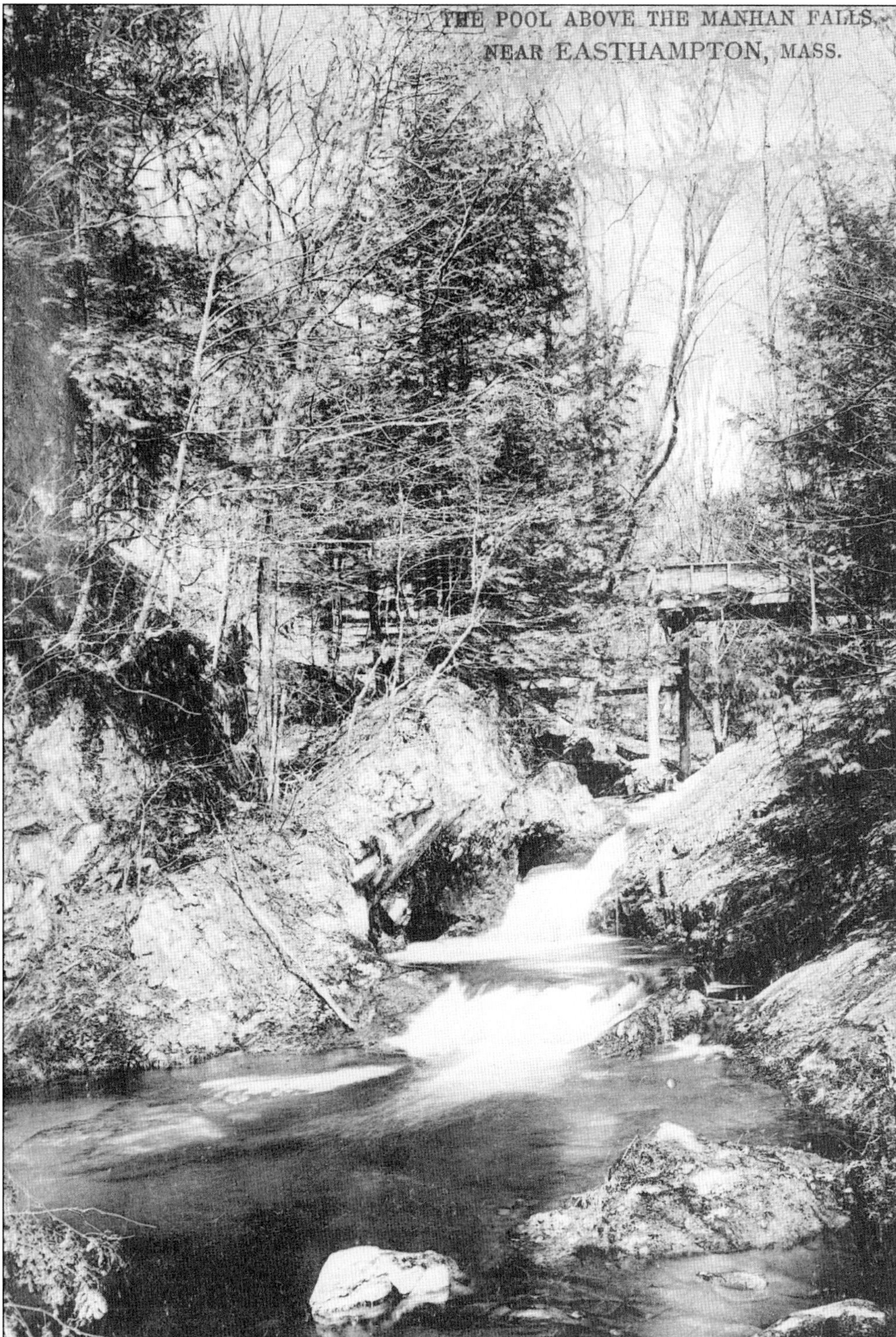

Pool above Manhan Falls, Fomer Road. Shown is the old bridge over the Manhan River below White Reservoir. (Keene postcard, *c.* 1910.)

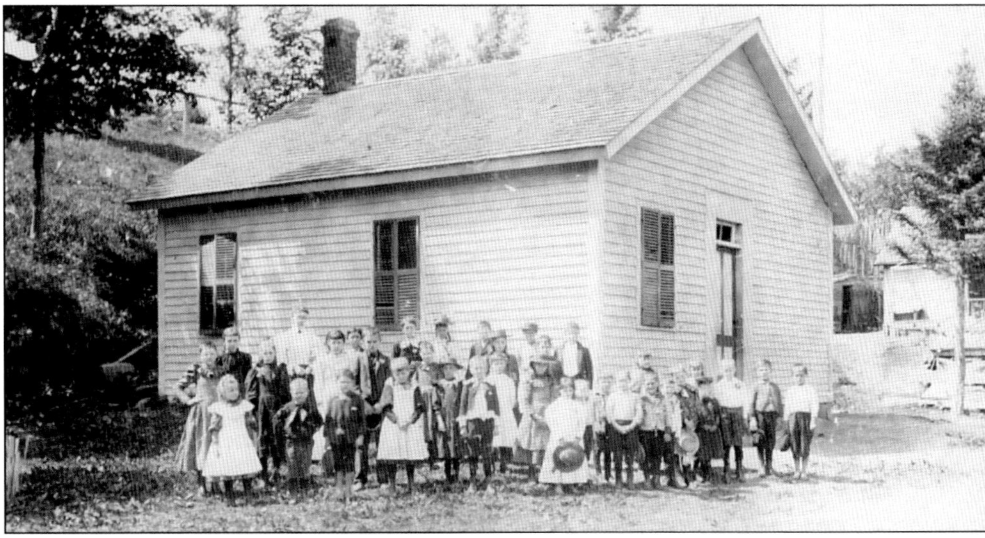

Foamer District School No. 7, corner of Fomer and Manhan Roads. (In recent years the old spelling of "Foamer" was changed to "Fomer.") This old building was remodeled and relocated at least twice during its many years of use. In 1927 the students were transported to the old Sheldon School as the consolidation of schools was begun. (Judd photograph, c. 1895.)

Friday Evening, Feb'y 23, 1877.

District No. 7,

School Exhibition.

PROGRAMME,

Singing.

Declamation: The little Hero, Edward Clark.

Dialogue: Scene between Capt. Tackle and Jack Bowlin.

Singing.

Dialogue: The Rival Speakers, Edgar Bosworth, Edward Clark.

Recitation: Curfew must not Ring to night, Eva Fish.

Singing.

Recitation: Zara's Ear-rings, May Osborne.

Dialogue: Temptation Resisted, Two Characters.

Tableau: Tempted.

Singing.

Dialogue: Taking the Census, Eleven Characters.

Declamation. Arthur Searle.

Reading: Over the Hill to the Poor House, Ida Searle.

Singing.

Reading: Aunt Bethia's Courtship, Eva Fish.

Recitation: Lift him Up, Ida Searle.

Dialogue: Hoiden, Three Characters.

Singing.

School Programme, No. 7 School in the West Part. This interesting dramatic and singing program was planned for February 23, 1877.

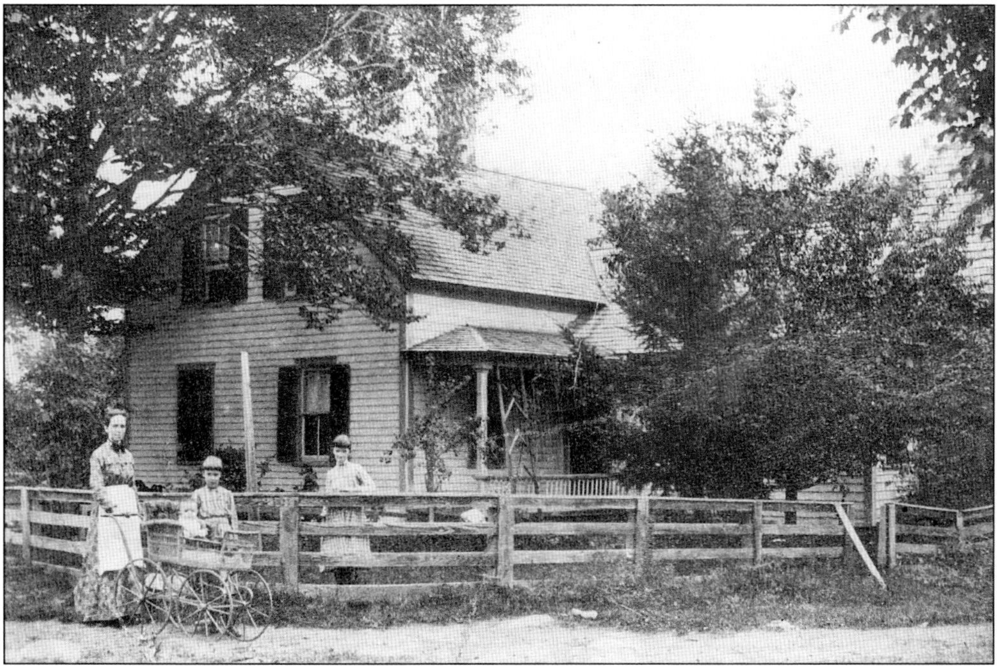

Edward K. Parsons Homestead, corner of Fomer and Manhan Roads. Pictured are members of the Parsons family. Their property was taken by the City of Holyoke in 1898 and the family moved to town. They built a large Victorian house at what is now 46 High Street. This is Sam Wright's "No. 28." (Corbin print, c. 1900.)

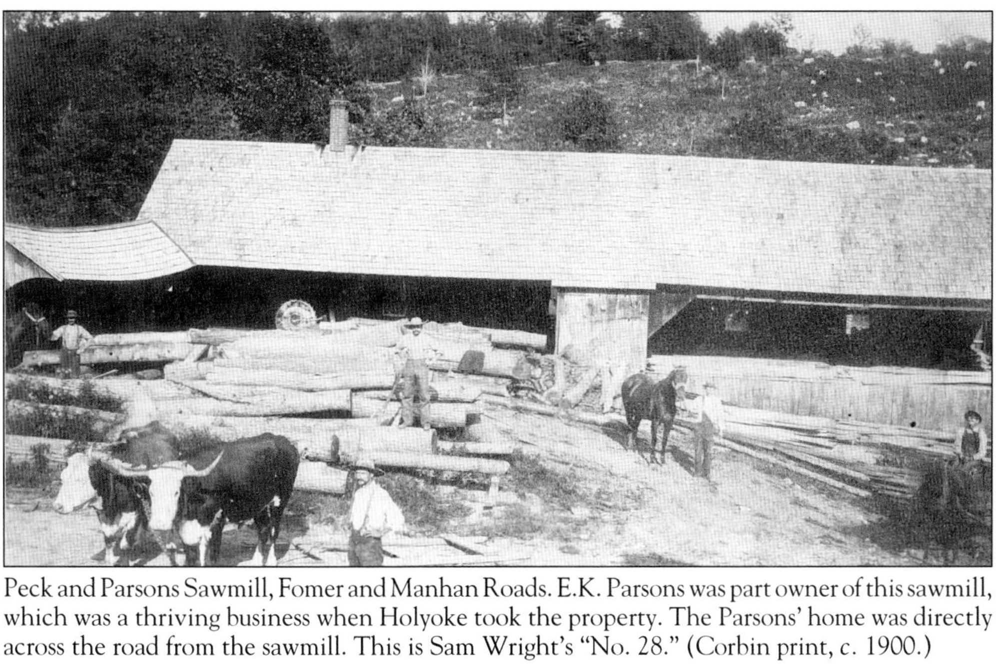

Peck and Parsons Sawmill, Fomer and Manhan Roads. E.K. Parsons was part owner of this sawmill, which was a thriving business when Holyoke took the property. The Parsons' home was directly across the road from the sawmill. This is Sam Wright's "No. 28." (Corbin print, c. 1900.)

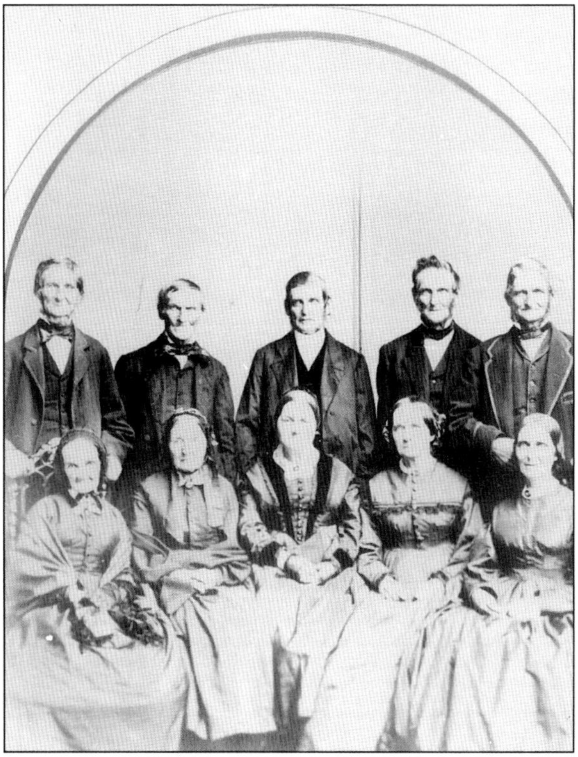

Clark brothers and their wives. These five brothers were born and raised on the homestead, which Sam Wright referred to as "No. 37." The brothers are as follows: Ancel (who migrated to Ohio), Edward (who served as a "six-month soldier" defending Boston in 1814), Noah (who was a tavern-keeper in Westfield), Strong (who stayed at the homestead), and King (the youngest, who became one of the wealthy farmers of the West Part).

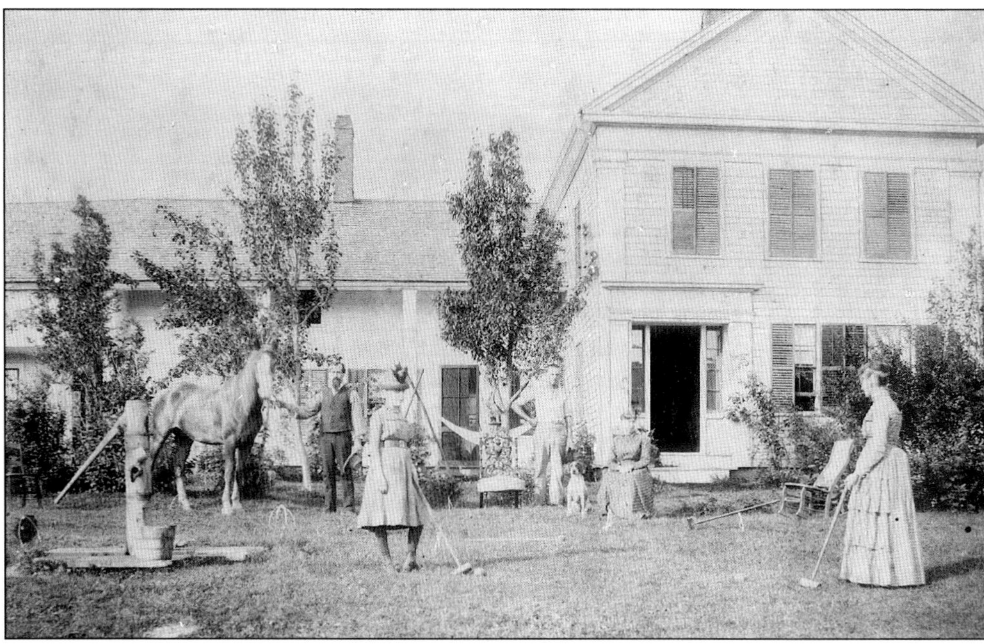

King Clark Homestead, Fomer Road. King, the youngest of the Clark brothers, came to live on this property about 1828. He stayed on to build this house and acquired extensive holdings. He was a fine manager and "owned many cattle and fattened considerable beef," according to Sam Wright. The property was eventually acquired by the City of Holyoke. This is Sam Wright's "No. 26." (Corbin print, *c.* 1900.)

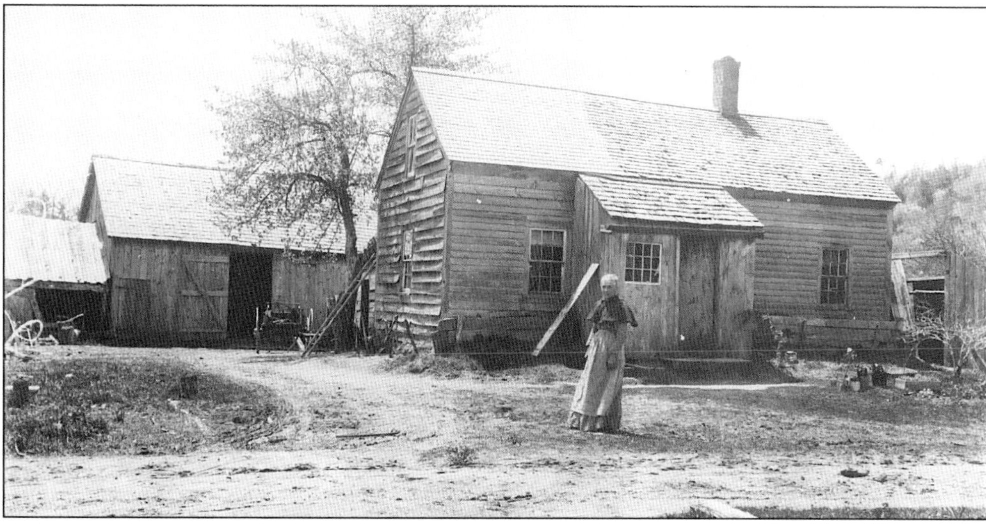

Boshan Home, Breakneck Road. Sam Wright wrote that this small house was built for hired help at the Isaac Parsons House. It was sold to John Boshan sometime after 1884. Mrs. Boshan is seen here shortly before the house was torn down. This is Wright's "No.19." (Howes Brothers photograph, 1900.)

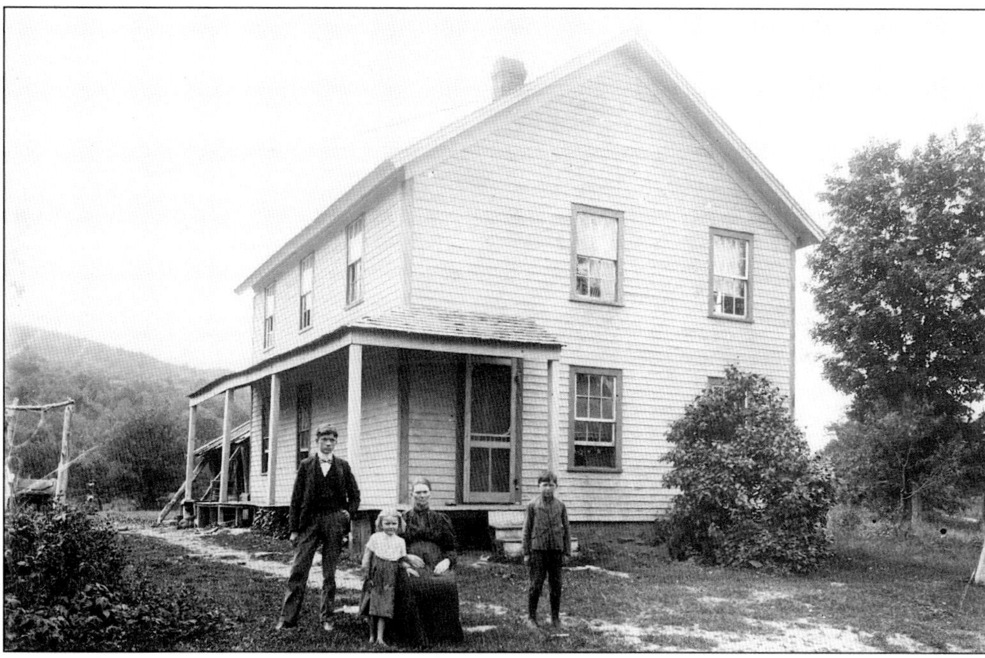

Clark-O'Conner Homestead, Manhan Road. Sam Wright recorded in 1890 that this property had been home to the five Clark brothers (see p. 50). Strong remained in the old house until his death in 1870. In 1883, Larry O'Conner purchased the property and built this newer house in 1886, having lost the old one to fire the previous year. Charles O'Conner, who now lives on Pleasant Street, is a grandson of Larry, and believes these folks to be family members. This homestead, Wright's "No. 37," no longer stands. (Howes Brothers photograph, 1900.)

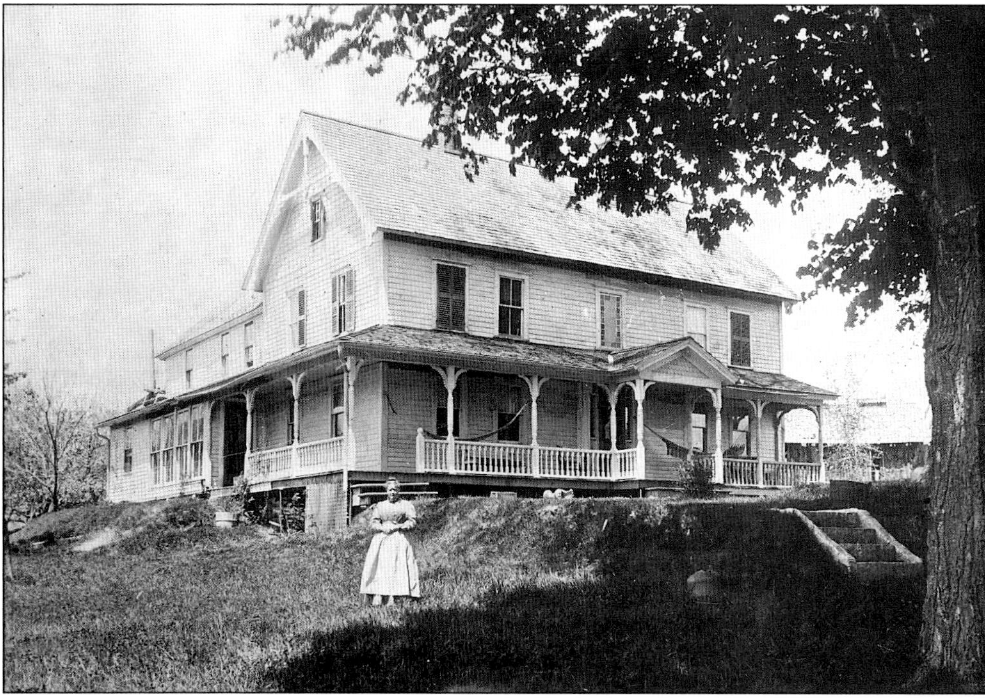

Parsons-Graves Homestead, Fomer Road. Isaac Parsons settled here in 1775 with a holding of 640 acres. He built this house in 1795. Sam Wright wrote that, for the century they resided there, the family was considered the wealthiest in the West Part. Holdings included a cider mill and a brandy still, and today remnants of the large orchards remain. In 1875 Isaac II sold to the Graves family, who occupied the property for 75 more years. This is Wright's "No. 18." (Howes Brothers photograph, 1900.)

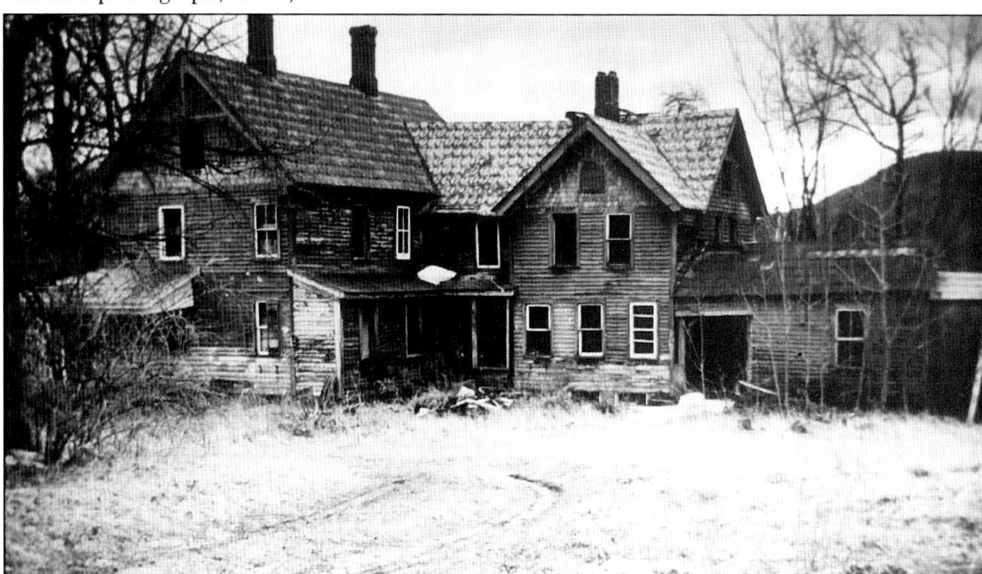

Parsons-Graves "End of an Era," Fomer Road. Most every town has its haunted house. Spooks were thought to inhabit the old Parsons-Graves House prior to its demise in the 1950s. (Hendrick photograph.)

Four

Center Expands

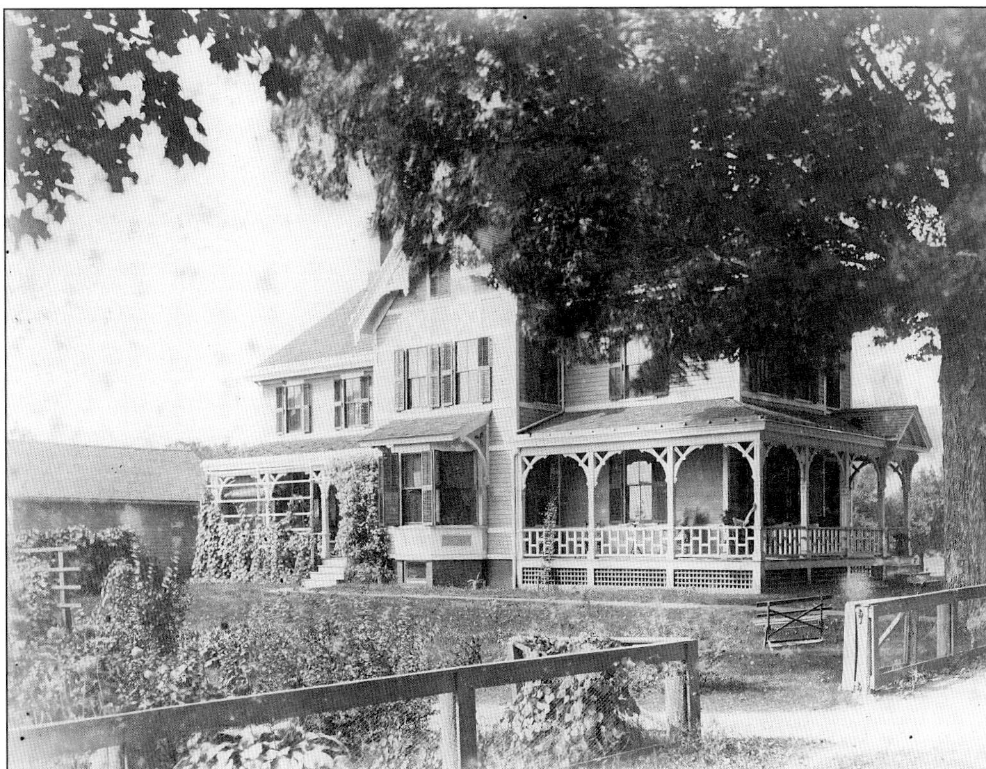

Anson Swift House, 14 East Street. During the 1800s the road we call East Street was called the Holyoke Road. At the same time High Street was referred to as Back Lane, and most public buildings were located on Main Street. The above area was known as the Center and was a desirable place to live. In 1884 Mr. Swift built this handsome home, and in later years it was the home of the Gaskill family. In 1987 the area was designated a historic district, giving recognition to its historic old buildings. This photograph was taken *c.* 1900.

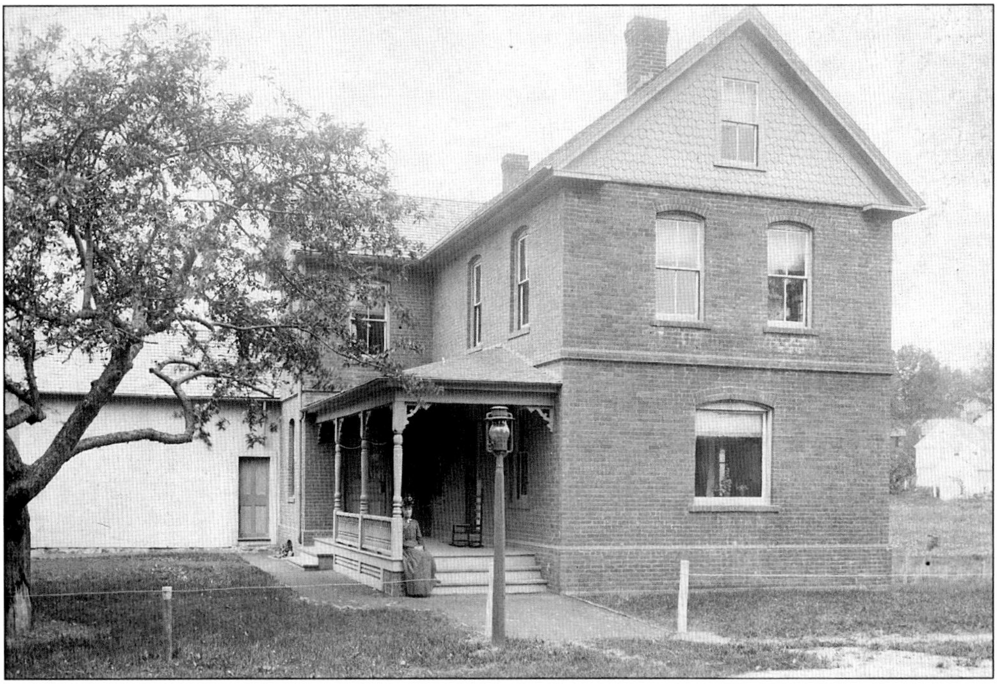

George Clark-Atkins Home, 12 East Street. This brick house with arched window lintels and decorative gable shingles was owned by Mr. Clark, and later Edward Atkins. Mr. Atkins operated a barbershop in the upper level of the barn. (Howes Brothers photograph, 1900.)

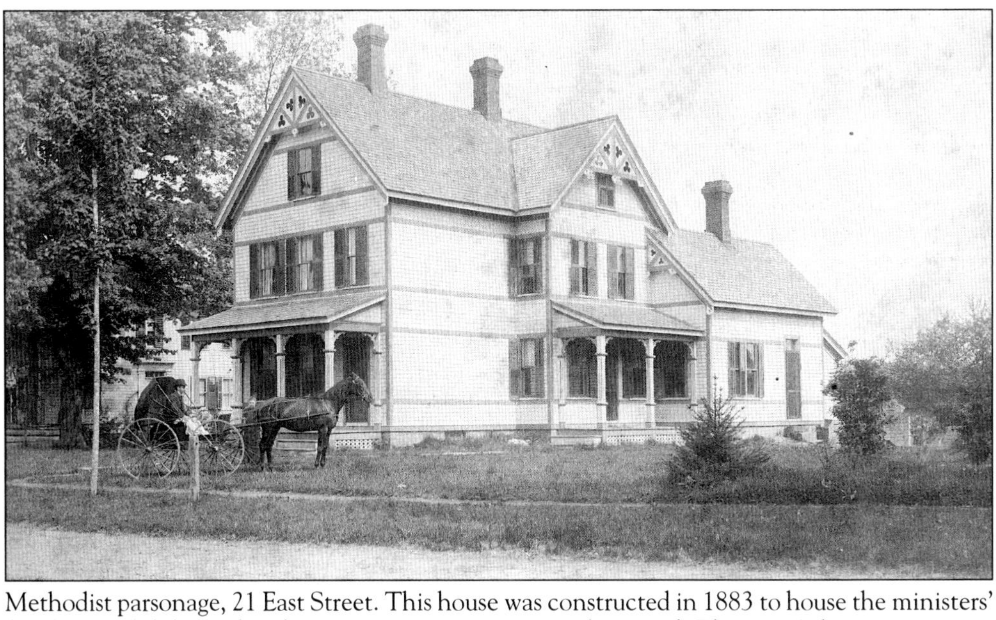

Methodist parsonage, 21 East Street. This house was constructed in 1883 to house the ministers' families, and did just that for 40 years. It is now privately owned. The town's historic resource survey notes that the Queen Anne style is typical of the better houses erected by contractors in the late 19th century. (Judd photograph, *c.* 1895.)

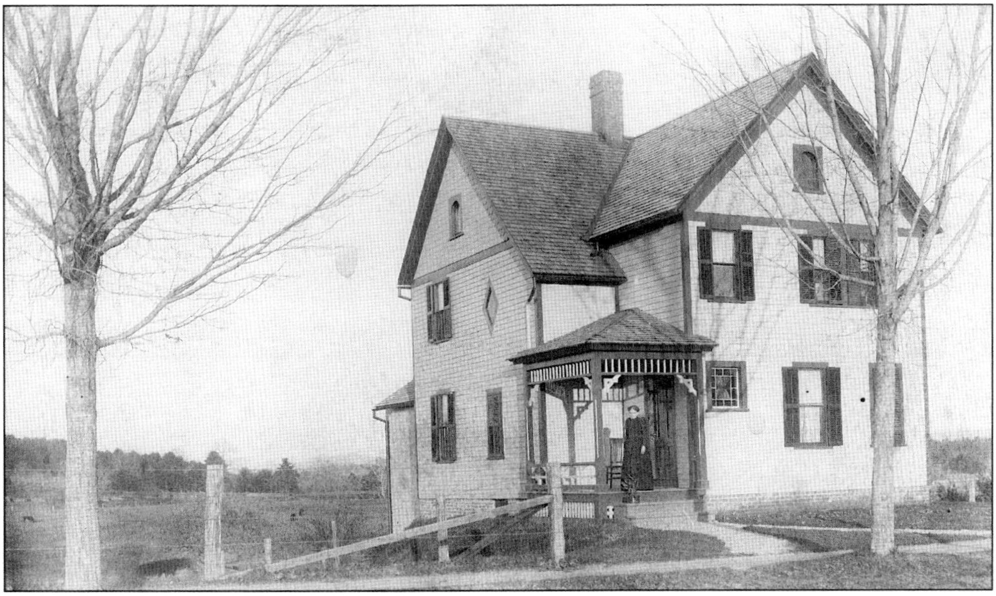

Caroline Edwards House, 11 East Street. The original house on this location burned in 1873. In 1893 Caroline Edwards bought the lot and had the house built. She had lived in Kansas, Colorado, and other parts of the country, and many of her letters to the editor of the *Gazette* were written during that era. Miss Edwards was also the proud owner of the town's first flush toilet. (Howes Brothers photograph, 1900.)

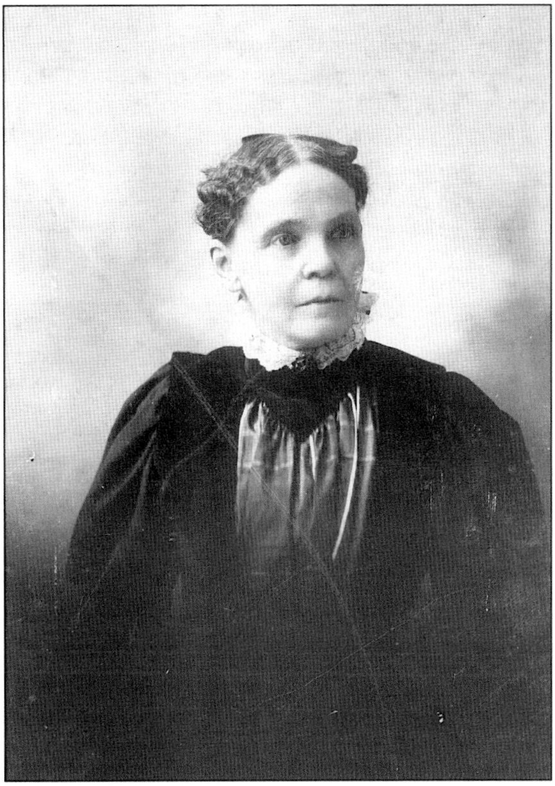

Caroline Edwards. Born in 1833, Miss Edwards was well known for her numerous newspaper articles. Her scrapbooks are perused for local historical information, and her writings are available at the Edwards Library.

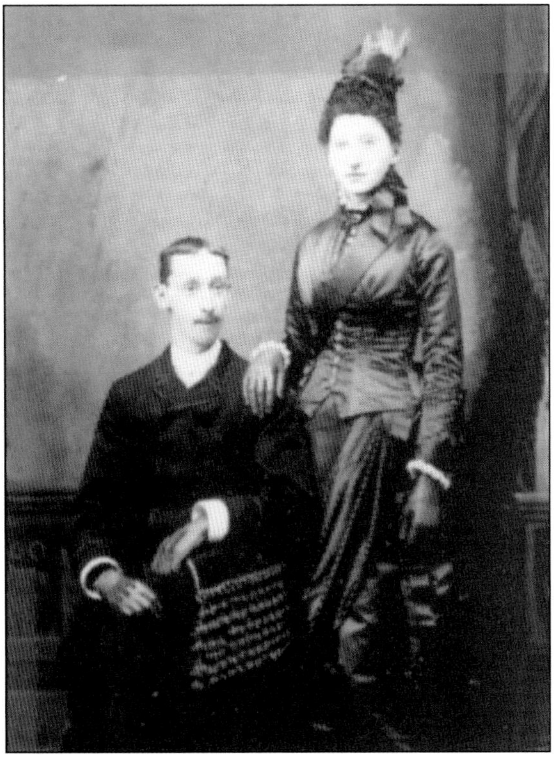

Thanksgiving Day, 1887. Emma Ranger Lyman and Willfred J. Lyman are seen on their wedding day as they embark on 62 years of marital bliss.

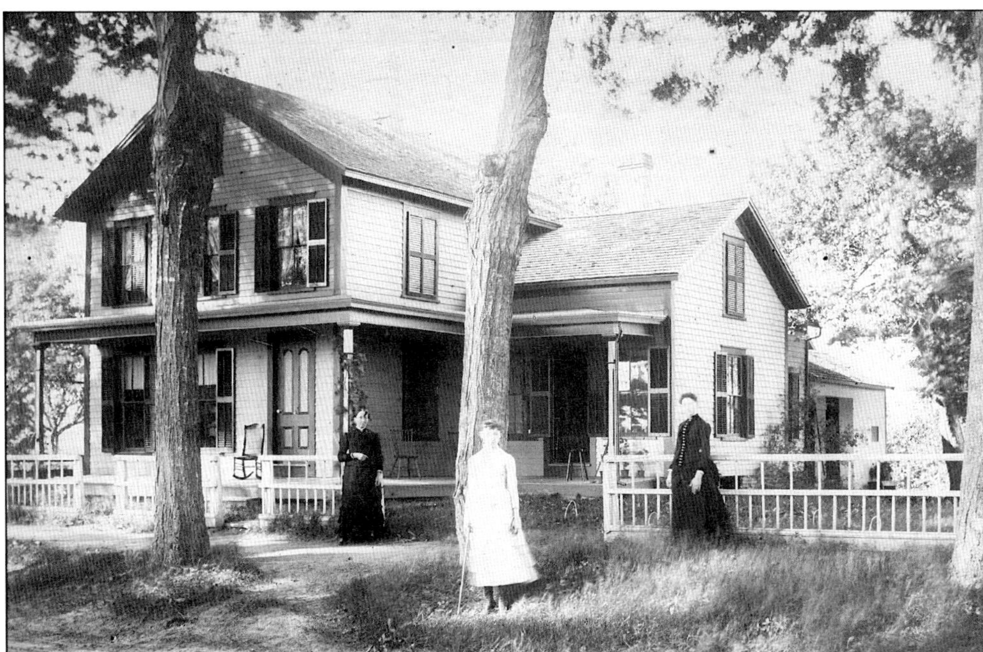

Ranger-Lyman Home, 11 East Street. When Mary Ranger purchased this partially completed house in 1874, she was a recent widow with three young children. She and two of her daughters—Lilla and Emma—are shown in this *c.* 1890 photograph. Emma married W.J. Lyman, and the couple lived in this house for their 62 years together.

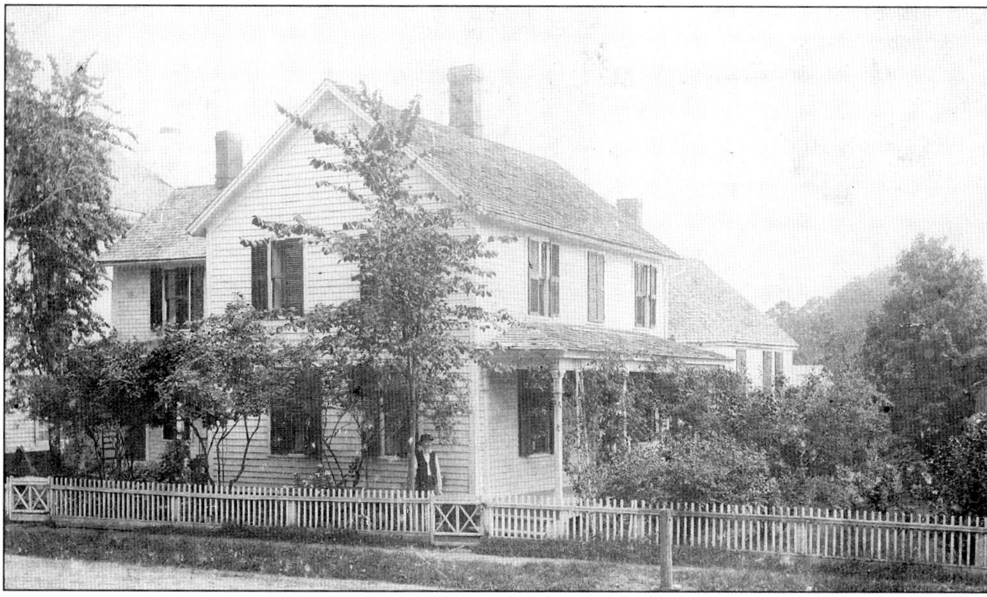

William Boyd Residence, 217 College Highway. The center of town suffered greatly when the disastrous fire of December 1914 spread rapidly through the buildings on the east side of the old Main Street. This building was completely burned, along with the Methodist church building next door. (Judd photograph, *c.* 1895.)

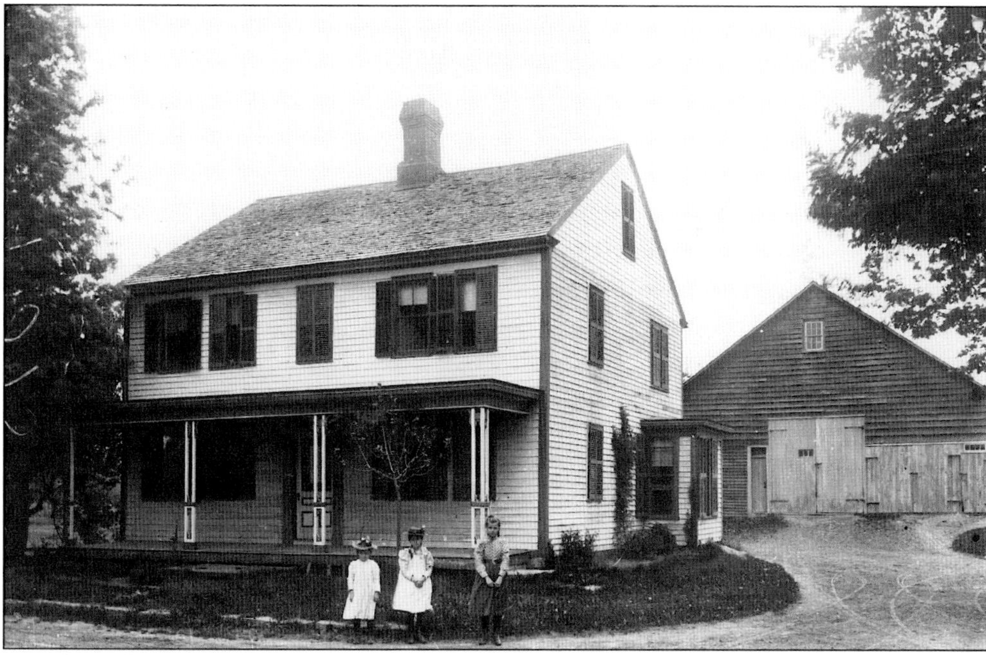

Dr. Blair-Edward Clark House, 231 College Highway. It appears that the first owner of this house was the town's second doctor, but records are not entirely clear. After being owned by at least two other families, it was purchased by Edward Clark in 1906. Most of the land that surrounded this farm now comprises Conant Park. (Howes Brothers photograph, 1900.)

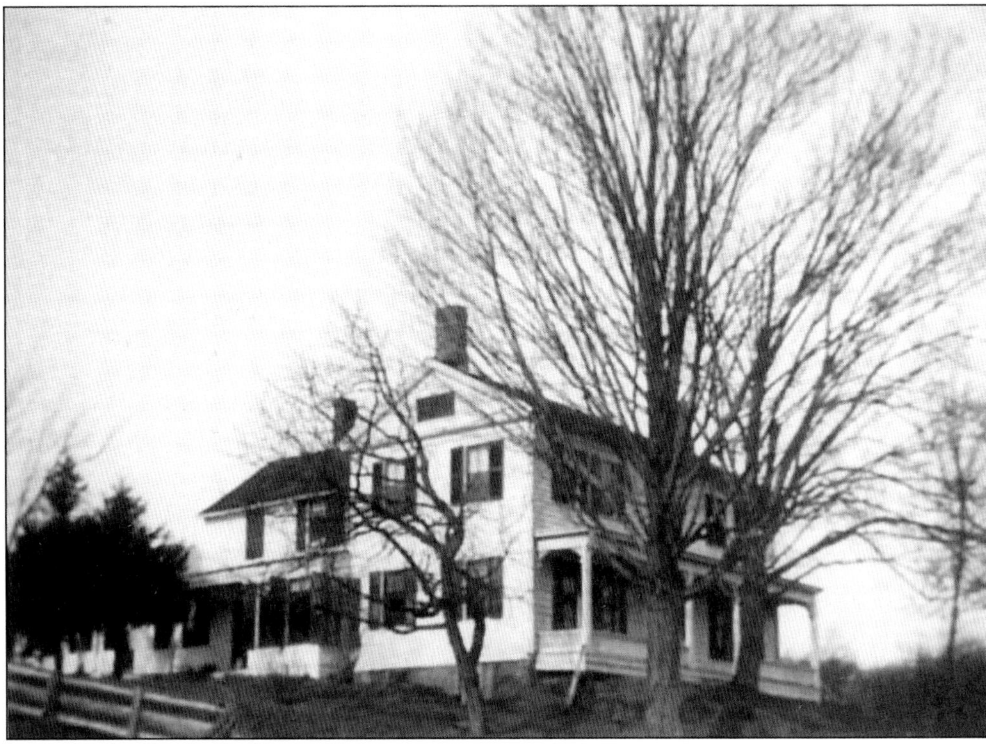

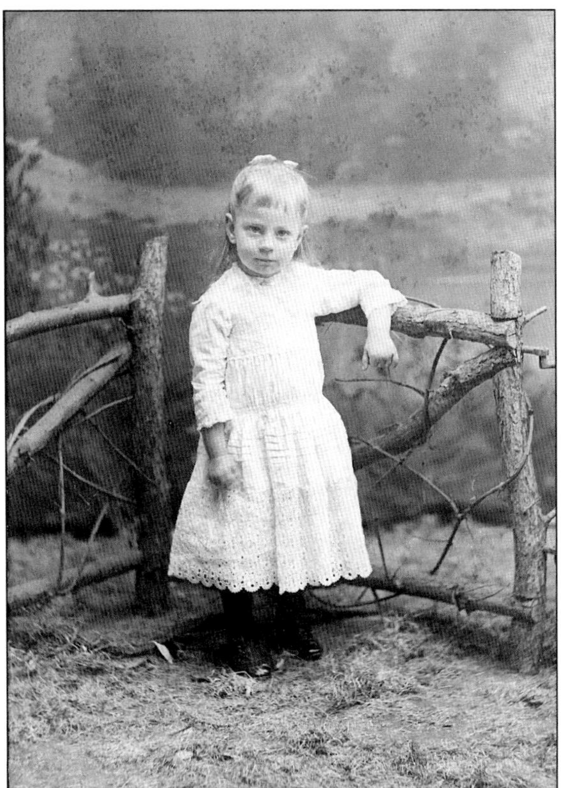

Wolcott-Tiffany House, 68 High Street. Stephen Wolcott purchased the lot in 1813, and in 1868 Lyman Tiffany acquired the property. After his death it was inherited by his son Charles and daughter Ella, and eventually Charles's daughter Ethel was alone in the old house. Rarely does one see a home as untouched by time as this one; furnishings remained in place for many years. The seven-piece parlor set, which still remained in the parlor, was purchased at the household auction by the historical society. (Tiffany photograph, *c.* 1910.)

Ethel Tiffany at two and a half years. When she died in 1980, the house had belonged to the Tiffanys for 112 years. Many of her childhood toys were still in the house and her wicker doll carriage, wooden doll cradle, and several miniature playthings were given to the Clark-Chapman House. This photograph was taken in 1887.

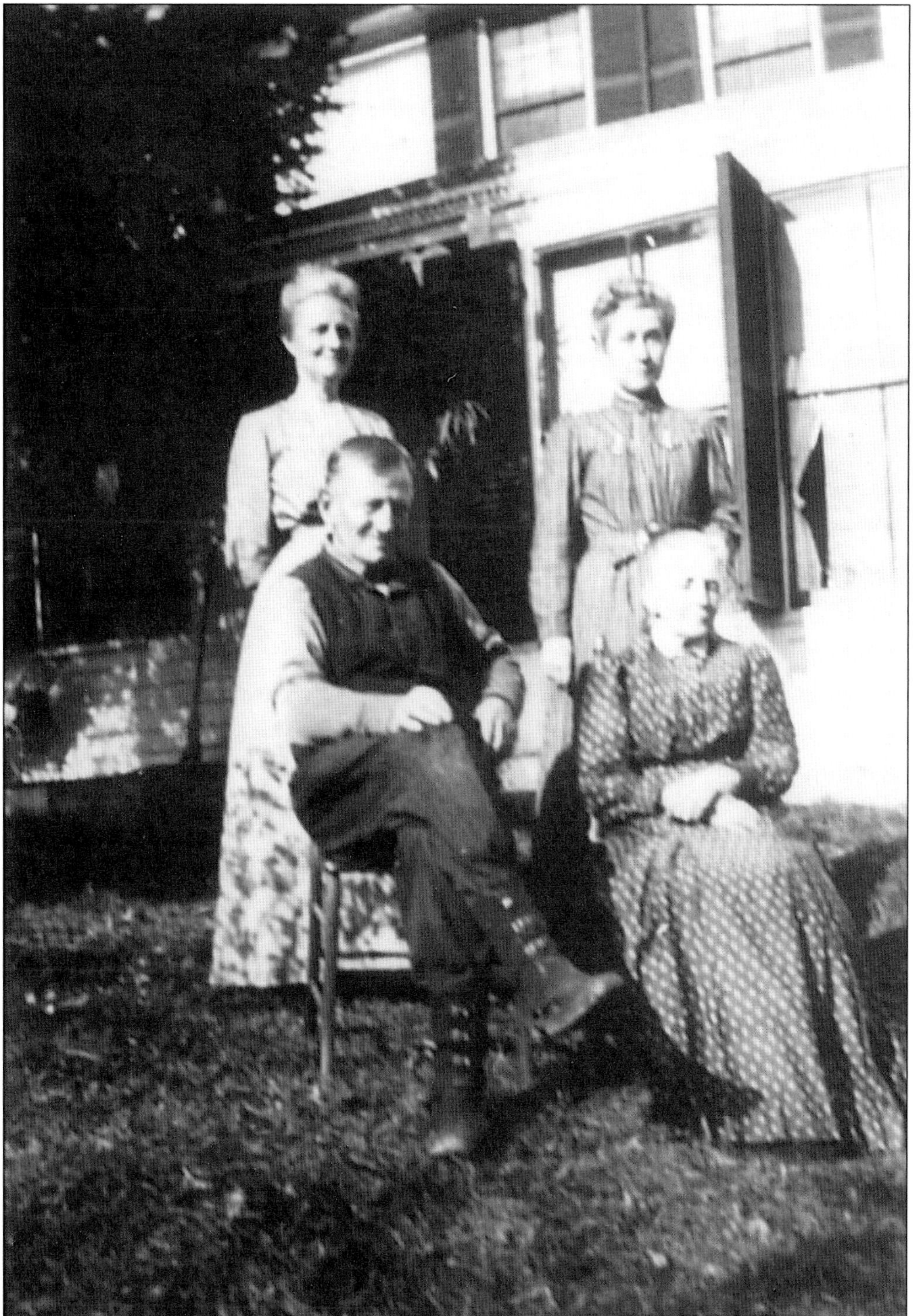

Tiffany family at home, 68 High Street. Seated are Charles and his wife, Kate (parents of Ethel). The older lady standing in the rear is Charles's sister Ella; Ethel stands to Ella's left. (Tiffany photograph, c. 1910.)

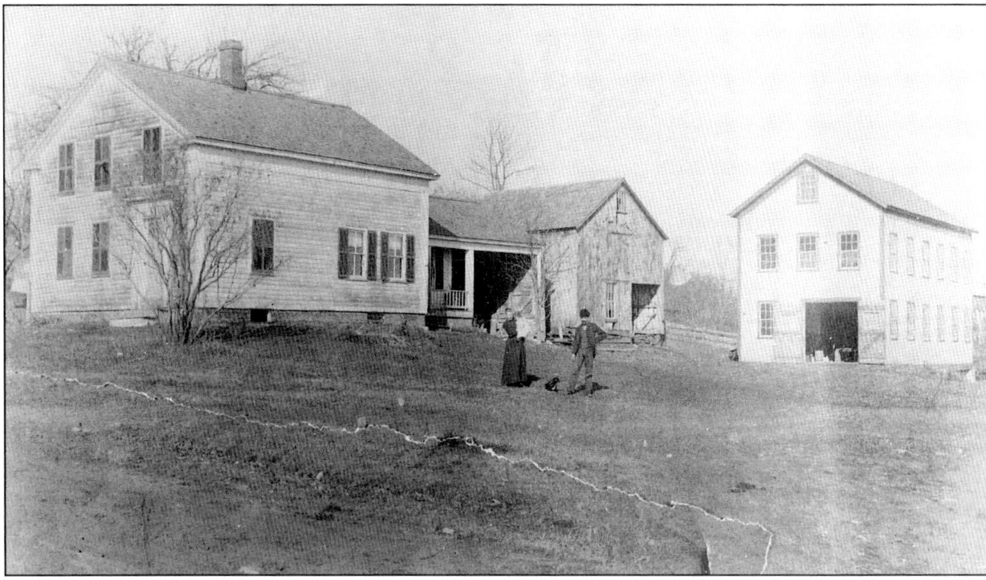

Simeon Sheldon House, 40 High Street. In 1854 Mr. Sheldon built this house to be used as a Methodist parsonage. A later owner, Charles Leonard, who purchased the land and buildings in 1883, was a wagon painter and his shop can be seen to the right in the picture. The building was owned by Mahlon Sheldon from 1911 to 1938 and many old-timers still refer to it as the Sheldon House. This picture was taken *c.* 1885.

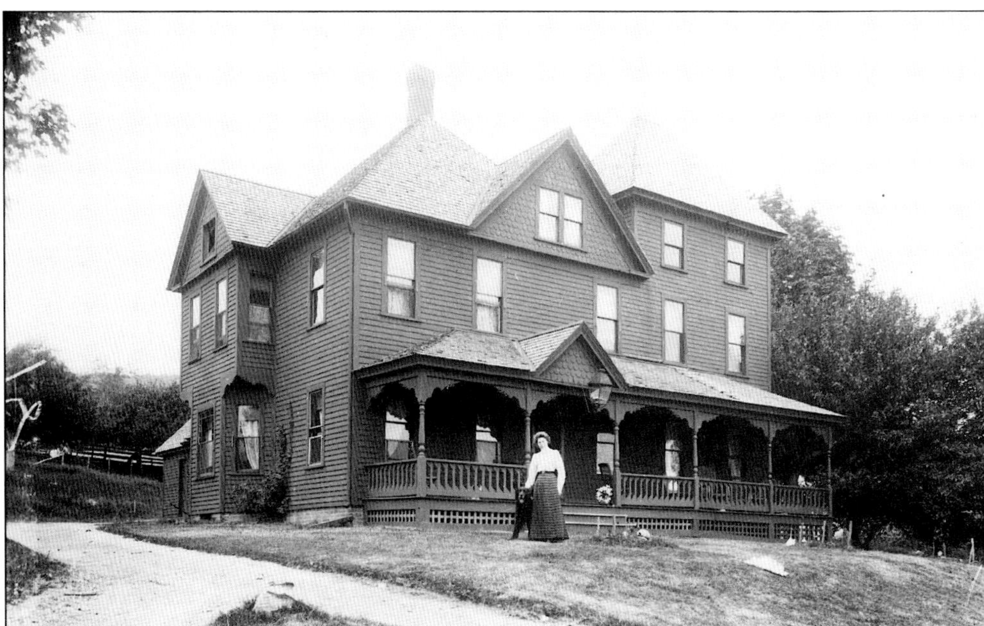

Sewell Hobbs House, 56 High Street. Mr. Hobbs was a well-known entrepreneur whose businesses were located in Holyoke. As a hostler he ran a livery stable, and later he was a restaurateur and caterer. His house was noted as one of three High Street showplaces. It was consumed by fire in 1915. (Howes Brothers photograph, 1900.)

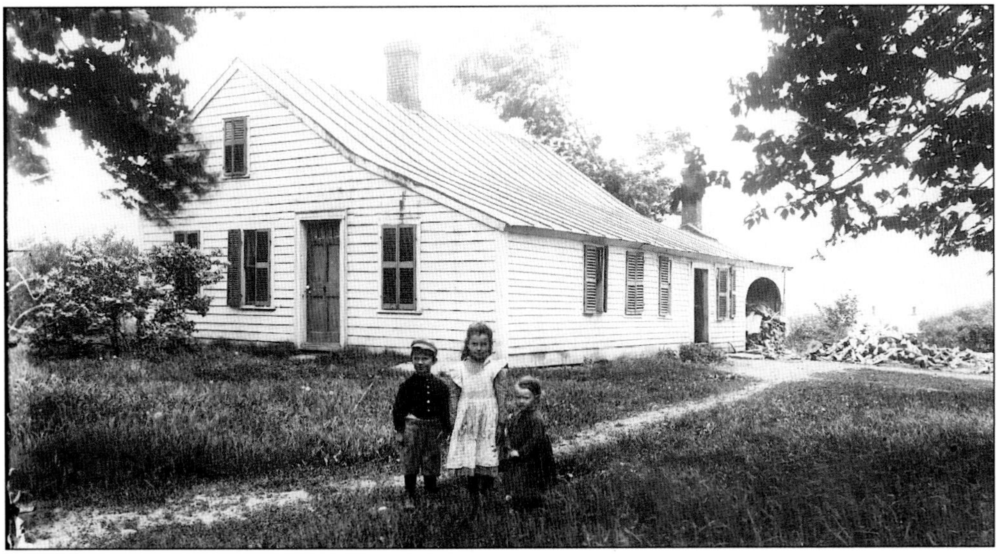

Norris Family Home, 73 High Street. When John Norris purchased this property in 1893 there were already 14 previously listed owners. Norris was employed as a boss on the New York, New Haven, and Hartford Railroad. His six children were raised here and in 1930 the house was enlarged. One son, Edward, was the highway superintendent, and George had a dental practice in Westfield for many years. William became the principal of the Norris School, which was named in his honor. (Howes Brothers photograph, 1900.)

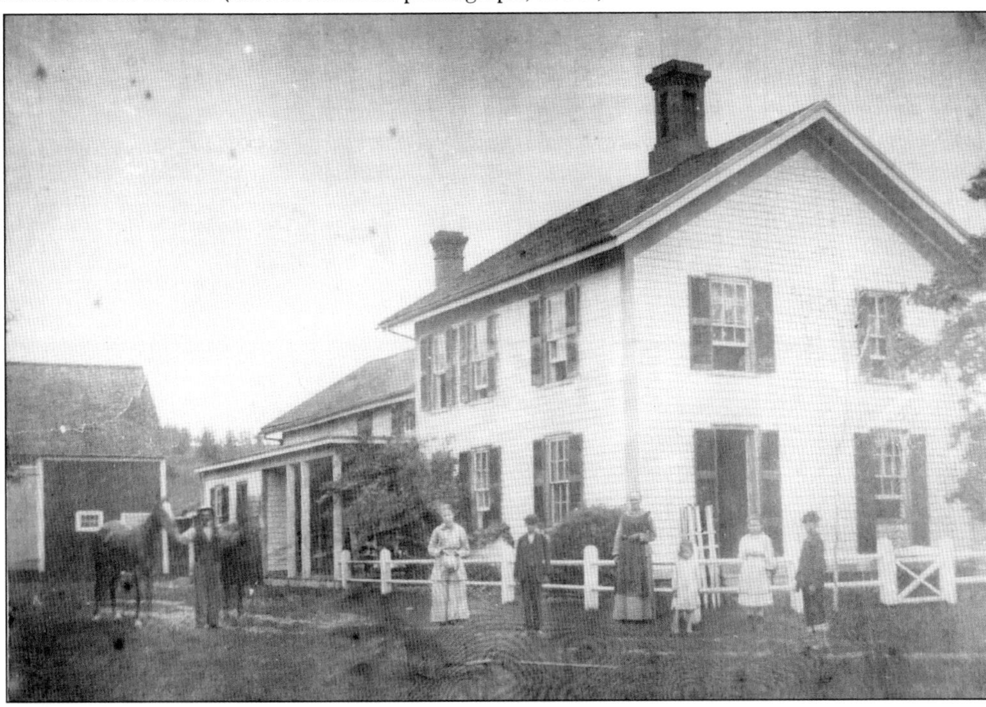

Zopher Searle-Foley House, 68 High Street. Through the years this house experienced many changes as owners adapted it to fit their needs. Mr. Searle acquired it in 1831 and after a series of owners the Foley family lived here when this picture was taken. In later years the Beach family owned the property. (Foley photograph, *c.* 1900.)

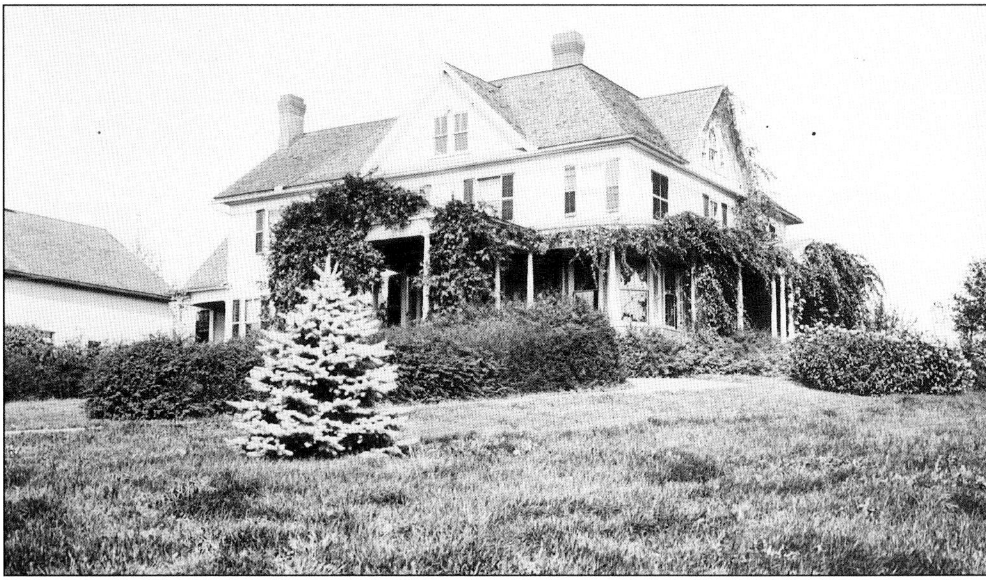

Swasey Mansion, 72 High Street. Edward R. Swasey acquired this choice piece of land in 1901. He went on to build this spectacular house, which he shared with his wife, Mitta Piper Swasey. Presumably his wealth was inherited from a Civil War leather business. (Swasey photograph, *c.* 1913.)

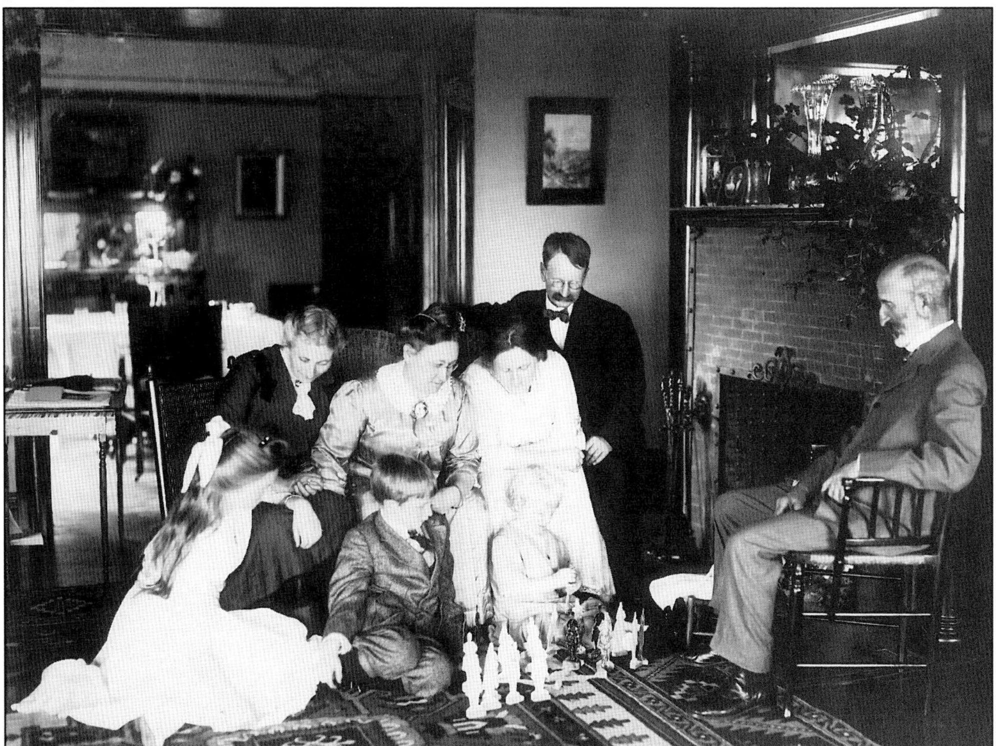

Family gathering in the mansion. Mr. and Mrs. Edward Swasey appear with members of the Piper and Parsons families. (Swasey photograph, *c.* 1913.)

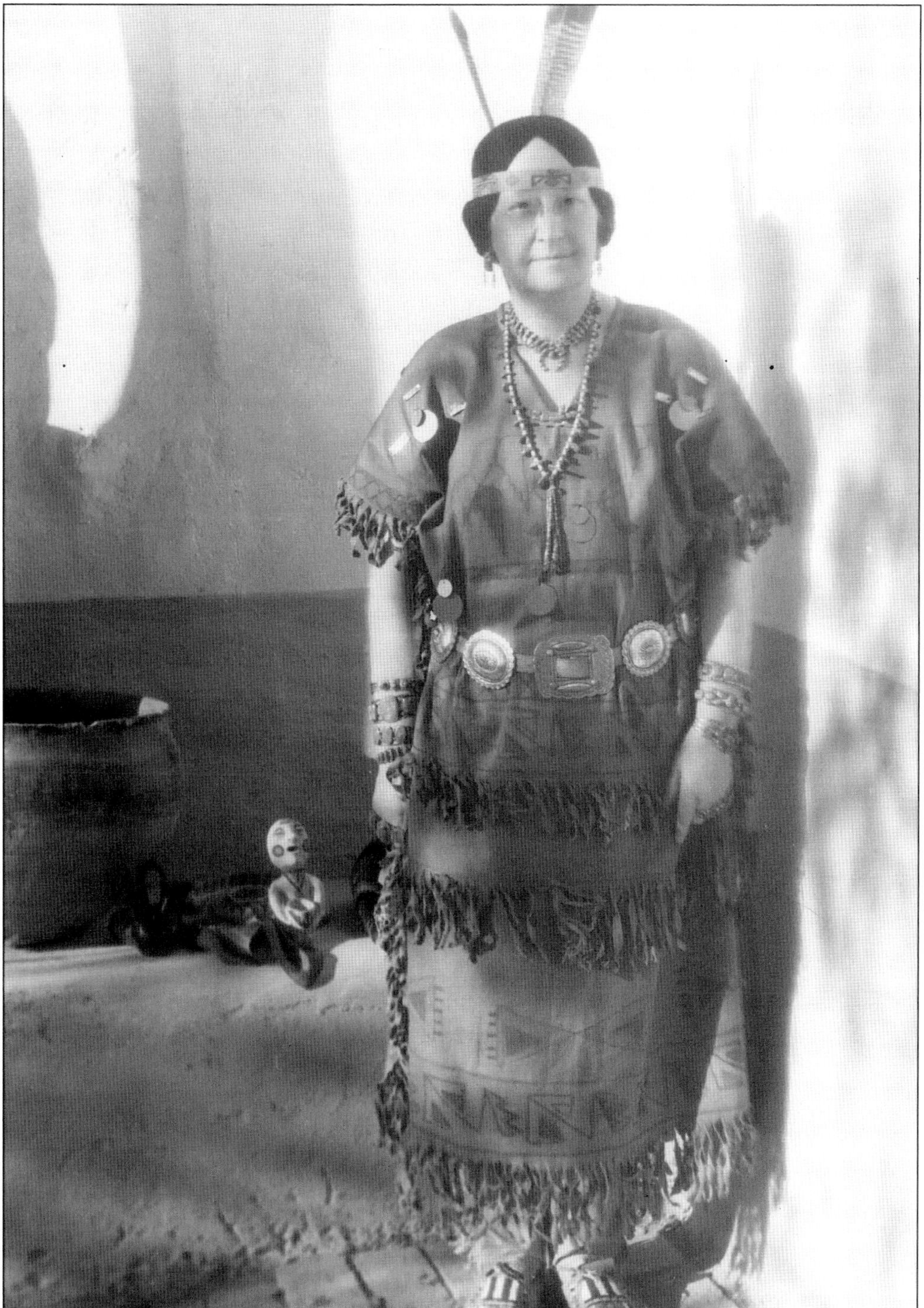

Mitta Piper Swasey. Mrs. Swasey had a keen interest in the welfare of Native Americans and took several trips to the Southwest. Affectionately called Aunt Mitta by many who knew her, she would speak to local groups about her travels; here she appears in Native American attire. (Swasey photograph, *c.* 1913.)

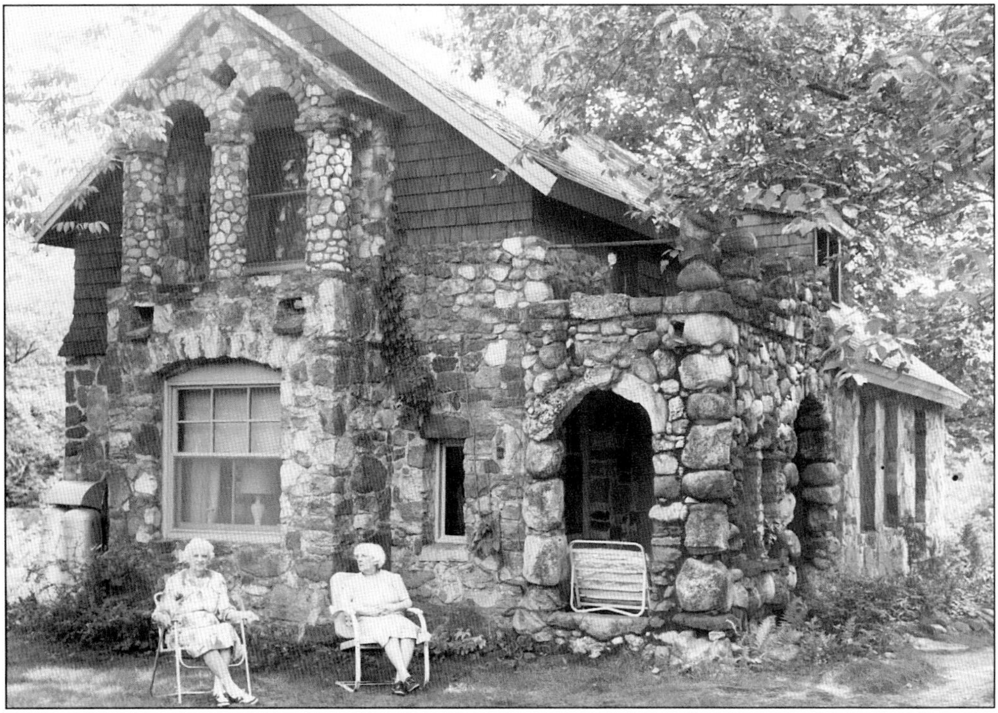

Rufus Anderson's Stone House, 62 Rattle Hill Road. Mr. Anderson was recovering from malaria when he first started collecting native stones for his planned home. He searched the area for suitable shapes and sizes, which must have been a challenge, considering the columns, arches, and dormers involved. Completed in 1894, the house was featured in a 1905 issue of *Good Housekeeping* magazine. (Alice Banner photograph, 1956.)

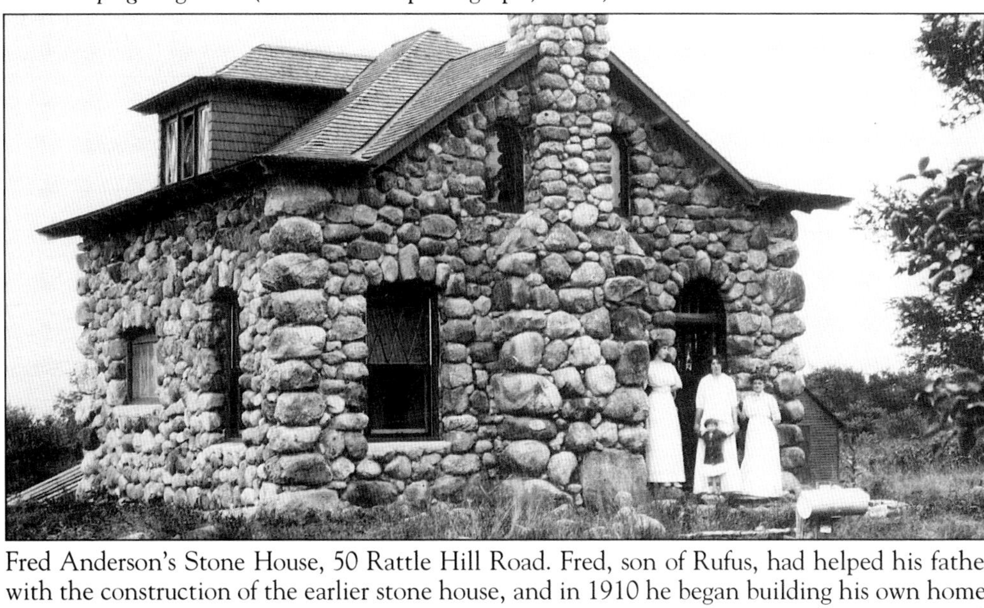

Fred Anderson's Stone House, 50 Rattle Hill Road. Fred, son of Rufus, had helped his father with the construction of the earlier stone house, and in 1910 he began building his own home. This time around, the father assisted the son in the search for just the right stones. The result is another distinctive structure, and succeeding generations continue to live in both of these stone houses. (Alice Banner photograph, *c.* 1915.)

Five

Places of Business

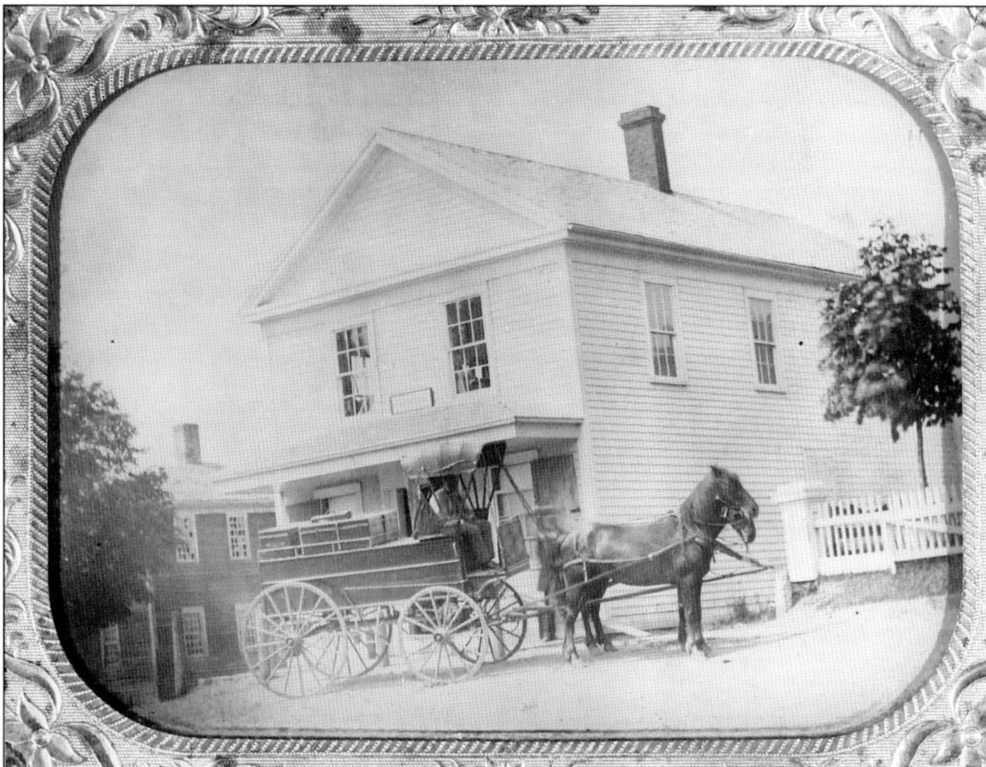

Judd Store, corner of East Street and College Highway. In 1850 the store next door was sold and this new building was constructed. The Judd family continued the business for 62 more years. The building showing at the left was the second schoolhouse and appears to sit in the space now occupied by the College Highway. It was removed when the new brick District School No. 1 was built in 1863. In 1904 Caroline Edwards wrote that the land was considerably altered to accommodate the new school building, and the highway may have been relocated at that time. (Helen Judd Coleman daguerreotype [see p. 24], *c.* 1860.)

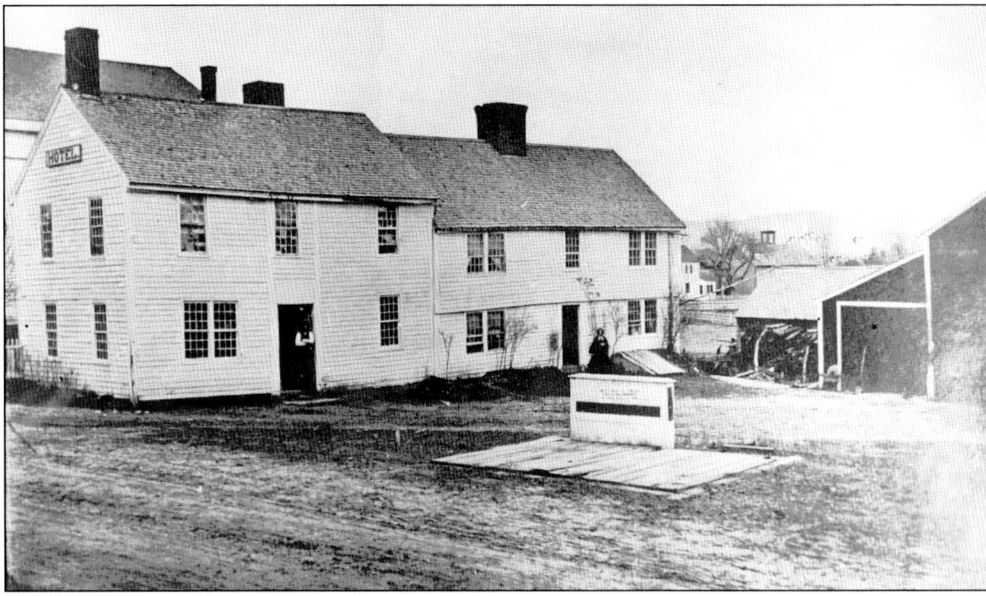

Perez Clapp Tavern, 217 College Highway. Located just south of the old Methodist church (Grange Hall) was the Bascomb House, set back from the road and facing south. In 1788, when the present church was constructed, the old meetinghouse was moved across the way and joined with the Bascomb House. The newly enlarged building was then operated as a tavern with Perez Clapp being the proprietor. It burned in December 1914, along with other neighboring properties. (Buchholz & Hendrick photograph, 1866.)

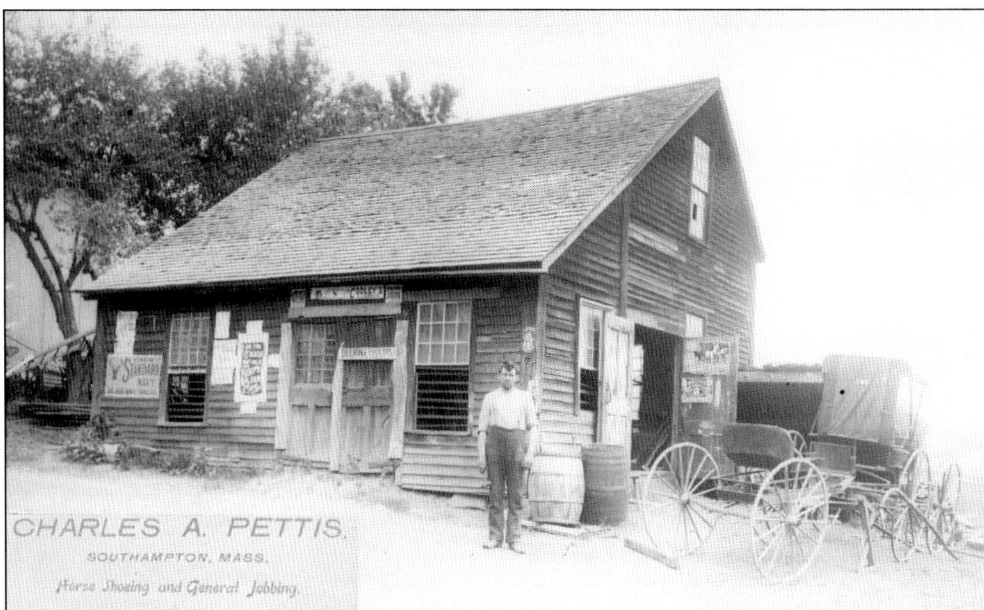

Pettis Blacksmith Shop, 4 Maple Street. Built in 1850, this building was in continuous use until the mid-1940s. Besides being used for blacksmithing, it was a convenient place for smokers, drinkers, and penny-ante players. It breathed its last when the space it occupied was needed for the new Center school. In the 1700s and 1800s there were at least ten such businesses in the community. (Howes Brothers photograph, 1900.)

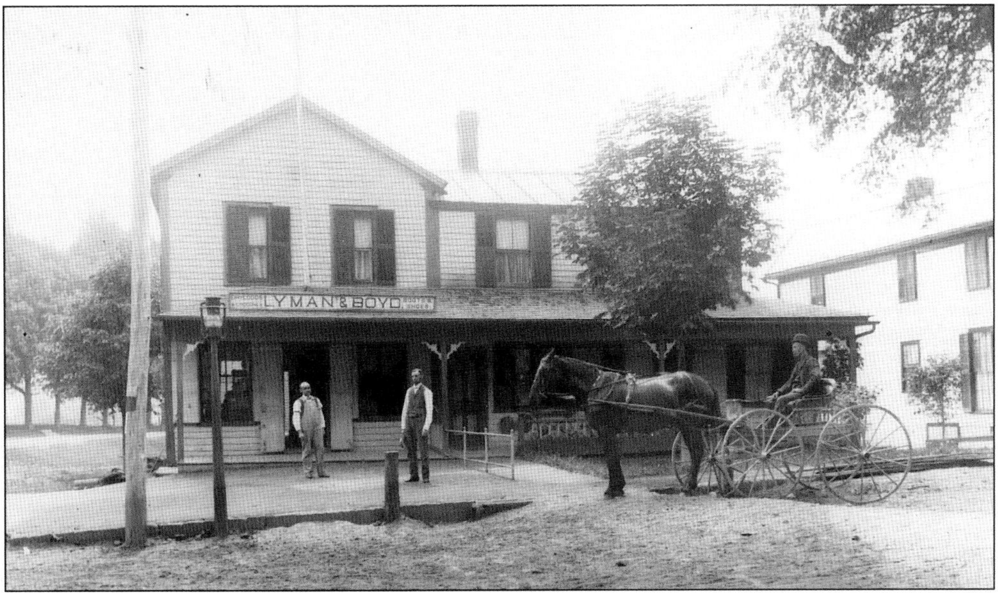

Lyman and Boyd General Store, 211 College Highway. This established store was relocated in 1828 from the Green across the street to its present location. Over the years it had many owners and was enlarged. During the 1850s a manufactory of pocketbooks and wallets was conducted on the second floor. Frank Boyd and W.S. Lyman became proprietors in 1894 and the business was subsequently known as Boyd's Store until after World War II. In the picture are Billy Boyd, Stephen Lyman, and Frank Boyd (in the buggy). (Howes Brothers photograph, 1900.)

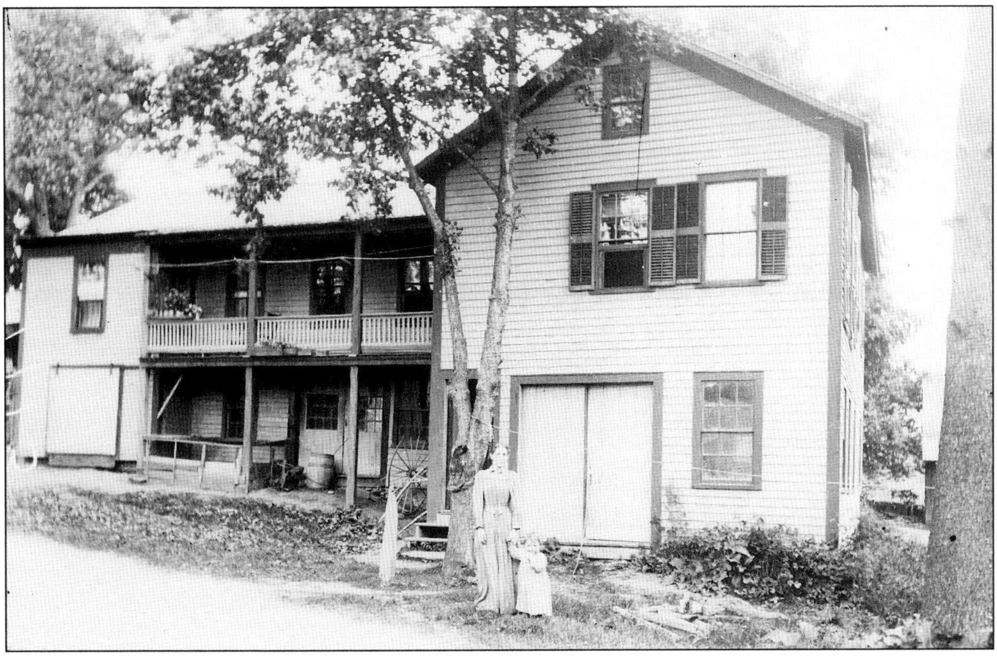

Charlie Tyler's Tenement House, Maple Street. This building was wedged into the triangle at the rear of Sheldon Academy. Originally known as Otis Clapp's Wagon Shop, it evolved into the multi-use building you see here. After it was torn down, the location became the playground area for the Sheldon School. (Howes Brothers photograph, 1900.)

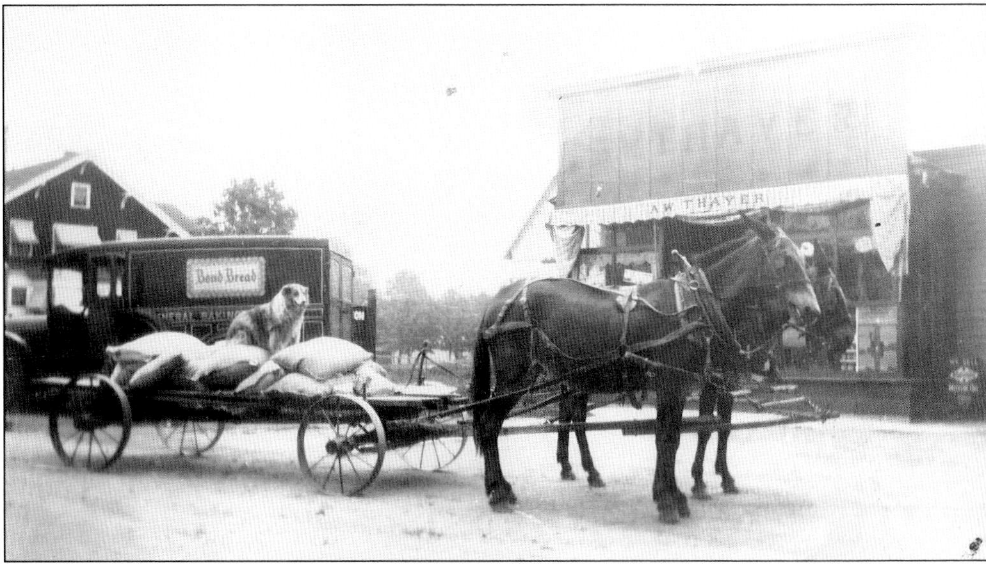

Thayer's Grocery Store and Meat Market, 221 College Highway. Arthur Thayer established his store here in the 1920s. He also built his large house, which stands today adjacent to the old library building. Mr. Thayer, in addition to running his food store, sold coal and pumped gasoline. During the Great Depression he was the welfare agent in charge of dispensing surplus foods to the "worthy poor." (Thayer snapshot, *c.* 1930.)

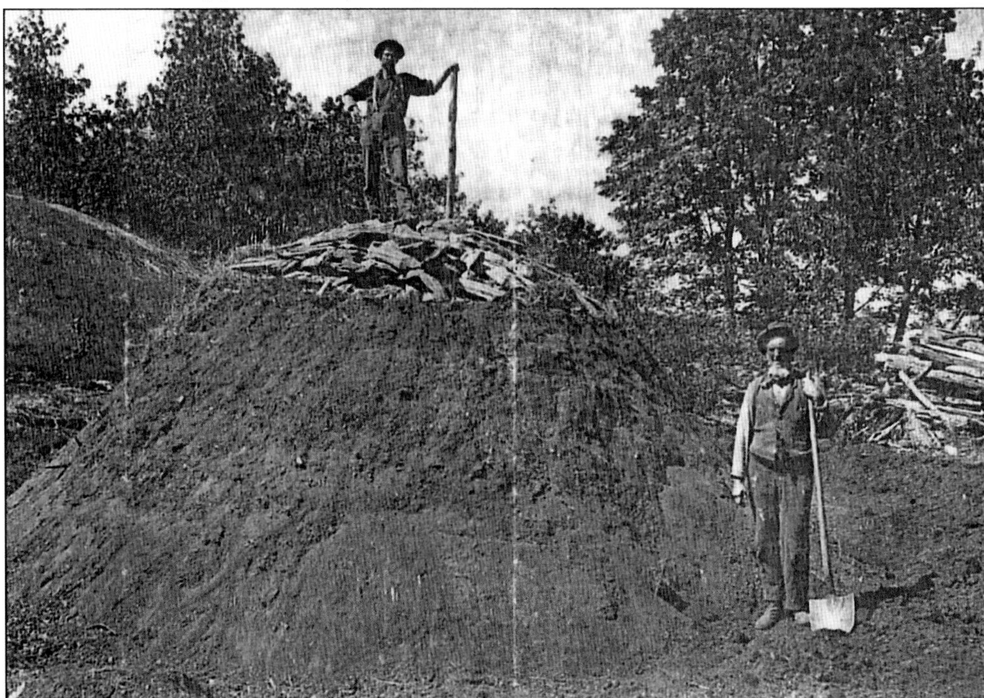

Gib Hall's charcoal pile, 80 Maple Street. Gib is shown here as he prepares to fire up his kiln. He was a town character and was known to fire up his kiln with the help of a generous amount of local "bourbon." Several charcoal operations were located around town, and the procedure was described as a very dirty, miserable job. (Howes Brothers photograph, 1900.)

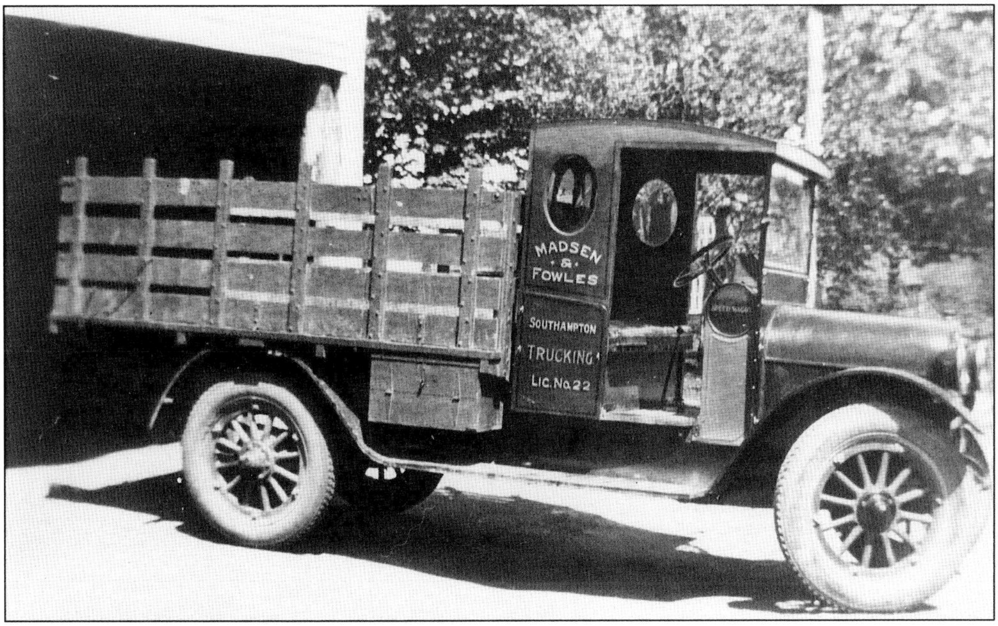

Madsen and Fowles Trucking, 5 Center Street. This was one of several vehicles used by Bernard (Bunny) Fowles and Axel Madsen in their trucking business. (Madsen snapshot.)

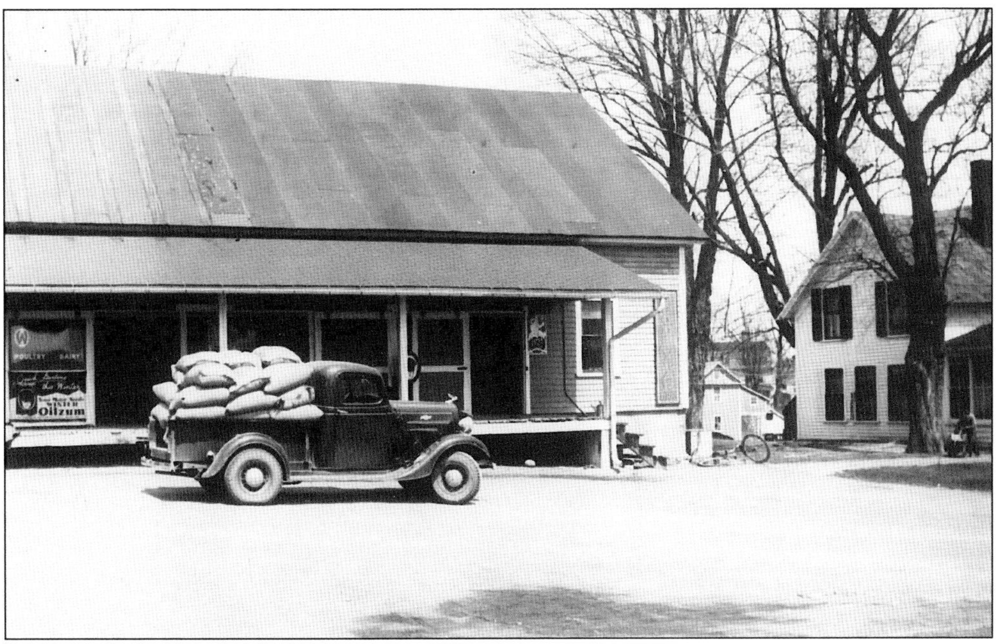

Madsen Grain Store, 4 Center Street. For many years Axel Madsen ran a grain business from this barn. He also stocked building materials in addition to being an insurance agent. These enterprises were conducted until after World War II. An addition to this building housed the town's fire-fighting equipment until the present fire station was established in 1949. (Madsen snapshot, *c.* 1930.)

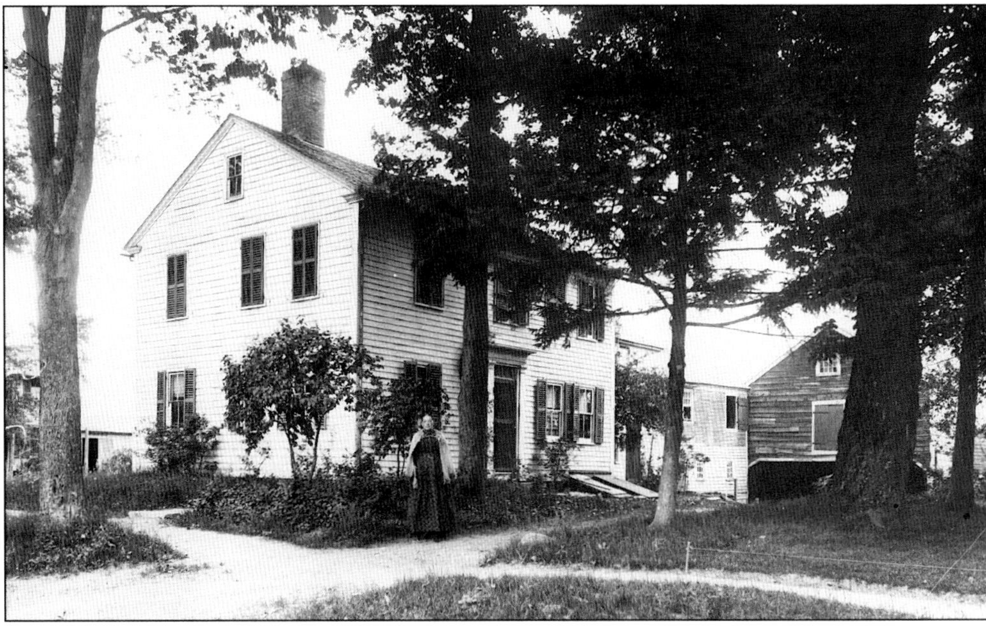

Dr. Josiah Gridley House, 19 East Street. Dr. Gridley purchased this house in 1830. He had a brief medical education, and, to quote Richard Frary (who now owns the property), "He had a lucrative medical practice, though some of his cures were his own patent medicines, including salves, liniments, bitters and pills." (Howes Brothers photograph, 1900.)

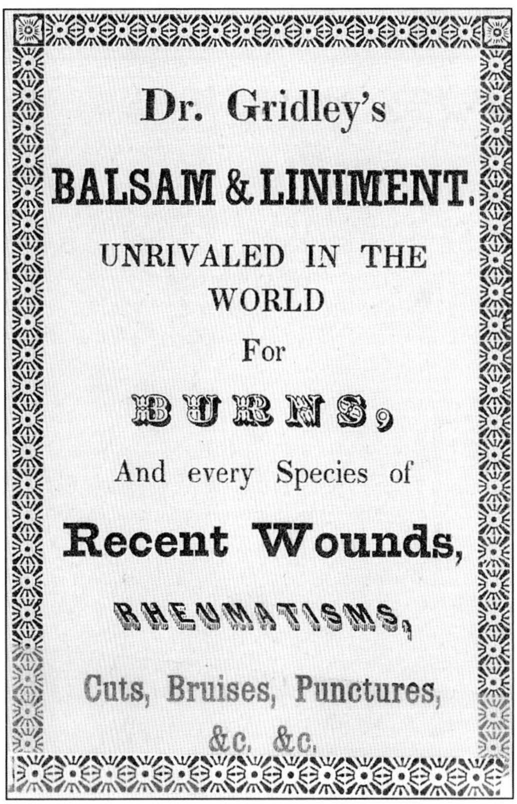

Dr. Gridley label. This label was found in the Gridley attic, and would have been used on the bottle of one of his cure-alls. He searched the fields and swamps for plants and berries, and he dug the roots of burdock, princess pine, and dock to be used in his concoctions.

Dr. Josiah Gridley (1802–1876). The historical society has his old ledger and black doctor's box. This is a typical recipe for one of his potions:

Hemlock	1 oz.
Olive Oil	3 oz.
Gum Camphor	6 oz.
Spirits of Turpentine	1 oz.
Oil Oregaeum	1 oz.
Alcohol	1 pt.

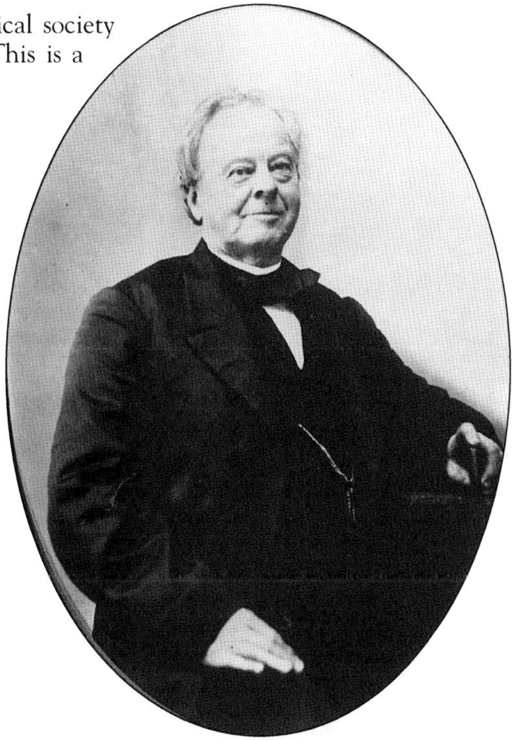

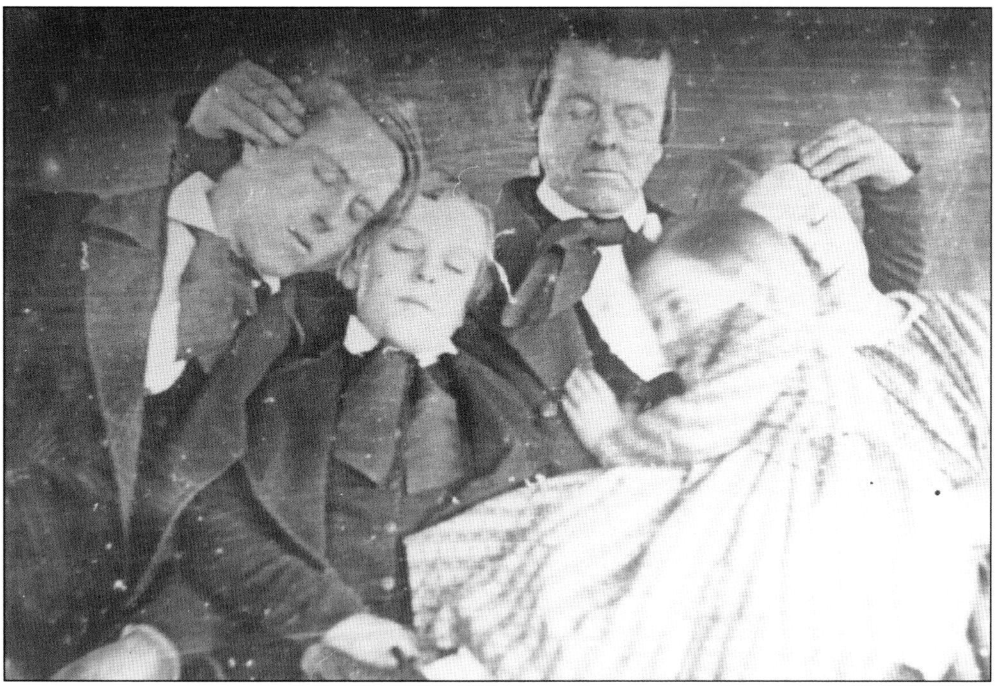

Gridley family seance. Dr. Gridley became quite involved with Spiritualism and is shown here c. 1860 attempting to communicate with the spirit of his son, Albert Jr., who died at age 19. The Clark-Chapman House museum owns a copy of his book, *Astounding Facts of the Spirit World.*

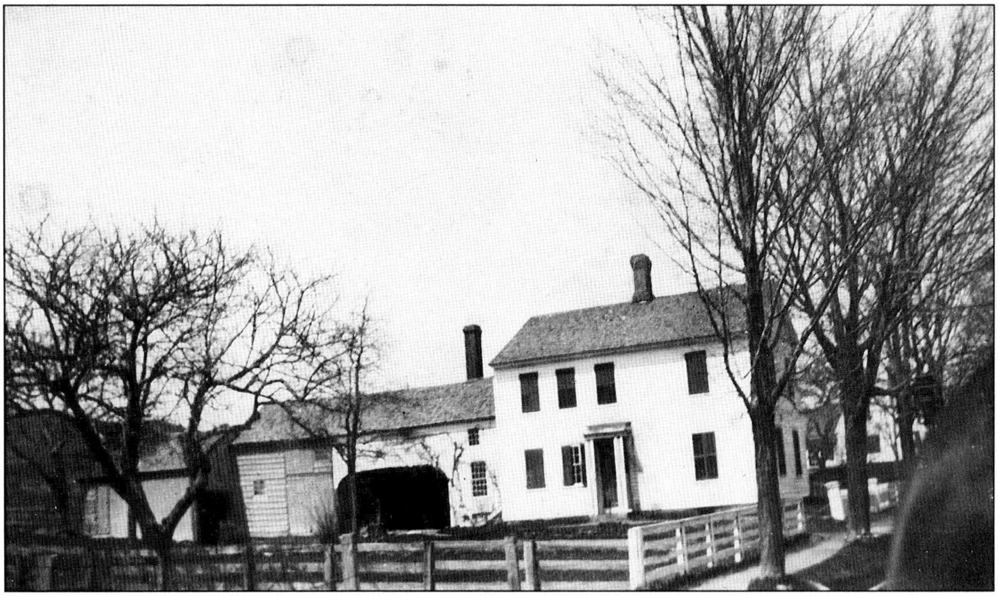

Clark-Chapman House, 234 College Highway. Sardis Chapman built his new house in 1827, the same year that he married Dolly Searle. After his death at age 89, the property passed through several families. In 1935, George and Mary Clark purchased the property for a family residence. They deeded it to the historical society in 1971, and it now houses the society's collection of memorabilia. This image was captured *c.* 1895.

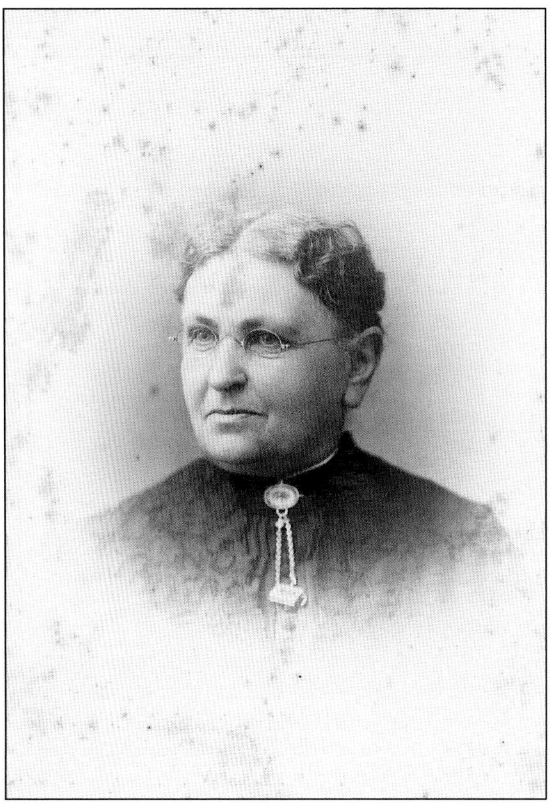

Harriet Chapman (1830–1896). She was the daughter of Sardis and Dolly, and was known for her concern for the welfare of Southampton folks. She was frequently seen with her horse and buggy, attending to the needs of her neighbors. Her will provided $1,000 toward the purchase of the handsome iron fence that encloses the burial ground.

Sardis Chapman, shoemaker (1803–1892). Mr. Chapman was very involved in genealogy research in his later years, leaving a wealth of information on local families. These records are available at Northampton's Forbes Library. He was also an abolitionist, and Caroline Edwards wrote in 1900 that Sojourner Truth had stayed with the family when she visited the area to tell her story.

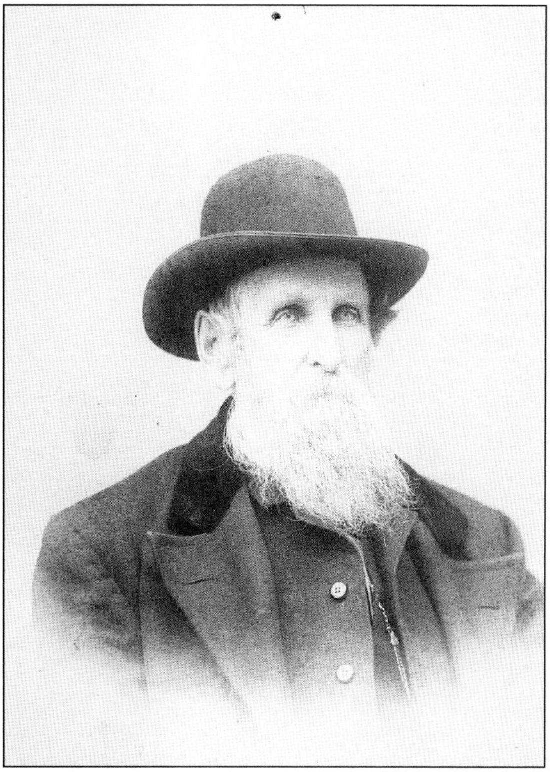

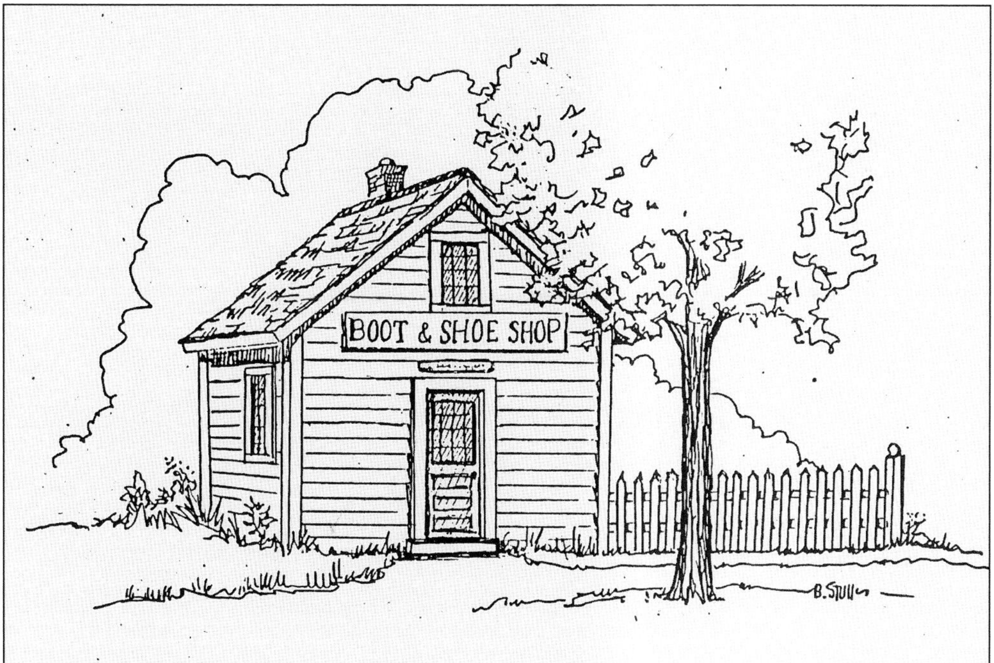

Chapman's Boot and Shoe Shop, 234 College Highway. In 1890 this shop was moved up the highway and became an addition to the Bernard Fowles House at 38 Pomeroy Meadow Road. (Sketch by Betty Stull Schaffer.)

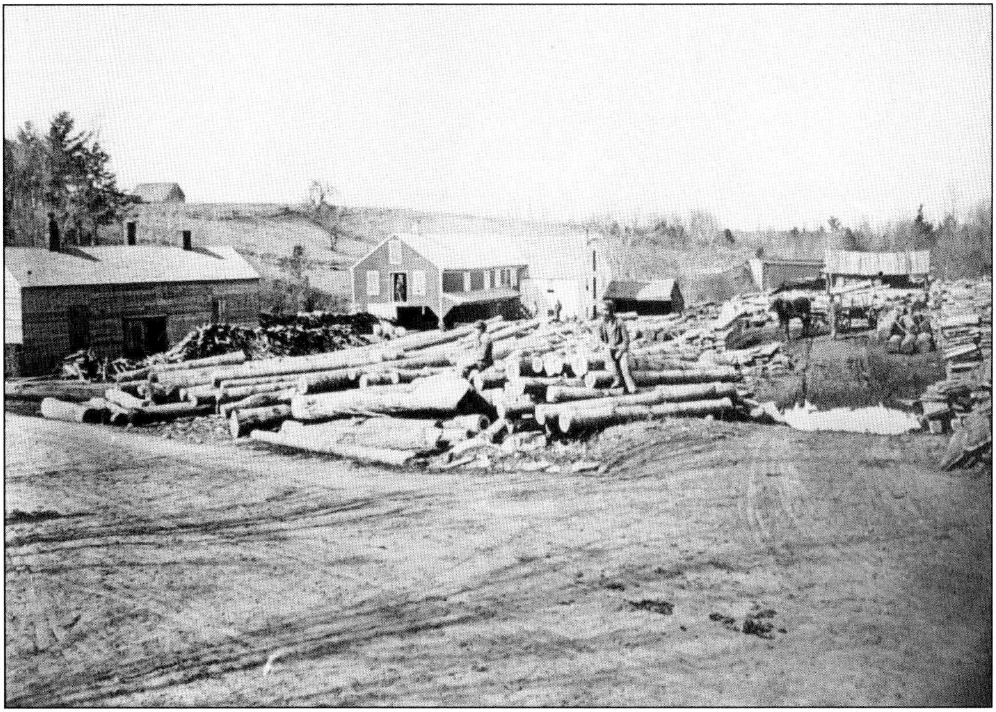

Ancient mill on the Manhan, 283 College Highway. Apparently this was the first of many mills in Southampton. It was authorized in 1732, and was to be built on the south side of the river. There have been many owners over the years, and several of them built houses in the area. At various times it operated as a sawmill, a shingle mill, a gristmill, and a piano-leg factory, and was eventually lost to fire and floods. (Buchholz & Hendrick photograph, c. 1866.)

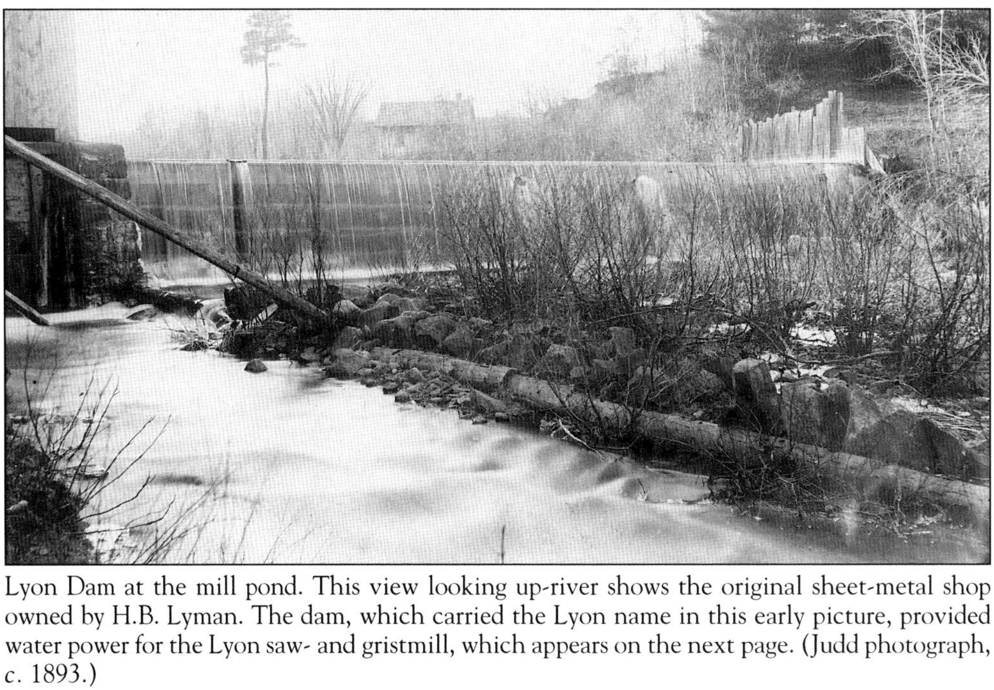

Lyon Dam at the mill pond. This view looking up-river shows the original sheet-metal shop owned by H.B. Lyman. The dam, which carried the Lyon name in this early picture, provided water power for the Lyon saw- and gristmill, which appears on the next page. (Judd photograph, c. 1893.)

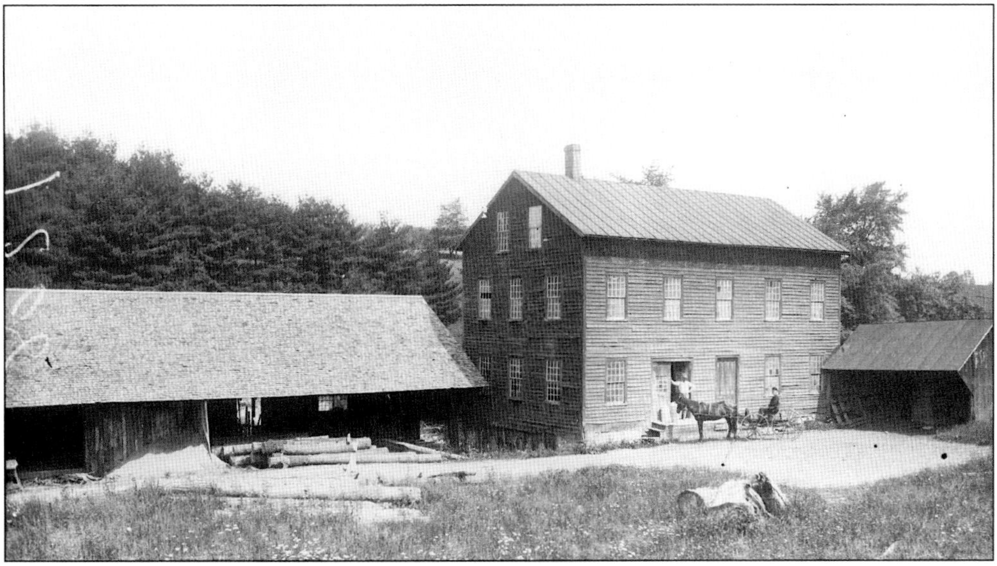

Old Red Mill, 238 College Highway. The picturesque mill building was the site of many manufacturing operations and had a short life as a tenement house called the Beehive. It was surreptitiously moved across the railroad tracks one dark night, and was then moved into position on the site of the earlier mill (p. 74). After the move, it had a new life as the Lyon Mill until Holyoke's dams diminished the waterpower and the mill had to close. (Howes Brothers photograph, 1900.)

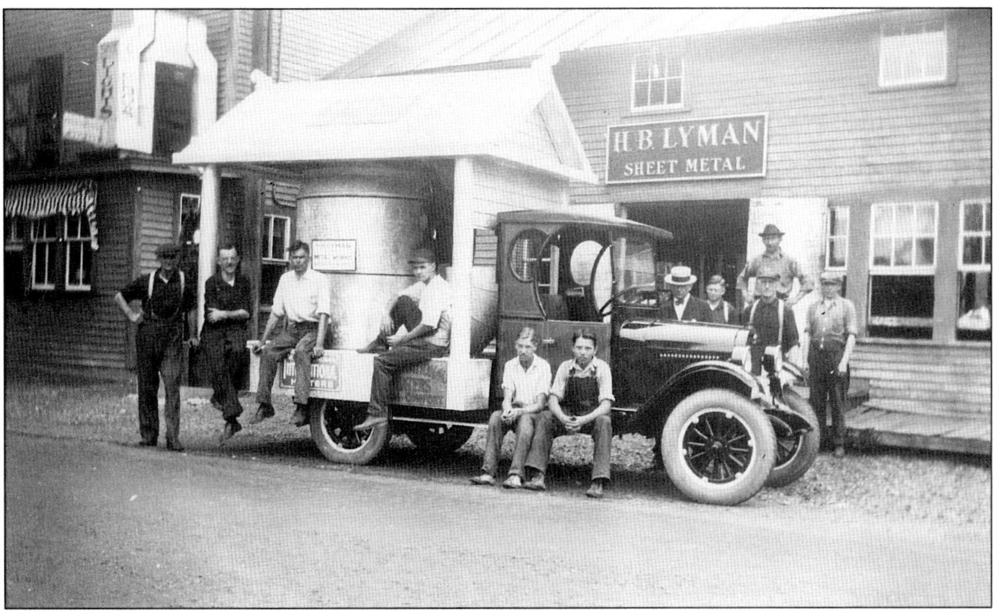

H.B. Lyman Company, 281 College Highway. In 1902, Herbert B. Lyman purchased the blacksmith shop that sat across the road, moved it to this site, and joined it to the shop he had built in 1893. Thus a very successful business was born, one that continues to flourish to this day. It appears that these shop employees are preparing a furnace display for an Old Home Day parade c. 1930.

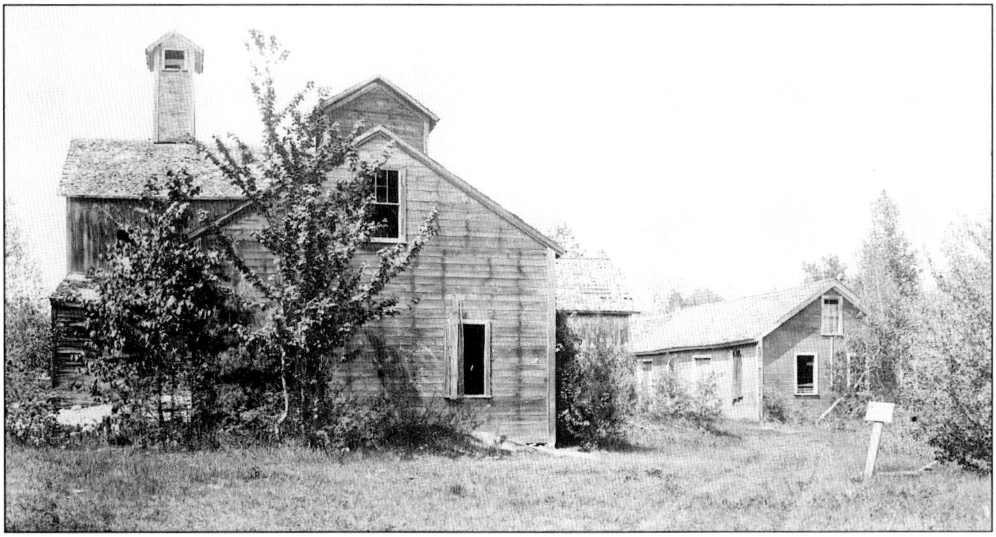

Old Lead Mine Building, 64 Lead Mine Road. Fortunes were made and lost from 1678 (when lead was first discovered) through the Civil War. Speculators bought and sold their rights as they attempted to retrieve the lead. In the end it was impossible to remove the lead and still show a profit. (Keene photograph, 1897.)

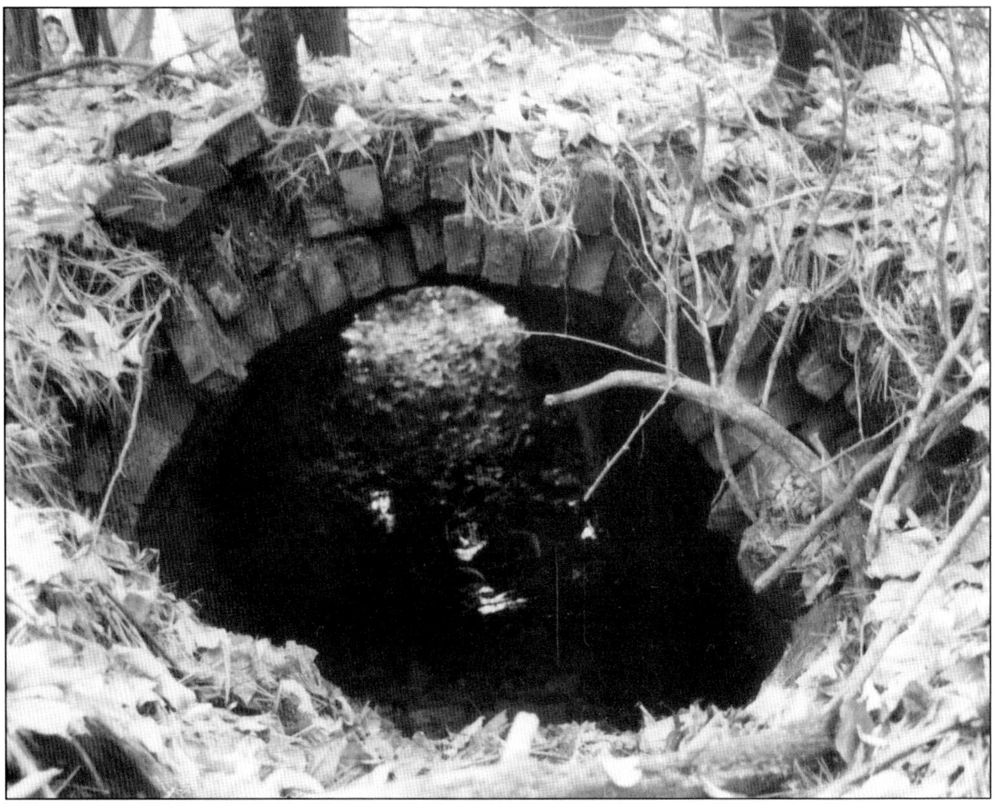

Remains of the smelter at the lead mine. This is all that remains of the smelter and smokestack, which had been located down by the Manhan River. The image depicts a 1989 conservation commission hike.

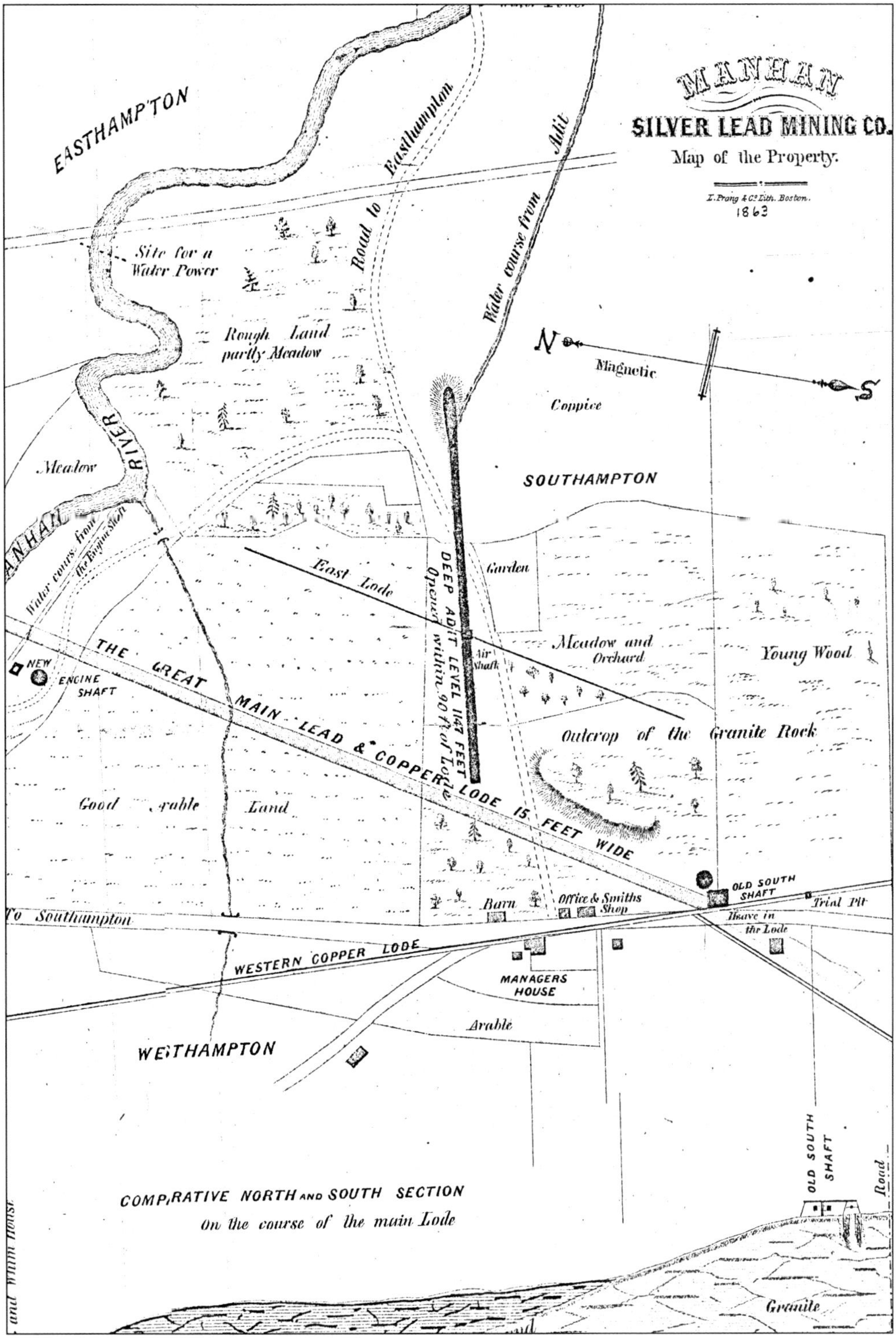

Lead mine survey. This survey was recorded in 1863 as the site was being offered as a good investment to prospective purchasers.

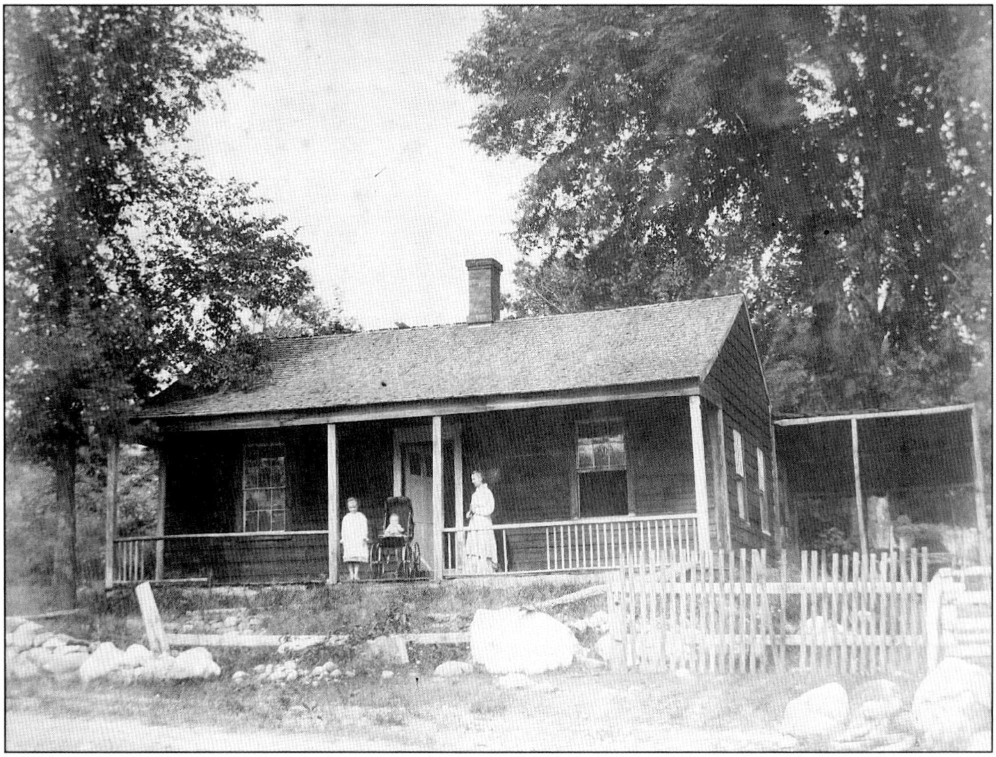

Russell's Whip Shop, 10 Manhan Road. The whip shop industry was one of several that operated on the Manhan River in the Russellville area. The two front rooms of this building had been part of Charles Russell's whip shop, which in 1891 was moved up the river and across the road, where it became the home of the Horace Williams family. It remained in the family until 1964. (Homestead View photograph, c. 1895.)

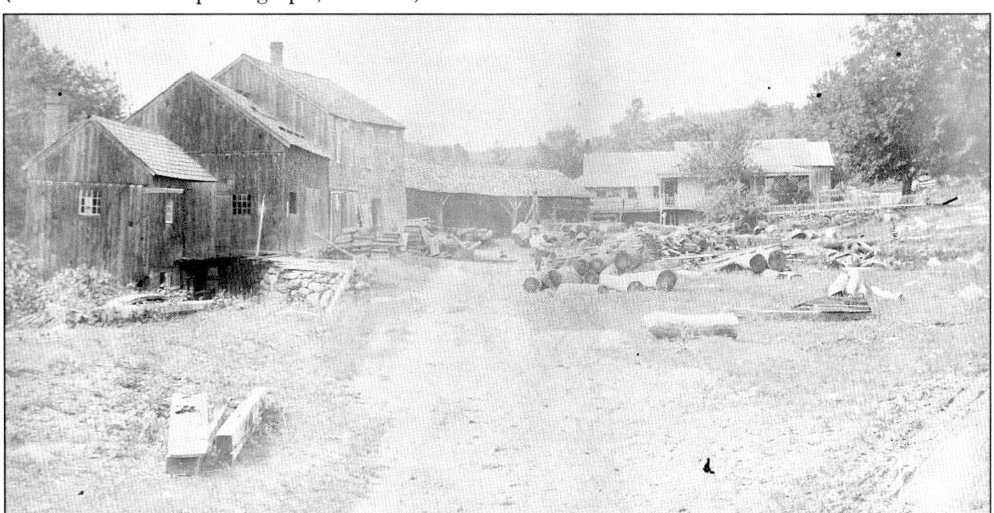

Wait's Mill, 11 Manhan Road. Charles Wait purchased this complex downstream from the Russellville Falls and ran a profitable business here from 1875 until 1897. At that time, the City of Holyoke obtained water rights for the first of three reservoirs, and in 1899 Wait settled with them for the loss of water to run his mill. (Homestead View photograph, c. 1895.)

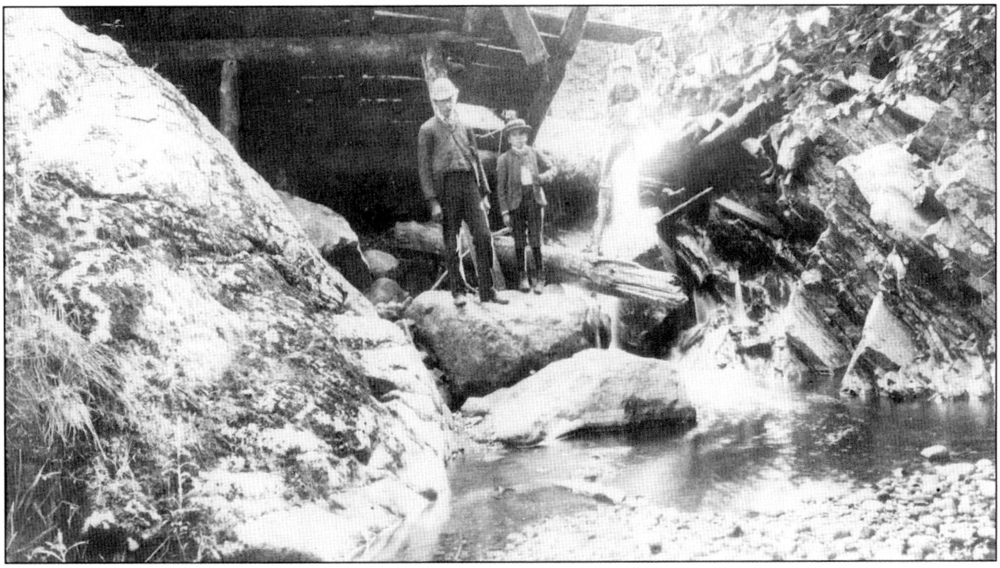

Remains of Jerry's Dam, Wyben Road. This site on Roaring Brook, shown c. 1891, was owned by Jerry Smith and Son, who had a whip shop here. The shop burned in 1881.

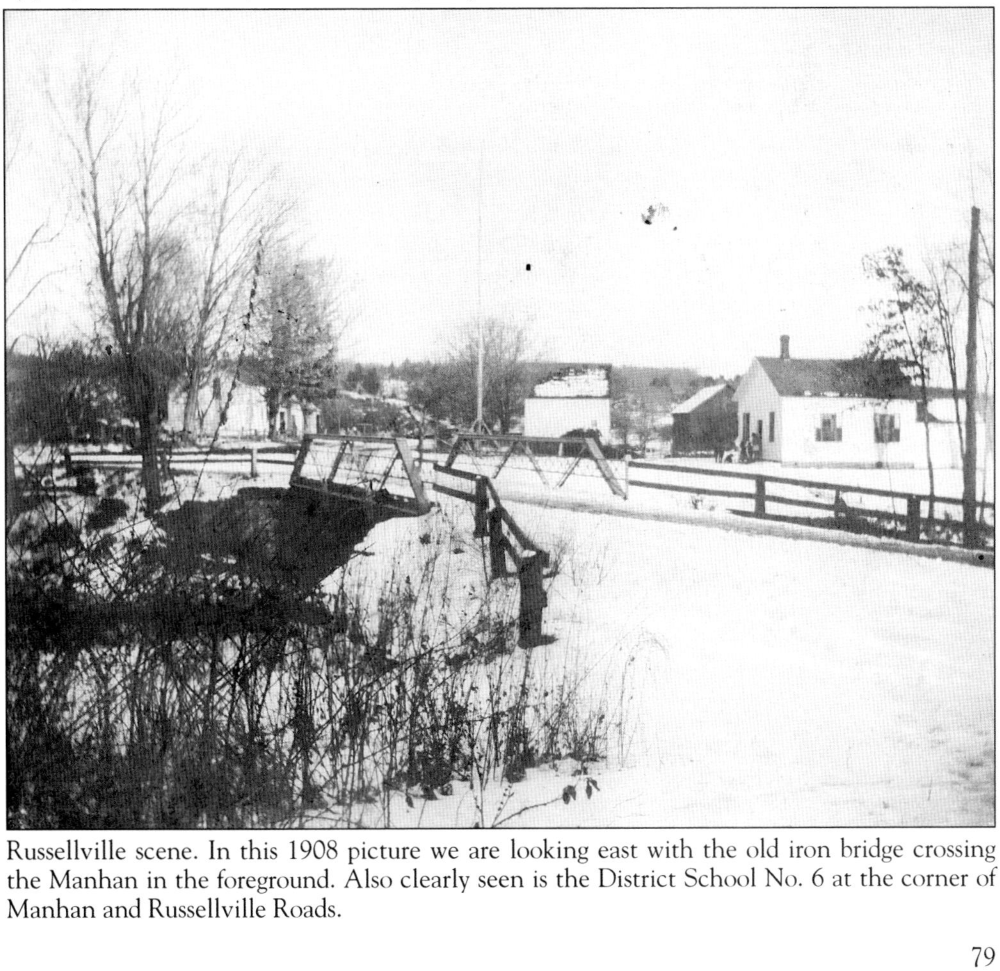

Russellville scene. In this 1908 picture we are looking east with the old iron bridge crossing the Manhan in the foreground. Also clearly seen is the District School No. 6 at the corner of Manhan and Russellville Roads.

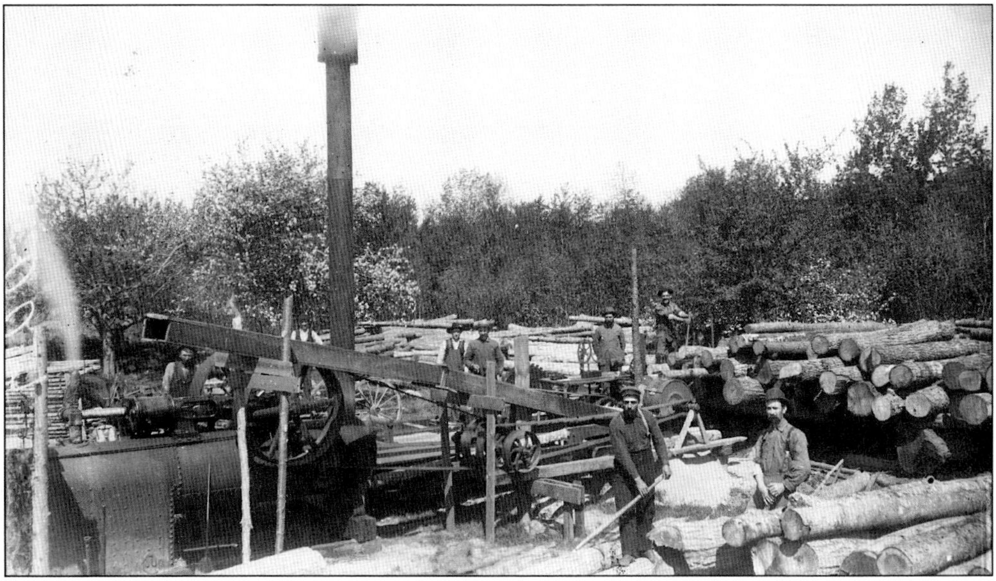

Peck and Healy's Sawmill, upper Maple Street. Steam-powered sawmills were portable, and were routinely moved from one locale to another. This operation was set up on Maple Street, west of Little Mountain. (Howes Brothers photograph, 1900.)

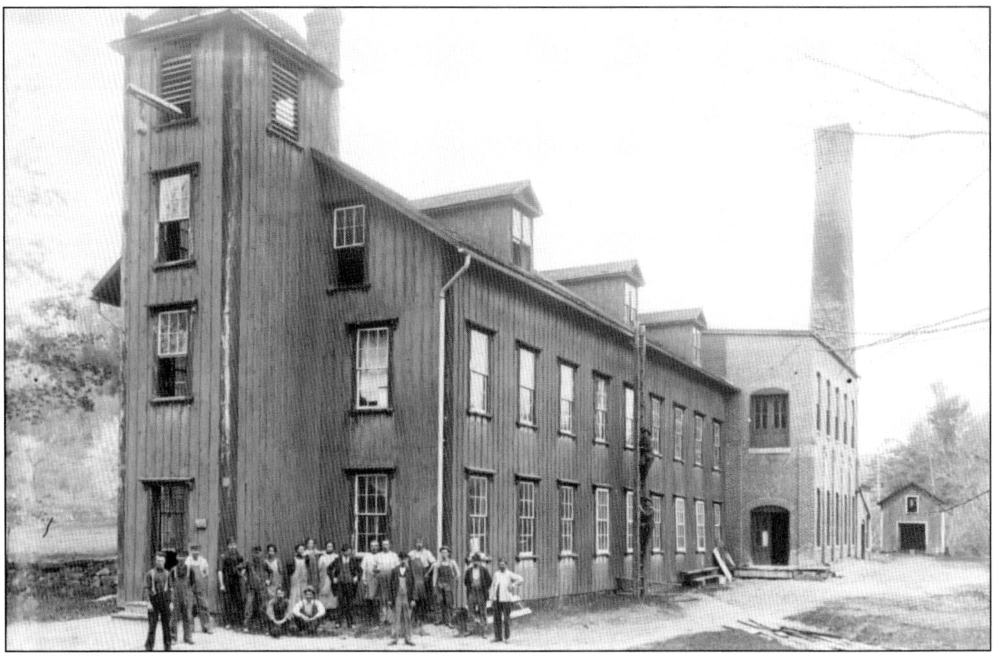

Elastic Web/Metro Engineering, 181 Glendale Road. Many different elastic materials were manufactured here from 1848 to 1912. The Glendale Village area was built up around the mill and its company housing, and a boarding house and schoolhouse were built across the river in Easthampton. Experienced weavers were imported from England and Germany, and at one time 45 people were employed there. The last webbing business went bankrupt in 1912. This is the present location of Metro Engineering. (Howes Brothers photograph, 1900.)

Six

Buildings for the Community

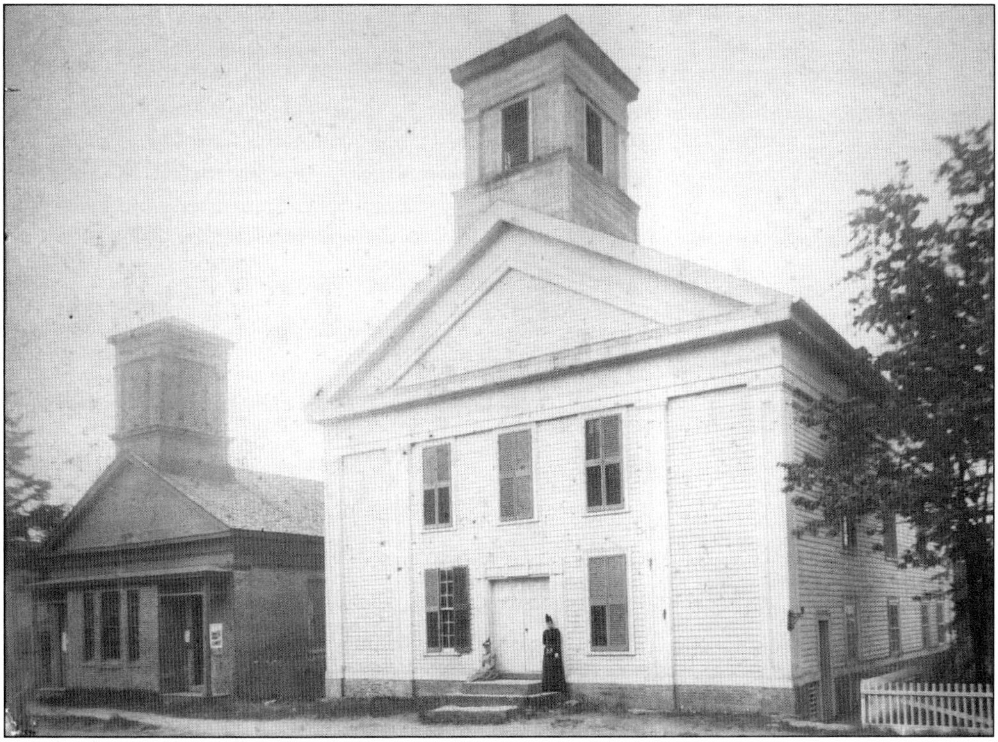

Original town hall and First Methodist Church, 215 College Highway. Before the brick town hall on the left was erected, town meetings were held in the upper hall of the second schoolhouse (see p. 65). The old building was replaced by the present town hall on East Street in 1904. The church was erected in 1844. It was enlarged and remodeled over the years and it burned in 1914. This photograph was taken c. 1890.

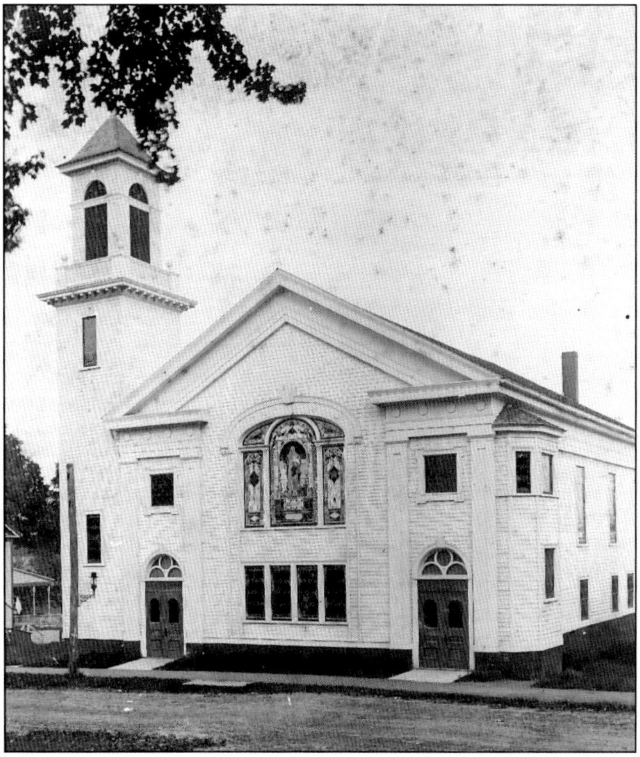

Remodeled Methodist church, 215 College Highway. The most obvious change during the life of this building was the addition of a traditional steeple in 1908 (this photograph was taken *c.* 1905). Only six years later, the fire which had started in the old Clapp Tavern (then William Boyd's home) spread rapidly and both buildings were lost.

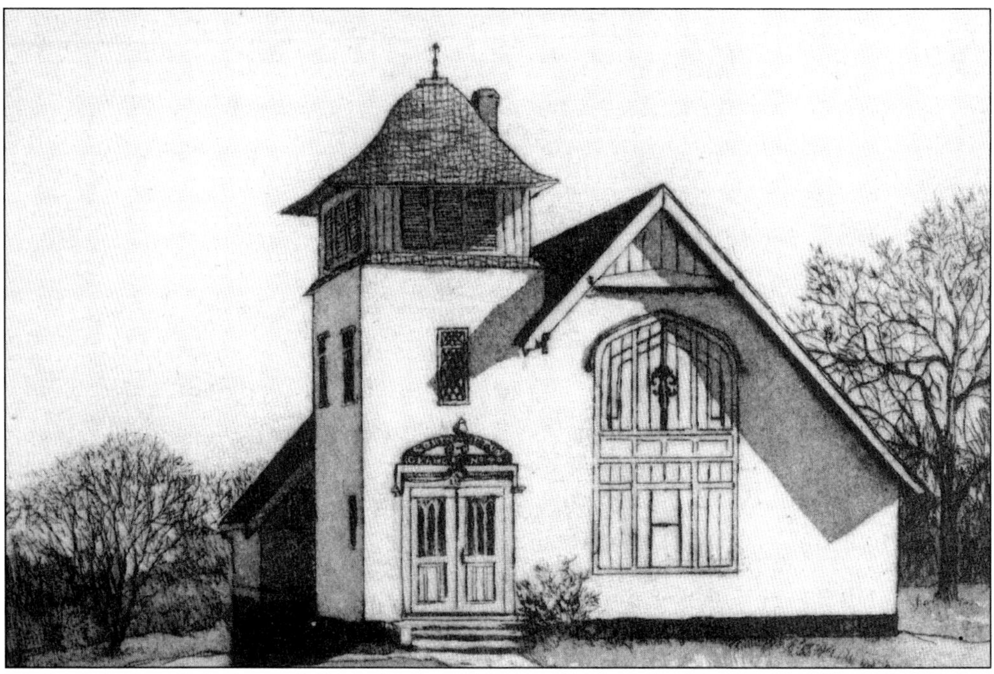

Methodist church/Grange Hall, College Highway. The new building was dedicated in 1916, but by 1924 the congregation had decided to no longer hold services here. Later, in 1938, the Grange purchased the facility. Back then the Grange was an active group, and many people remember attending dances and suppers held in the hall. (Drawing by Valerie McQuillan.)

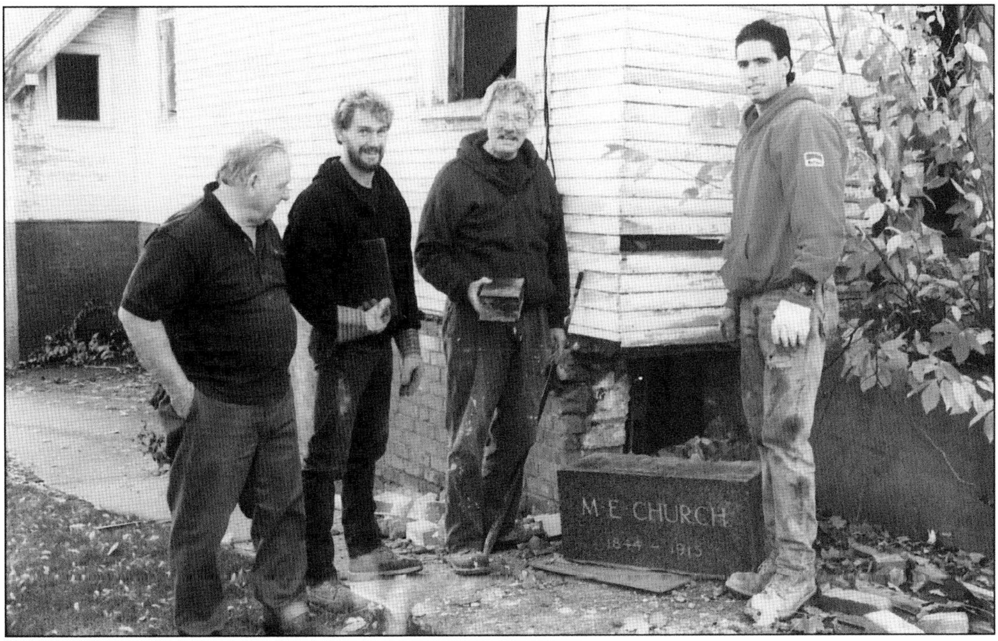

Wrecking crew, November 1997, 215 College Highway. Workers prepare to demolish the old Grange Hall. Richard Frary, president of the local historical society (third from the left), was present to examine the contents of the cornerstone.

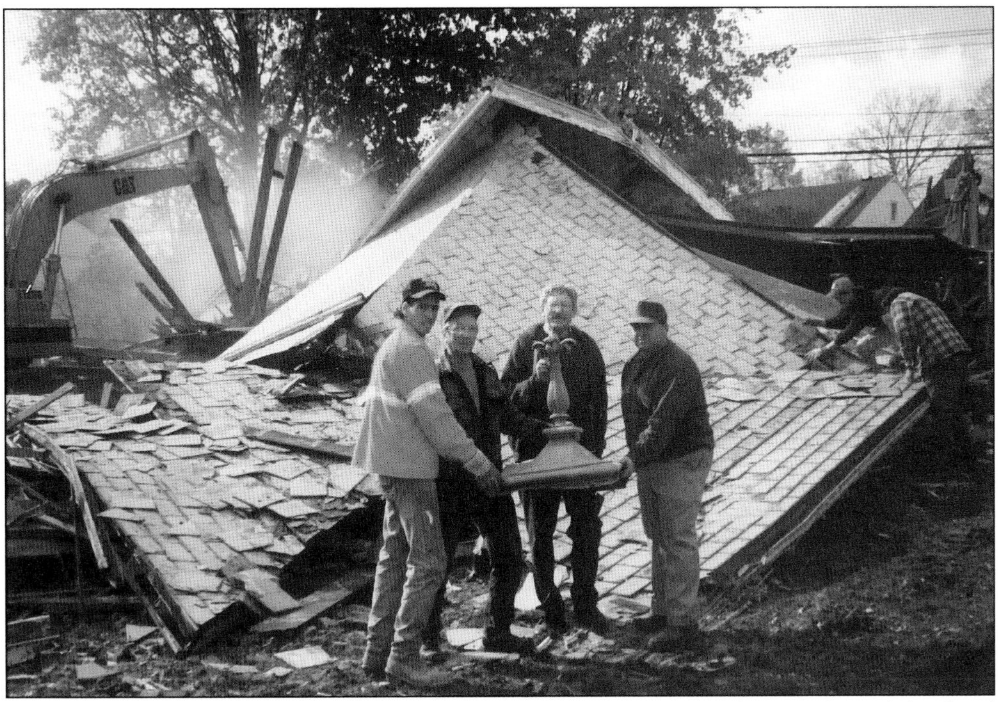

Grange Hall demolished. The old building was flattened and Richard Frary claimed the finial from the cupola for the historical society. The beautiful stained-glass windows were removed and presumably sold before the demolition. (Frary photograph, 1997.)

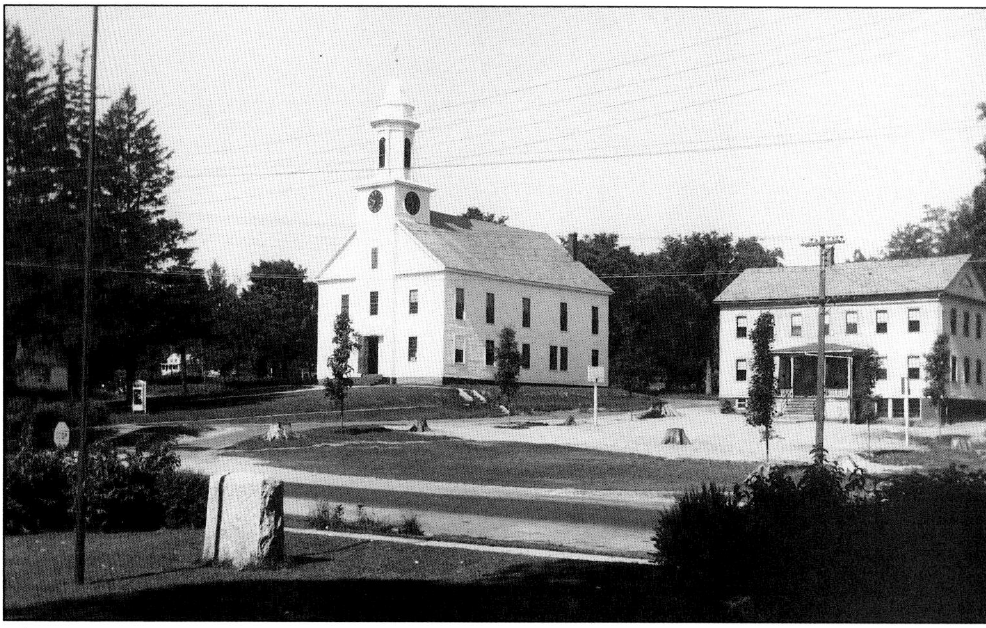

The Town Green, 210 College Highway. For many years this area in the town center was called the Green. When in 1829 the building of the Sheldon Academy was approved, it was to be situated there. The second meetinghouse, erected in 1788, faced the Green, but was turned one quarter turn to the east in 1841. (Hugh Scott photograph, *c*. 1945.)

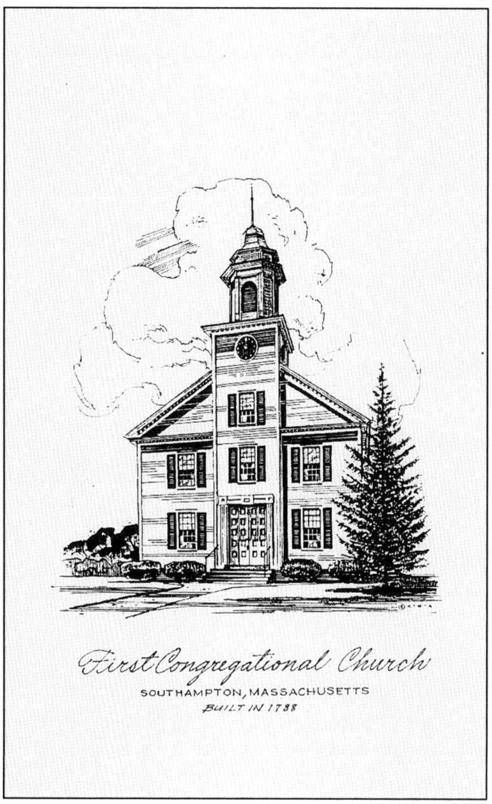

The Congregational church, 214 College Highway. No longer called a meetinghouse, the church acquired a bell in 1849, and in 1864 the town clock was installed. For 134 years it has reminded the townspeople of the time, and even today it is owned and maintained by the town. This church building is considered to be the oldest in continual use in western Massachusetts.

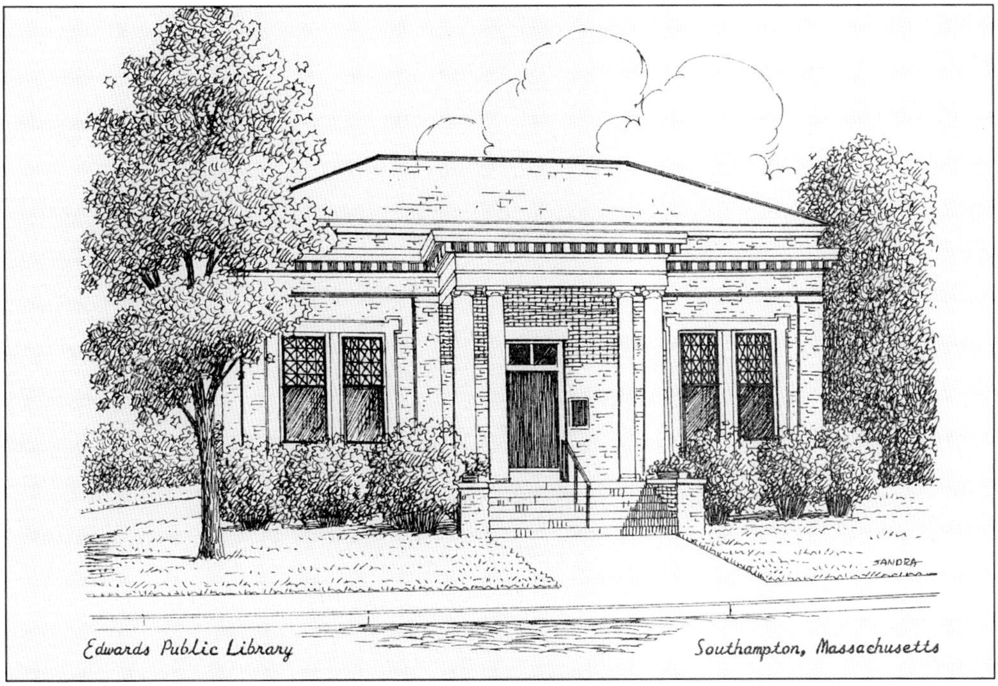

Edwards Library, 233 College Highway. A former resident, Rev. Henry Edwards provided $5,000 for this handsome building, which was dedicated in 1904. It housed the book collection for many years, but as the town grew the limitations of the small plot of land on which it sat meant that other arrangements had to be made. Thus, in 1996, a new Edwards Library was opened at the East Street entrance of Conant Park.

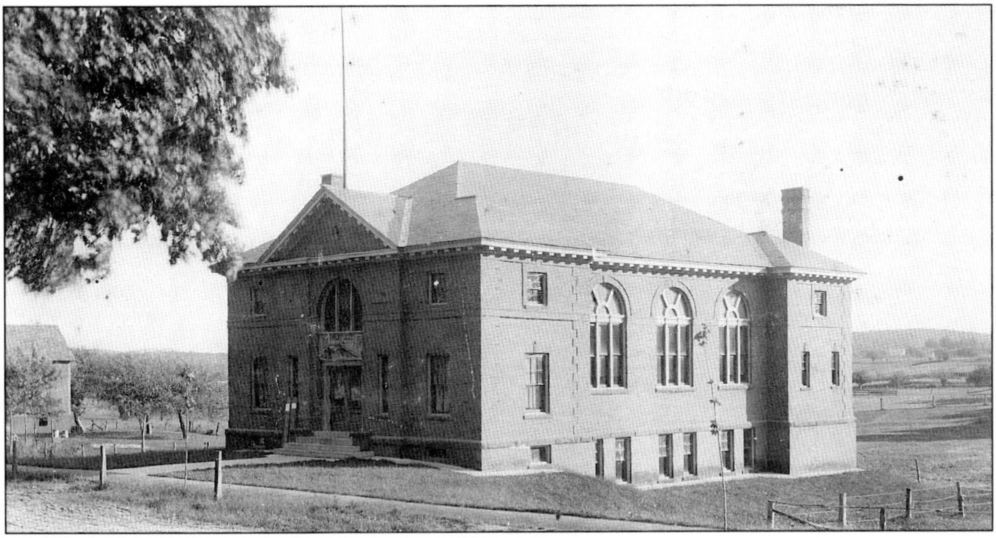

Town hall, 10 East Street. As previously noted, the growing community needed more meeting and office space, so the present building was constructed in 1904. Initially there were two offices, one on either side of the front door, and a large auditorium occupied the remainder of the first floor. There was a balcony for the audience, and a stage at the front of the room. Like the earlier hall, this one also housed a lock-up to accommodate tramps and law-breakers. (Keene postcard, *c.* 1905.)

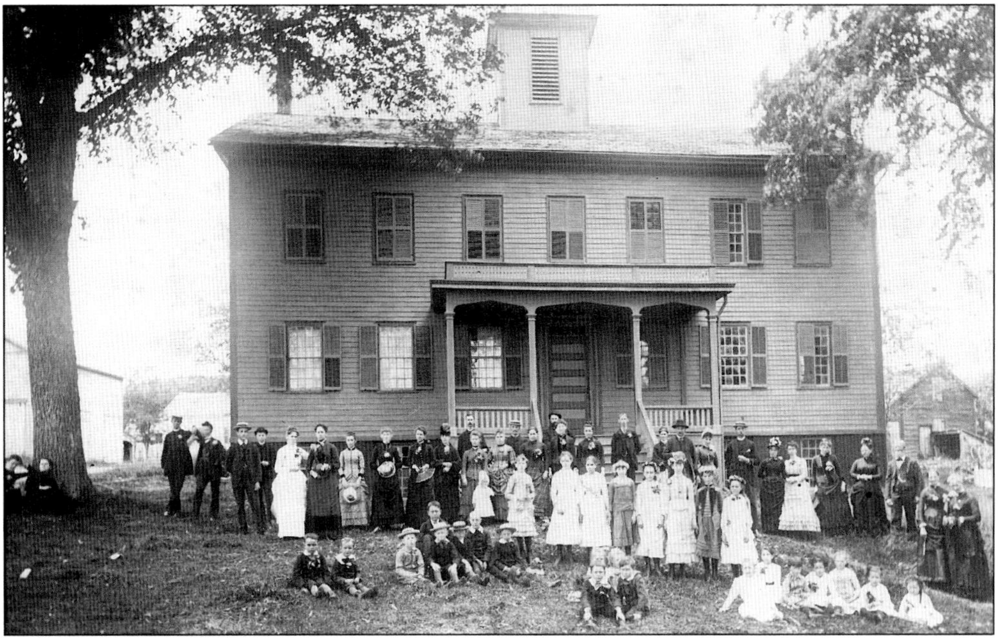

Sheldon Academy, 210 College Highway. The private academy was founded in 1829, and was declared a success from the start. Pupils arrived on the daily stage, and later on the canal boat from towns to the south. One hundred fifty-four pupils were enrolled here in 1832, but as communities developed their own institutions of higher learning, enrollment decreased. In 1927 the town approved the purchase of the building to bring all students from the town's many schoolhouses together under one roof. (Judd photograph, *c.* 1890.)

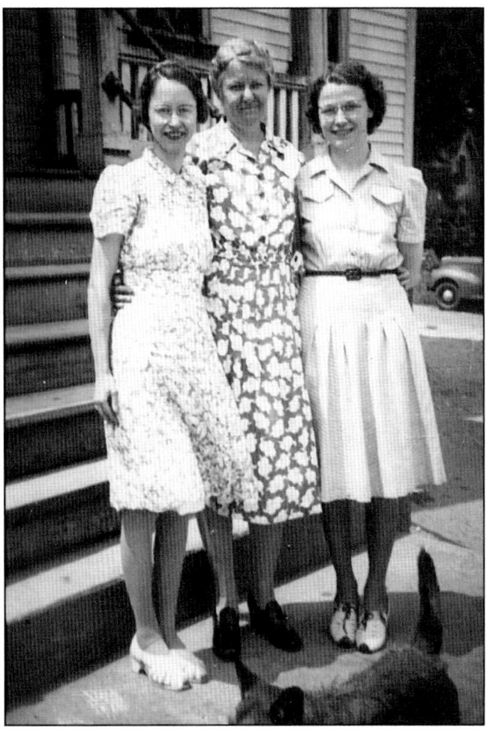

Teachers at the Sheldon School. Consolidation of the seven district schools was completed in 1930, so there were then four teachers at the new Sheldon School. Shown here *c.* 1943 from left to right are Beverly Larrabee, Margaret Zoudlick, and Helen Gunn Haller. Principal William Norris also taught the combined seventh and eighth grades.

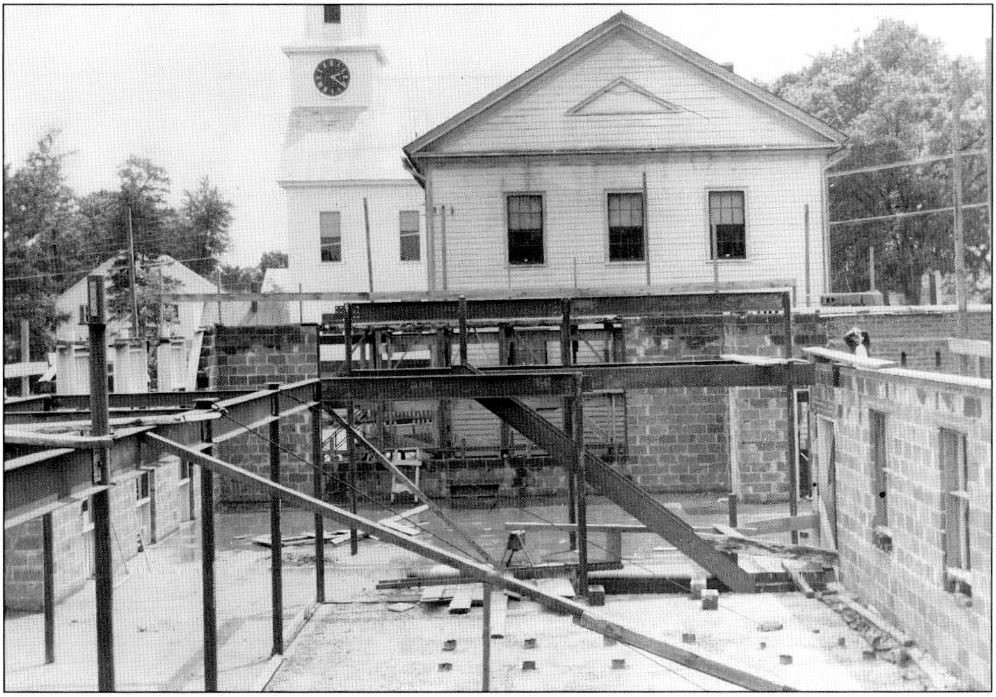

Construction of the new Center School. The Sheldon School classes continued as the new school was erected next door. We see here how close the construction really was. (Hugh Scott photograph, 1948.)

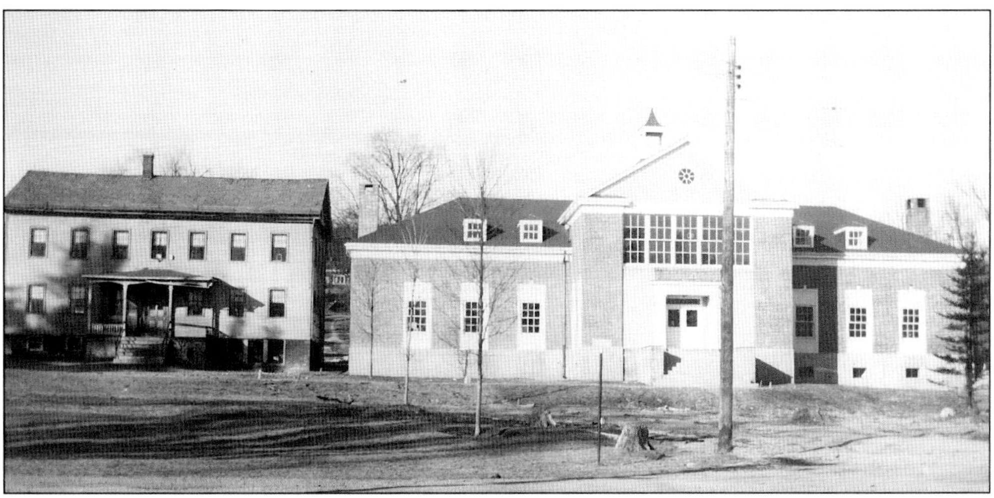

The new Center School. It was nearly completed and ready for students as the old Sheldon School waited for the demolition crew. The primary school was later named the Larrabee School in honor of Beverly Larrabee, who taught there and was made principal in 1966. (Hugh Scott photograph, 1949.)

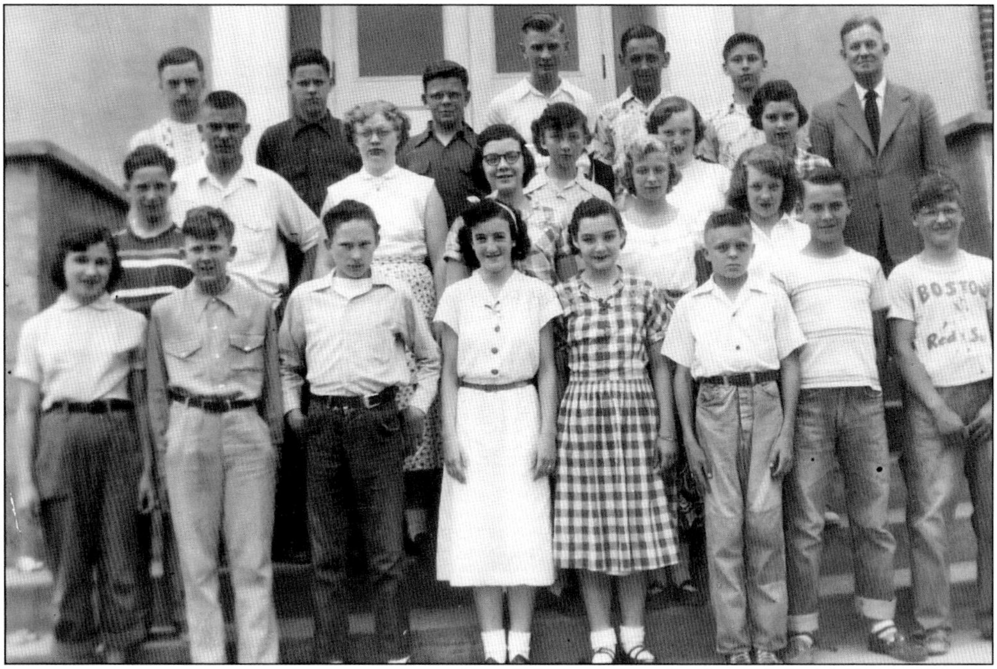

Eighth-grade Center School class, *c.* 1950. This was one of the earliest groups to graduate from the new school. Principal William Norris is shown with the students. He moved on to the junior high school when the Pomeroy Meadow Road building opened in 1957, and he was named the principal for that school also. The junior high was named in his honor after his death in 1960, and it remains the William E. Norris School, today educating all Southampton pupils from kindergarten through sixth grade.

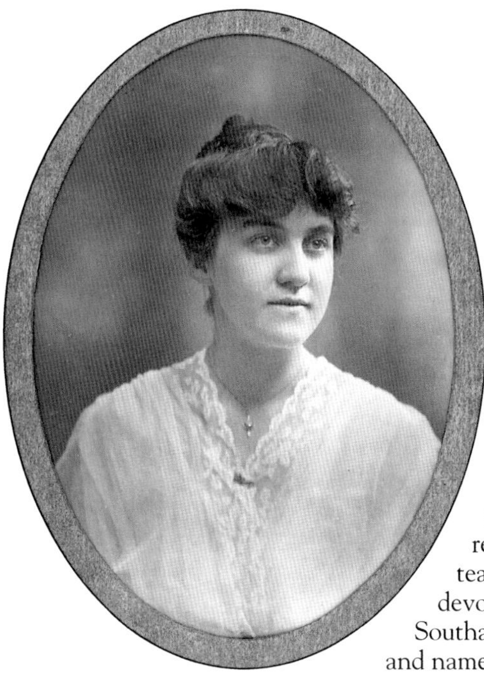

Mary Clark, teacher. A tribute to Mrs Clark appeared in the 1967 town report: "Mary Clark retired after many years of teaching. An excellent teacher, we wish to express our gratitude for her devoted service to Southampton." In 1971, the Southampton Historical Society acquired her home and named it the Clark-Chapman House.

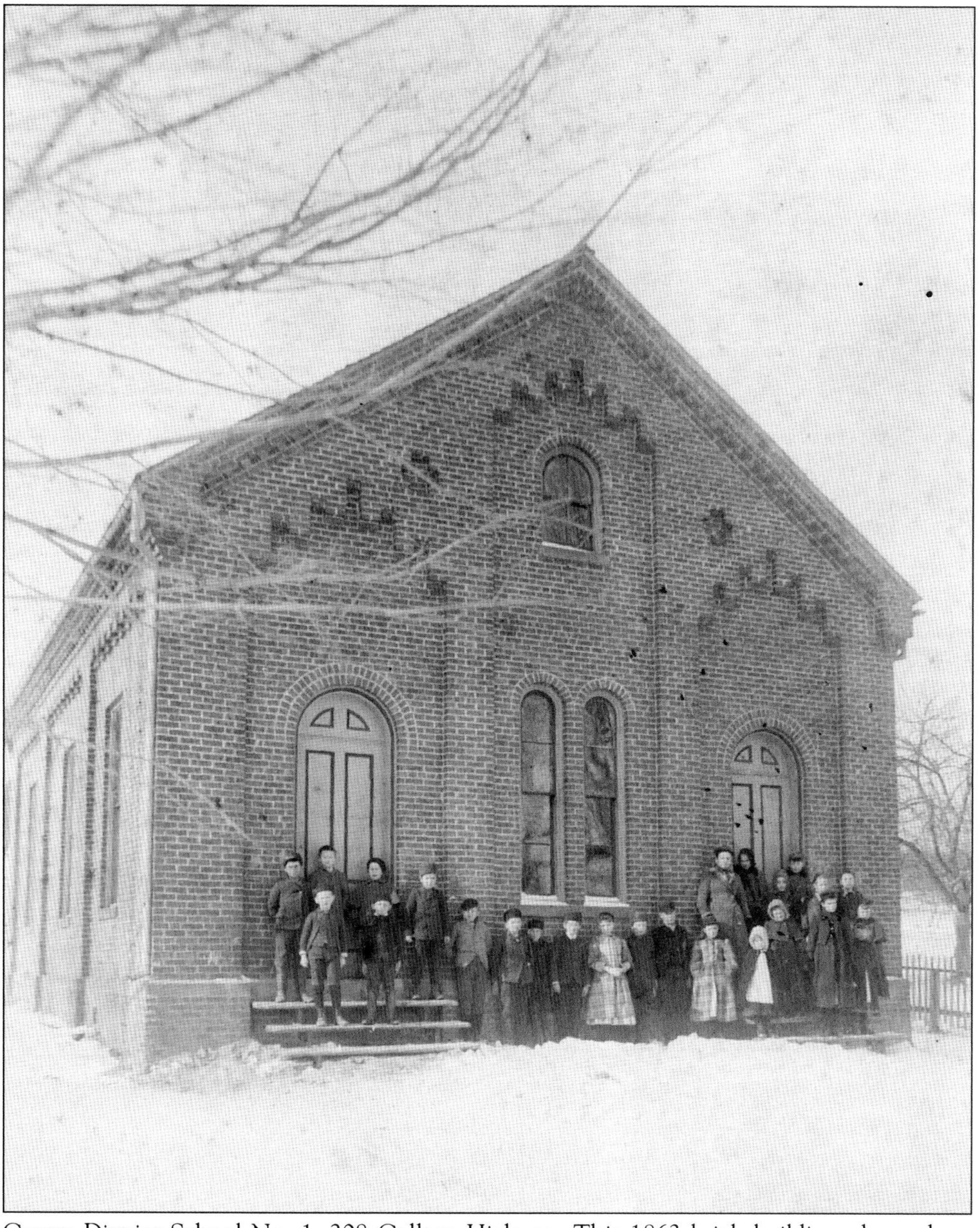

Center District School No. 1, 208 College Highway. This 1863 brick building, shown here *c.* 1891, was designed to serve the Center district for many years. Shown here is the teacher, Alice Adams (Brewer), with her students. In 1927 the consolidation of schools ended 65 years of this building's use. For the next 20 years, various groups used it for many different activities; in 1949, it was converted to a fire station.

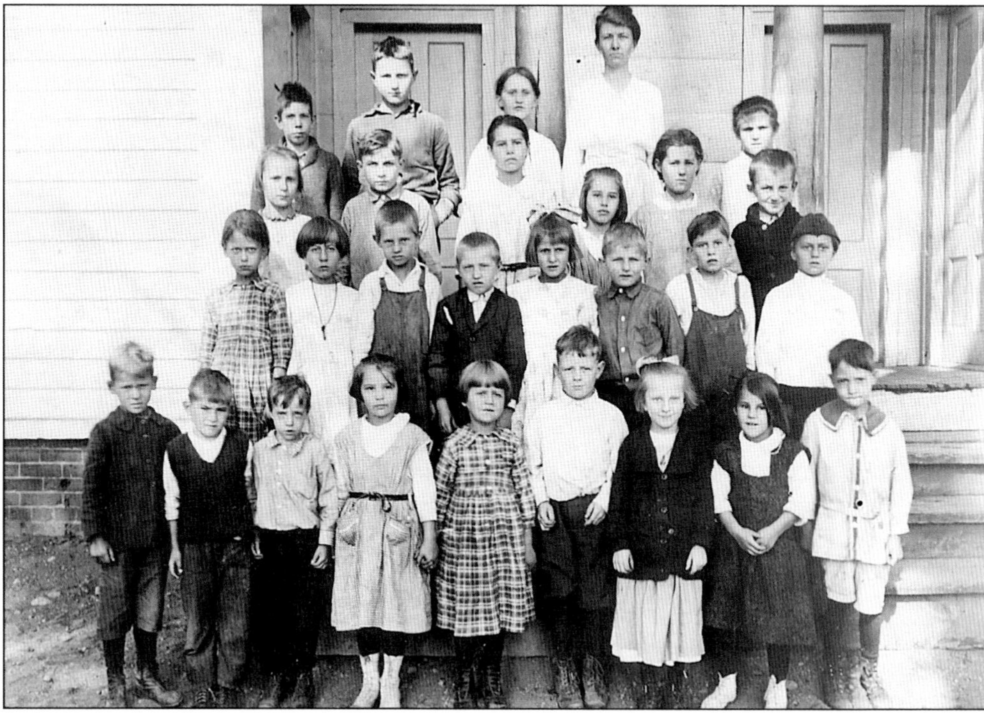

Students at District School No. 2, 121 Pomeroy Meadow Road. Margaret Zoudlick is shown with her pupils c. 1920. In the second row on the right is Max Garstka. Miss Zoudlick taught here from 1916 to 1930, when she transferred to the Sheldon School.

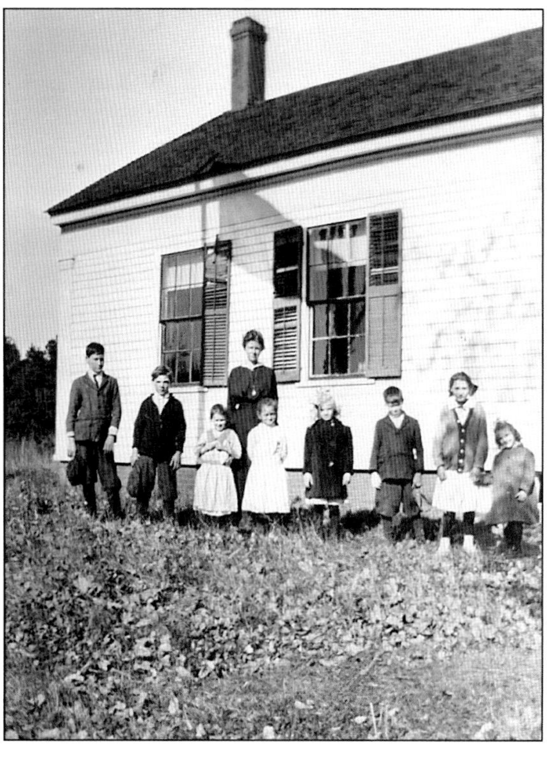

North District School No. 2. Not much is known about the beginnings of the education system, but it is recorded that after several years of dispute regarding the ownership of the land on which this building was situated, the school was relocated and rebuilt in 1845. The total cost of the project was $274.43, including the woodshed and privy.

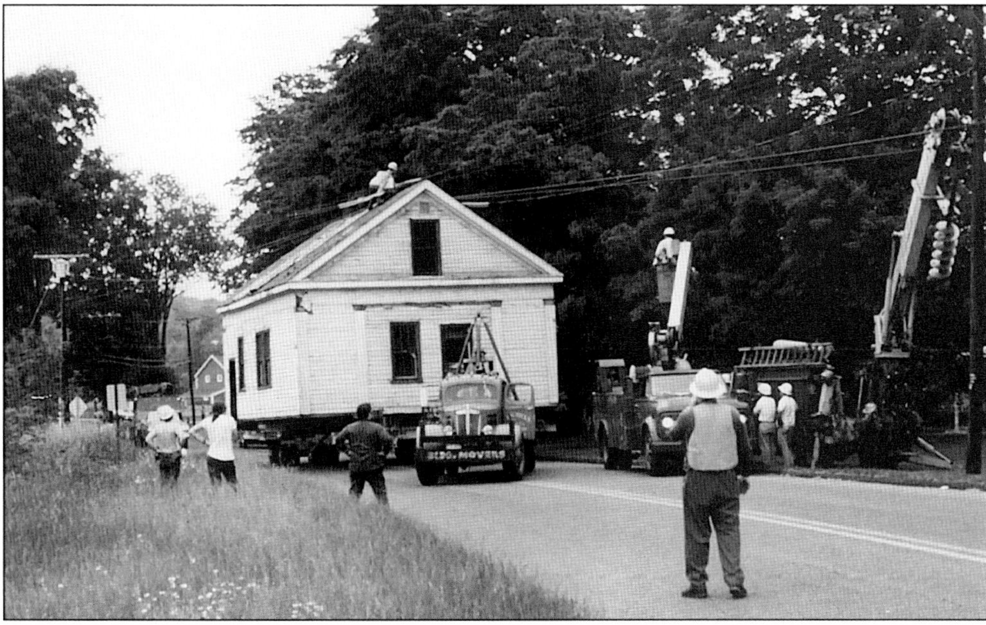

Moving day for No. 2. Many workmen and volunteers were involved in this 1975 project. Schoolchildren watched as the school moved past on Pomeroy Meadow Road, and interested folks lined the route along High Street, which was taken to avoid electrical wires. By evening the convoy had reached Conant Park. A good day's work!

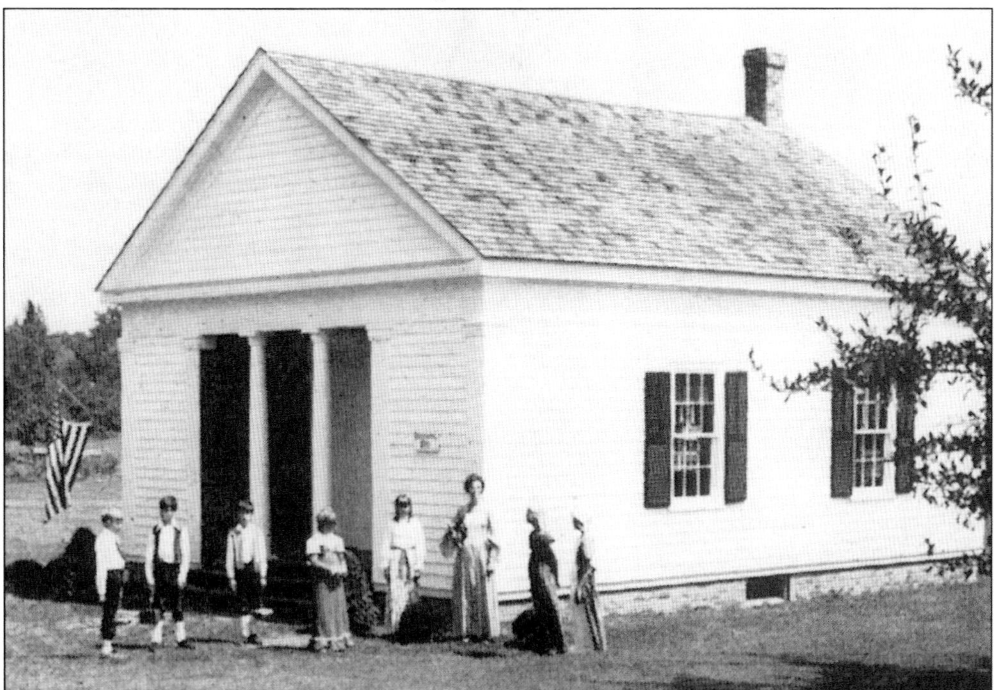

Open house at the Old North Schoolhouse, 237 College Highway in Conant Park. Now a museum under the jurisdiction of the Southampton Historical Commission, the former schoolhouse is visited by school classes and is open on Sunday afternoons during the summer.

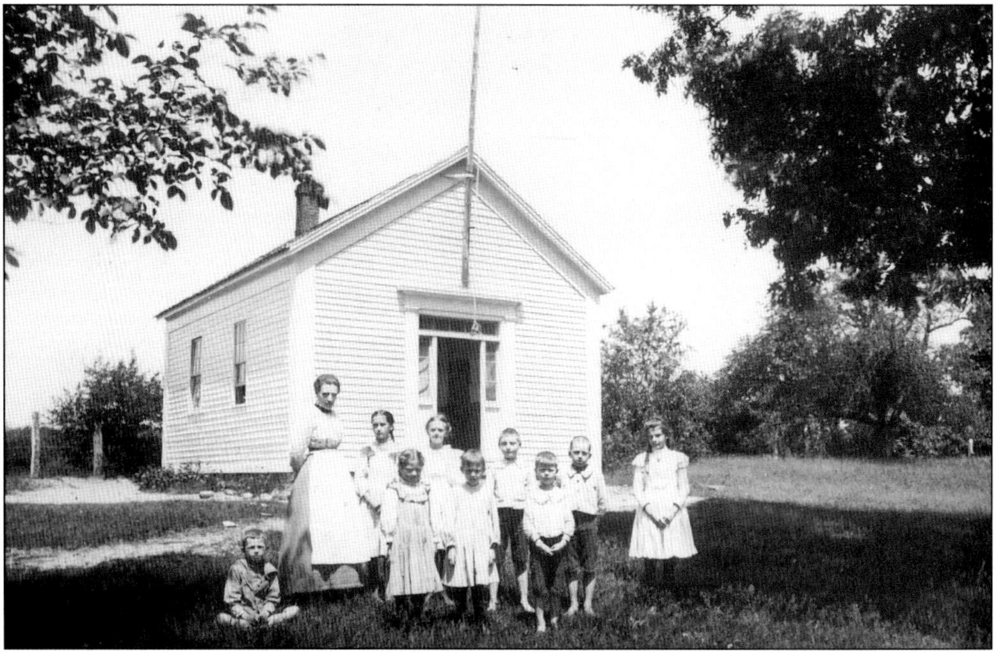

Bedlam District School No. 3, 95 Pleasant Street. Records indicate that this was in use by 1847 and continued until 1927. The street was renamed Pleasant in 1946 by a town vote. Residents desired a name that better described the area. (Howes Brothers photograph, 1900.)

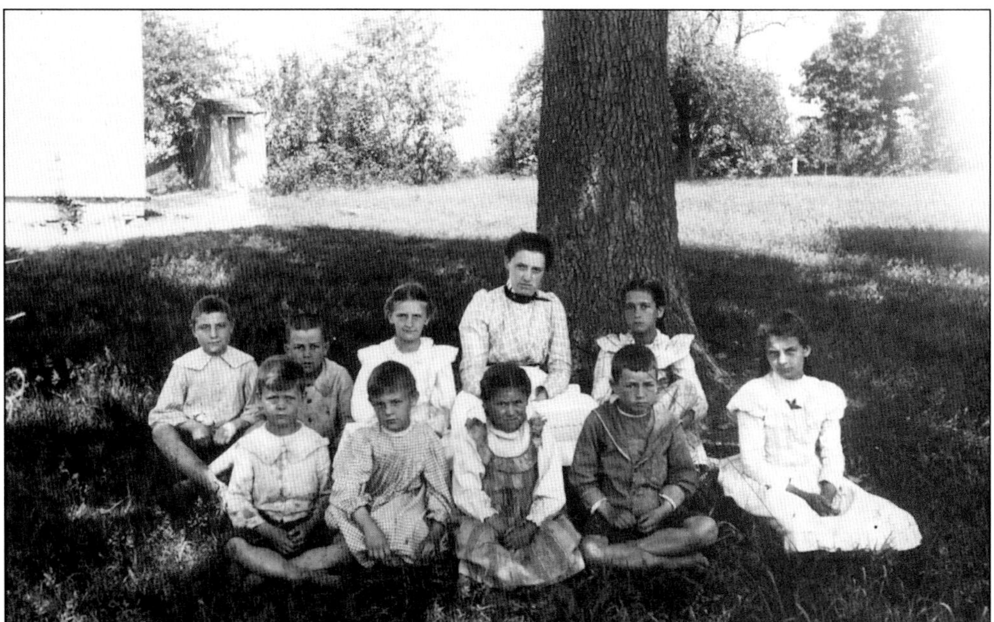

Pupils and teacher at No. 3. Apparently this school's enrollment was always small; the teacher's identity is unknown. Note the privy in the background, a necessity for all early school buildings. (Howes Brothers photograph, 1900.)

Foggintown District School No. 4, corner of Strong and Valley Roads. The building was situated in an area known for the dense fog that frequently surrounded it. This *c.* 1920 picture shows the teacher, Mira Poler, and identifies students Henry Sholl (top left) and Lora Paine (lower left).

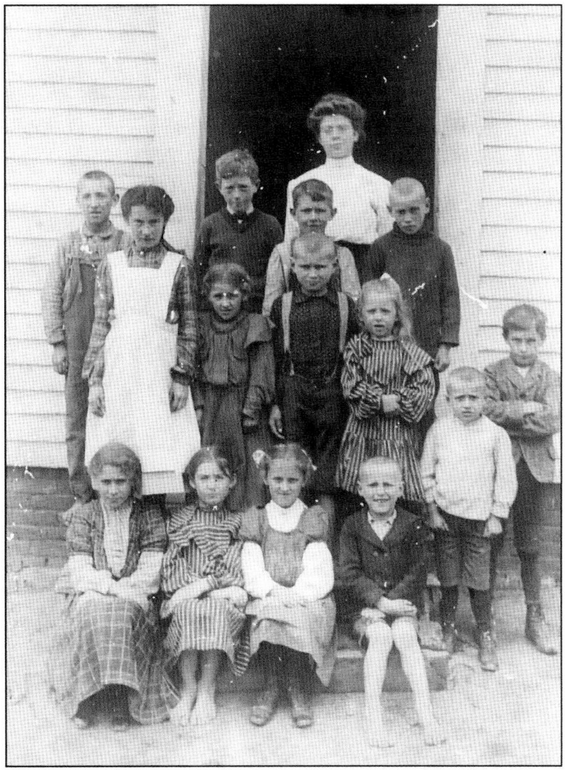

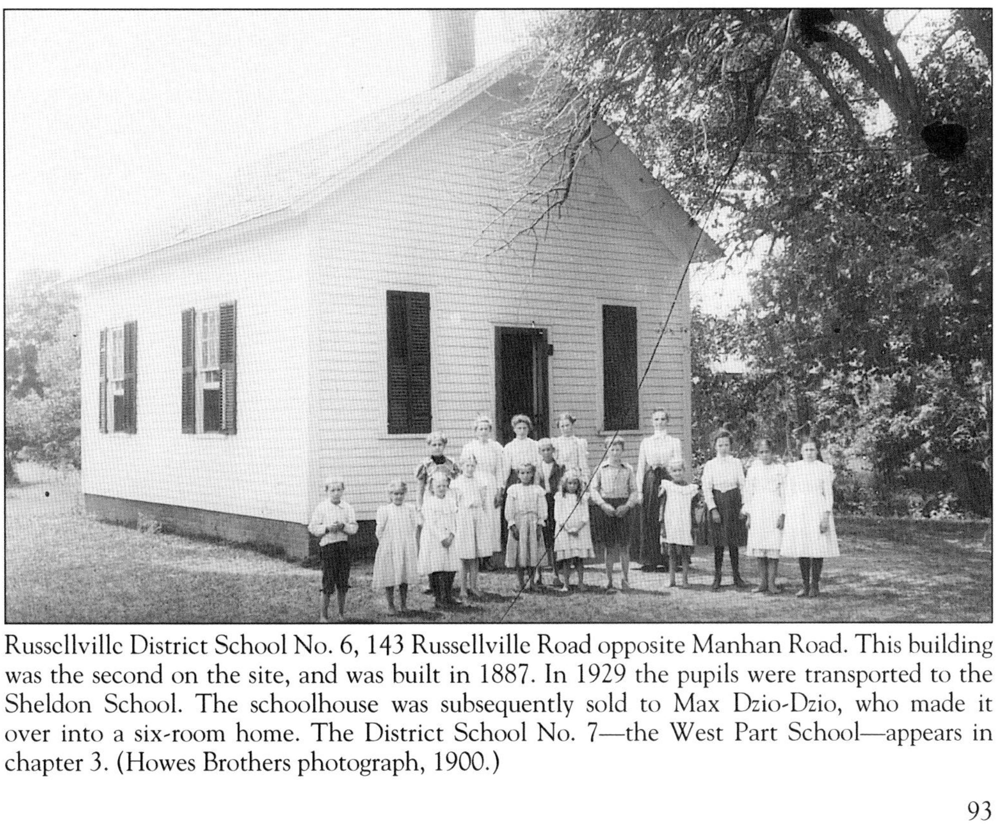

Russellville District School No. 6, 143 Russellville Road opposite Manhan Road. This building was the second on the site, and was built in 1887. In 1929 the pupils were transported to the Sheldon School. The schoolhouse was subsequently sold to Max Dzio-Dzio, who made it over into a six-room home. The District School No. 7—the West Part School—appears in chapter 3. (Howes Brothers photograph, 1900.)

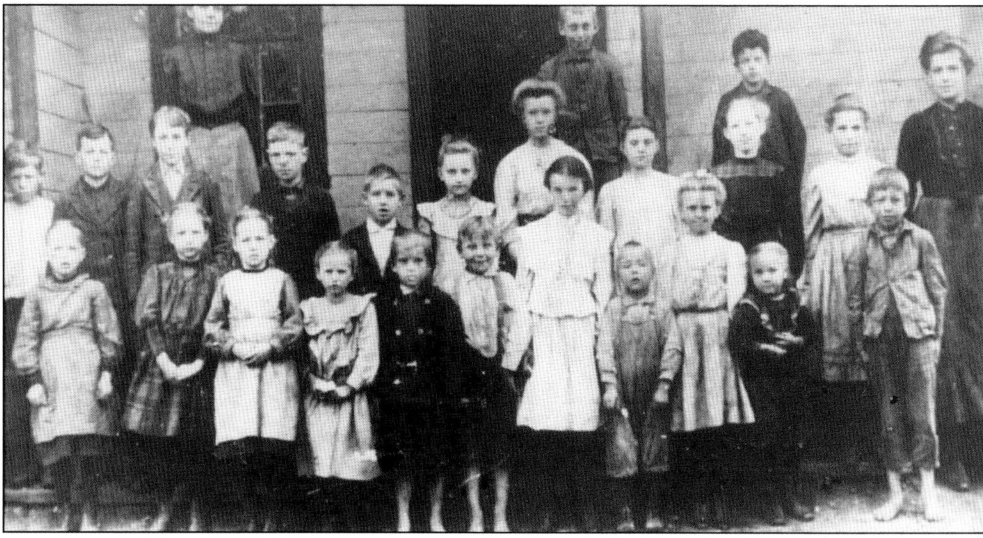

Southwest District School No. 5, 8 Fomer Road. Pupils are shown with their teacher, Julia Norris, in 1905. Grades one through six went to district schools near their homes, but grades seven, eight, and nine went to grammar school in Sheldon Academy.

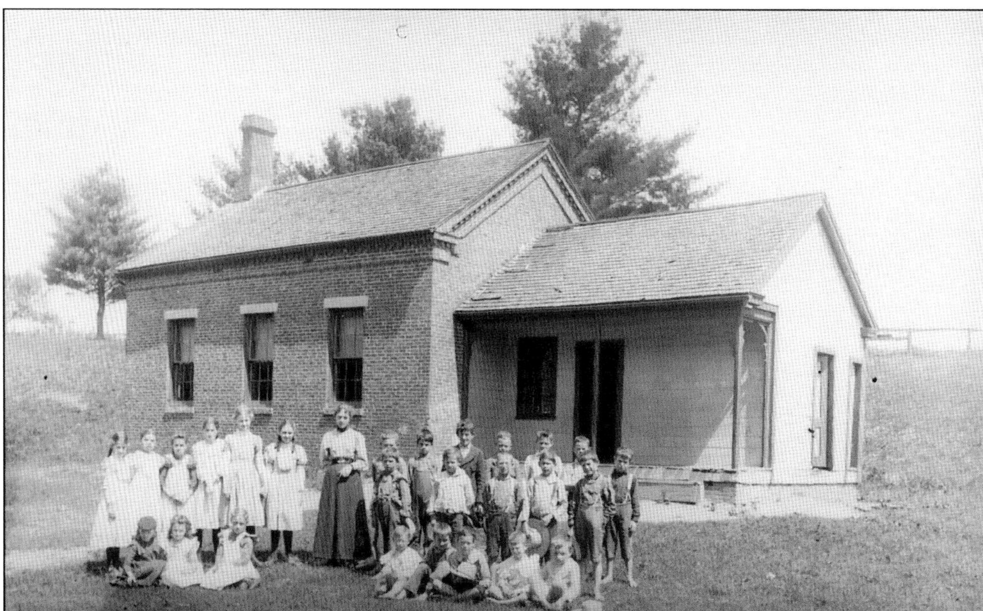

Southwest District School No. 5, 8 Fomer Road. This brick schoolhouse was built in 1866. Before that time, schools in different locations had served the area. After its closing before 1930, the building was used by the Jolly-Get-Together Club for its meetings. It was razed in 1952 and the town garage now occupies the site. (Howes Brothers photograph, 1900.)

Seven

Those Who Served

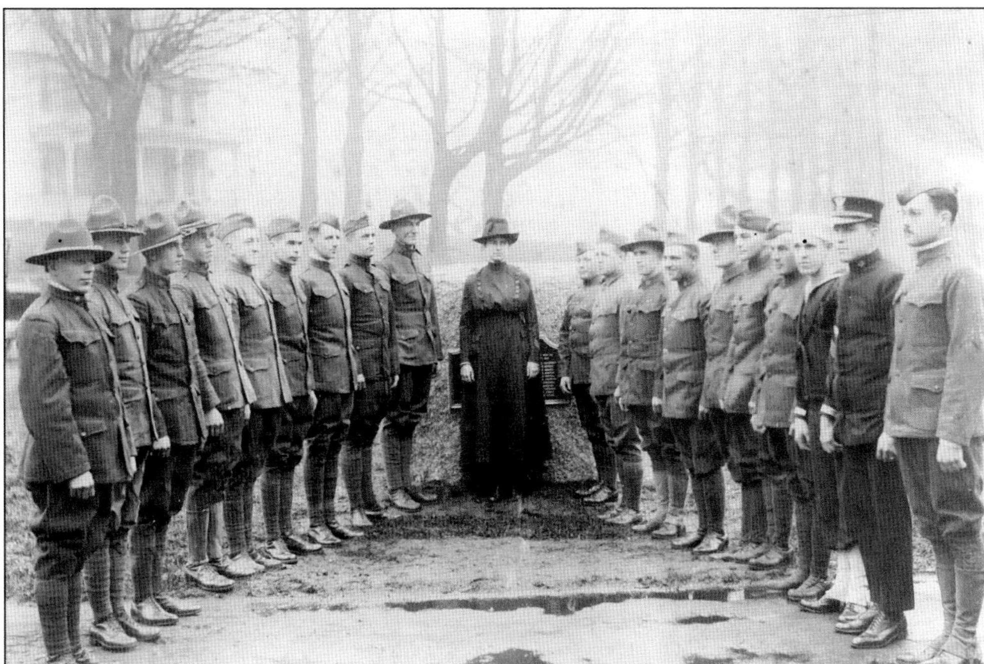

World War I veterans, Town Triangle, East Street and College Highway. These 20 veterans stand at attention in front of the monument in 1919, their images preserved for posterity. From left to right they are Edward Kupson, Frank Frary, David Hamlin, Edward Carlson, Alfred Stahly, Edward Stone, George Burbank, William Judd, Edward Norris, Army Nurse Helen Coleman, Fred Sherman, Sumner Coleman, Bernard Fowles, Frank Blow, George Norris, Frank Sherman, George Sherman, Harold Norton, Edward Norton, and Edward Pettis.

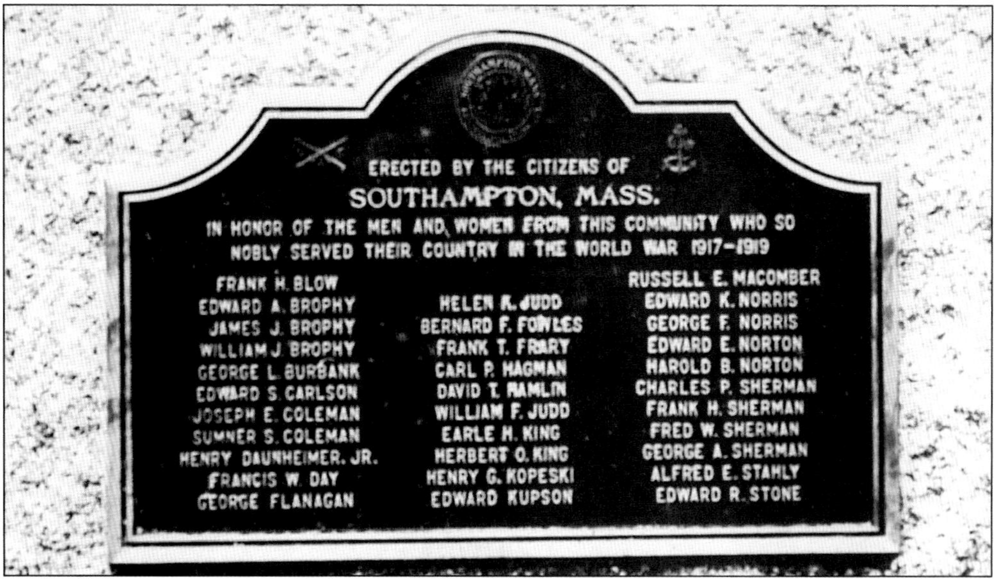

Monument to World War I veterans, Town Triangle. In addition to the 20 veterans previously pictured, the names of 12 others are listed as having served in the conflict. The reverse side of the monument holds a tablet containing the names of 119 Southampton residents who served in the military during World War II.

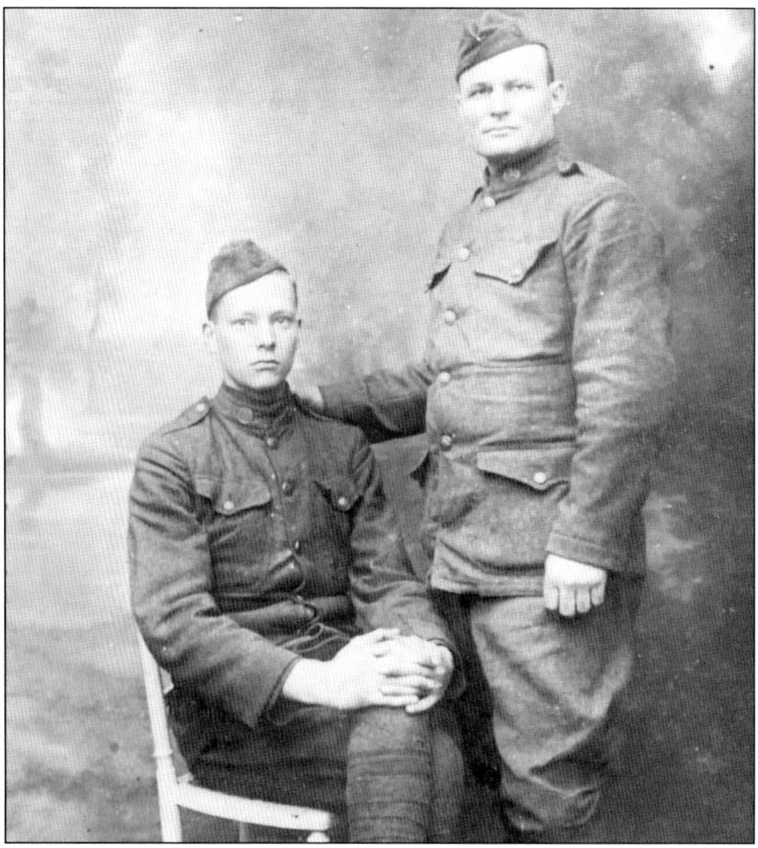

Henry Hatch, World War I veteran. Hatch appears here on the left, posing with his buddy while serving in France. Later he was a carpenter and cabinetmaker, and purchased the Jonathan Judd Sr. property (see p. 13) in 1927. His retirement years were spent restoring the old house.

Civil War veteran Ruben S. Searle. Searle enlisted from Southampton and served in the 37th Infantry from August 1862 to June 1865. "The town furnished one hundred and twenty-seven men, which was more than the number called for," according to Beula Bray's writings in *Southampton: Newtown on the Manhan*.

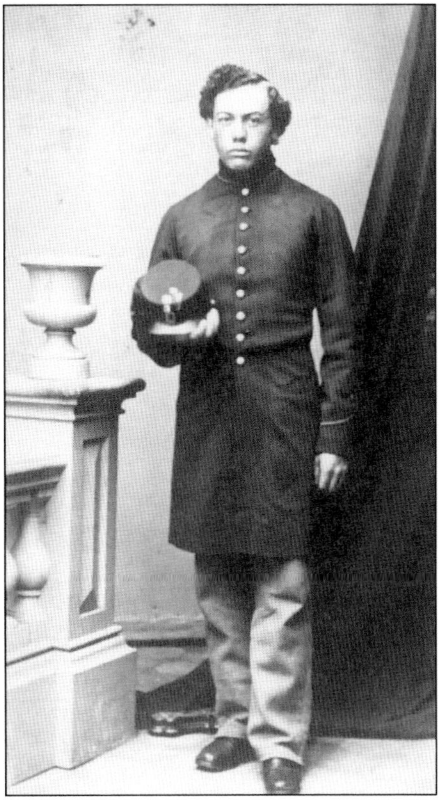

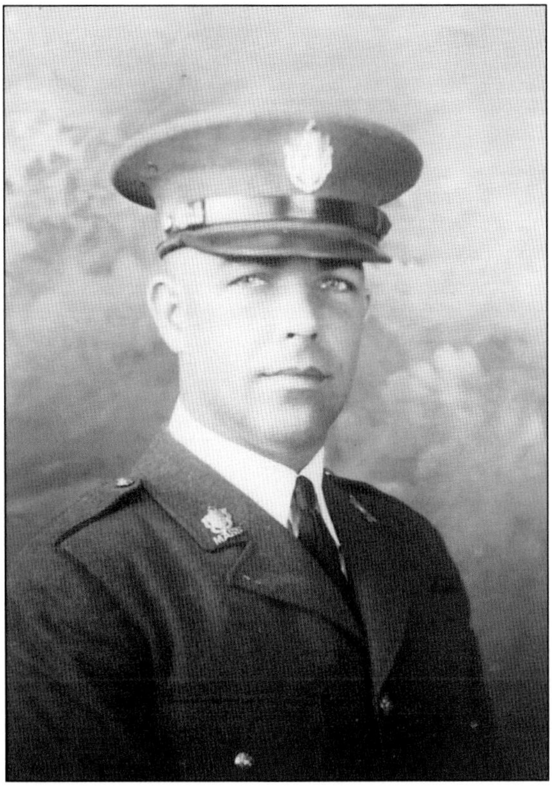

George Clark, career soldier. A Southampton native, Mr. Clark was an active member of the U.S. Army, serving in both world wars and also in the Korean Conflict. With his wife and children he resided in what is now the Clark-Chapman House.

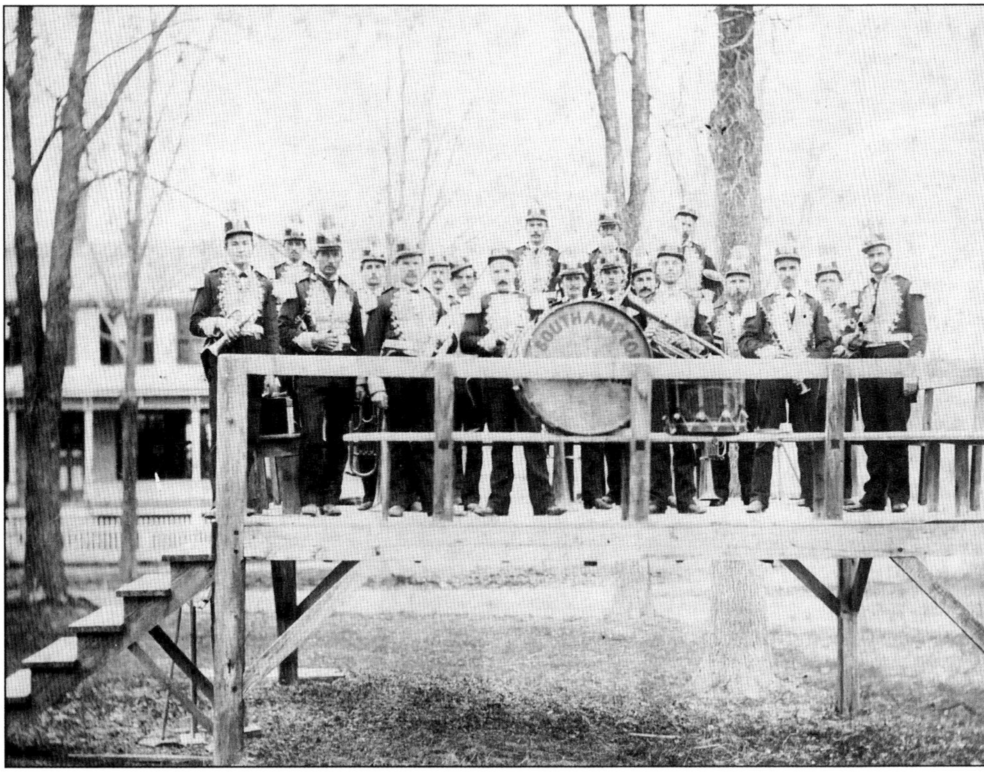

Band concert on the academy lawn. Little is known about the band, but this *c.* 1880 picture shows the Fred Judd House in the background. Standing to the left of the drummer is Henry Clapp, who also appears on p. 102.

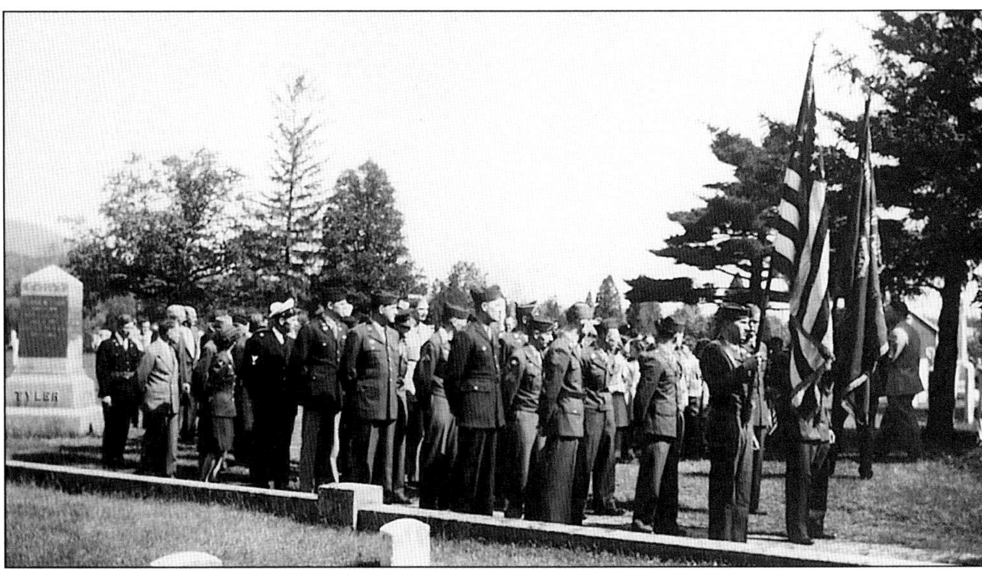

Memorial Day observance in the cemetery. Many of Southampton's recently returned veterans showed up to march in this annual Memorial Day parade. (Hugh Scott photograph, 1947.)

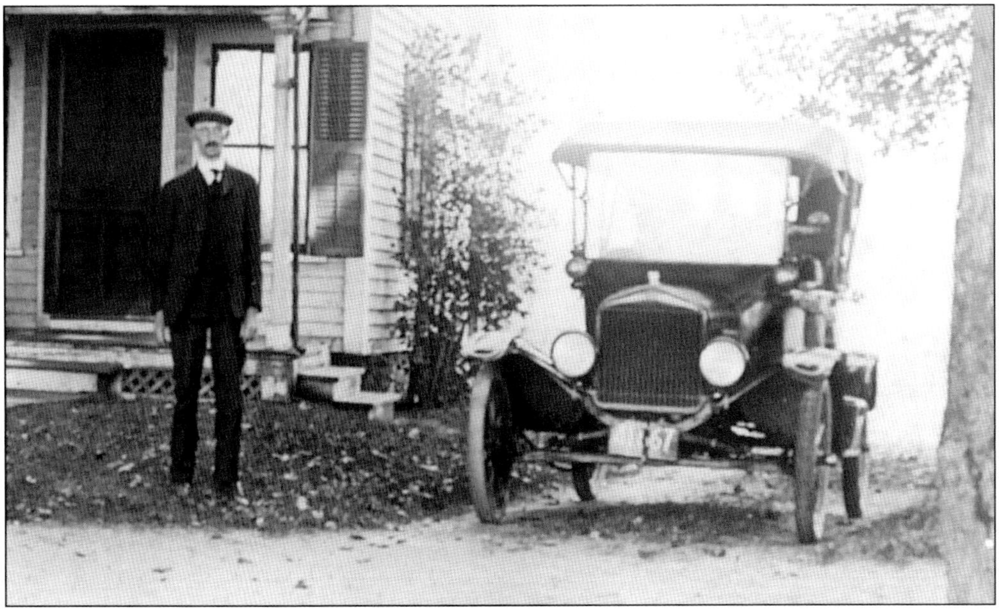

Police Chief W.J. Lyman, 17 East Street. Chief Lyman poses with the town's first cruiser. His specialty was raiding the bootlegger's stills during the Prohibition era. They were well-concealed in every corner of the town. (Lyman photograph, 1925.)

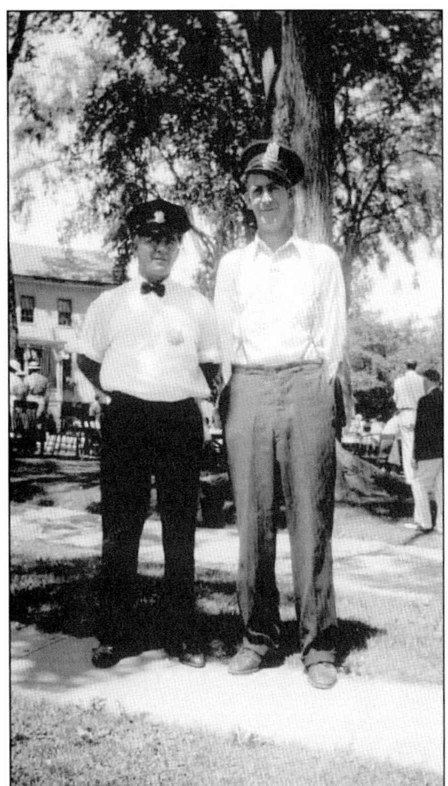

Policemen maintaining order on Old Home Day, Town Center. Reynolds Sherman, longtime policeman and chief in the mid-1940s, appears with his "deputy," Clifford Delisle. (Hugh Scott photograph, *c.* 1940.)

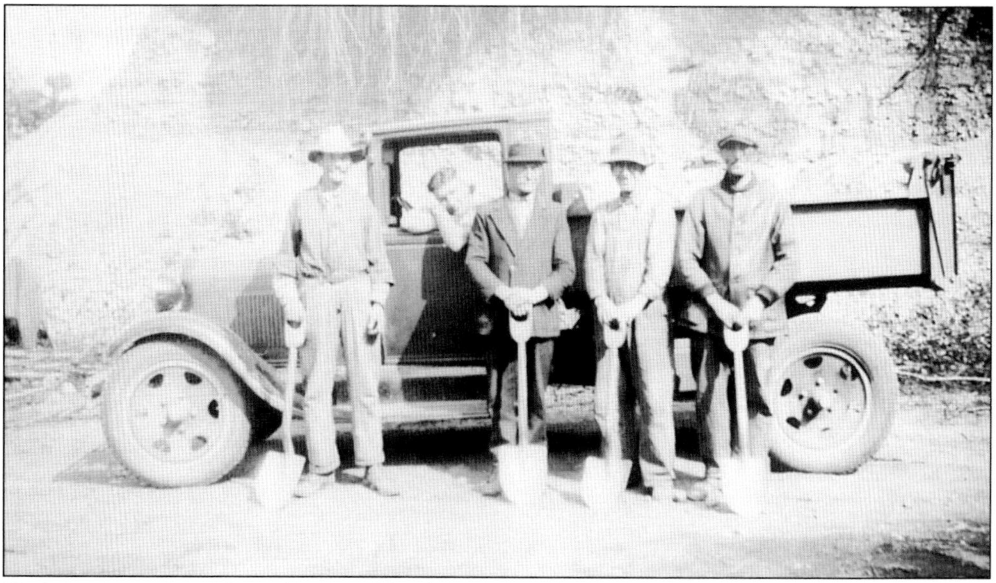

Highway crew at work in the gravel bank at 262 College Highway. Stash Deptula is asleep at the wheel and the worker on the right is Henry Sholl. In those days (*c.* 1929), the "equipment" consisted of a few shovels and a new dump truck.

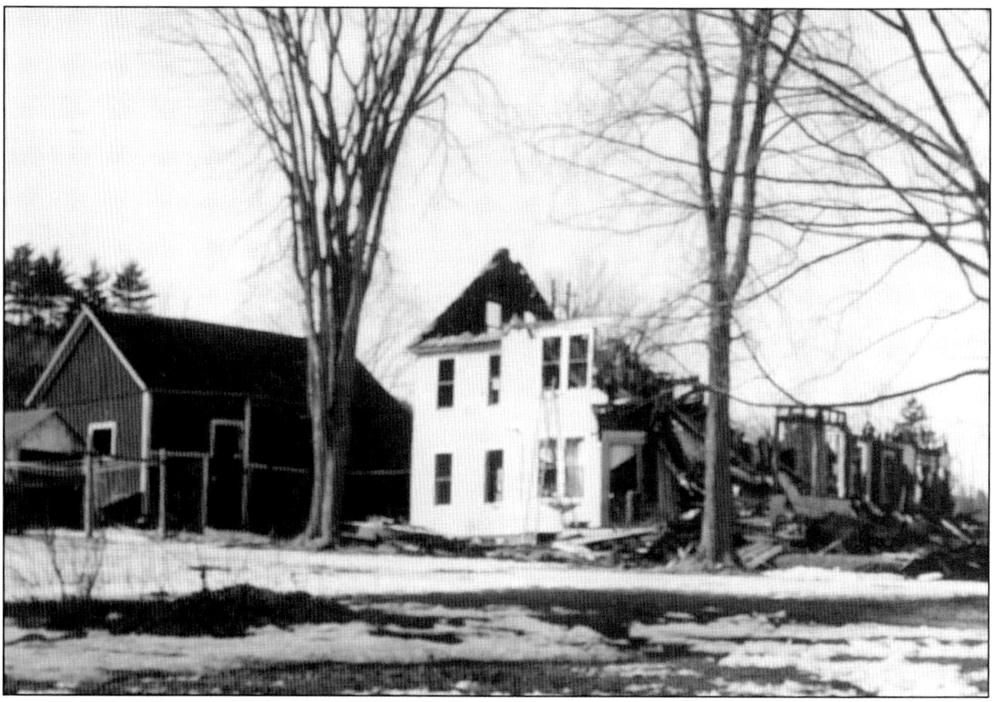

E.K. Parsons House, victim of fire, 46 High Street. One of three so-called High Street mansions, it was almost entirely burned in 1940. Built by E.K. Parsons after his West Part property was taken for the Holyoke Reservoir construction in 1898 (see p. 49), this structure was home to Parsons family for many years. It was owned by the Ray Douglas family at the time of the fire. (Bob Madsen photograph, 1940.)

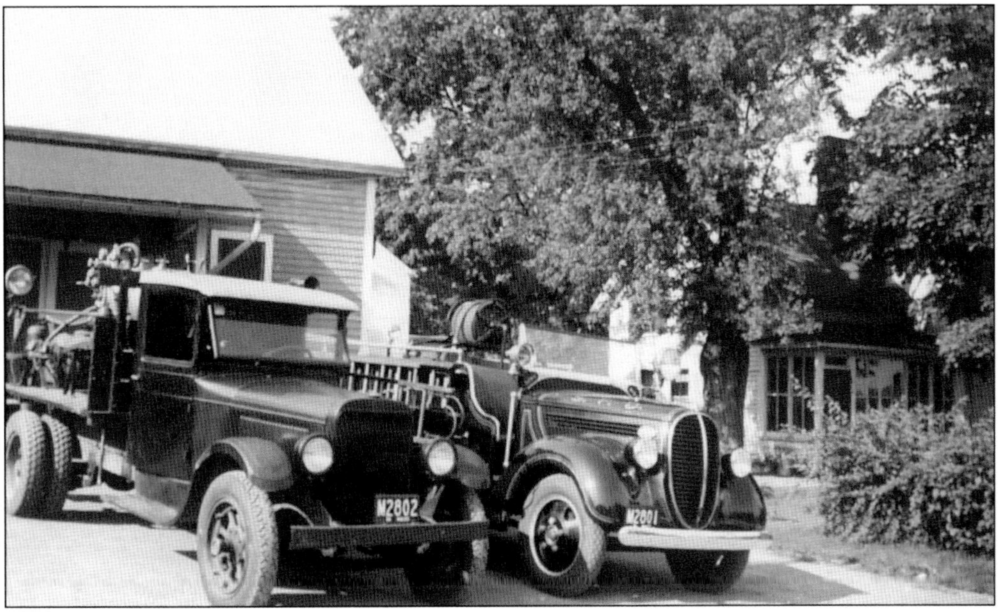

Early fire-fighting equipment, 4 Center Street. These vehicles were lined up outside the Madsen Grain Company, where they were garaged until 1949, when the District School No. 1 was adapted for the fire department's use. In 1947 the town obtained its first ambulance, a second-hand Nash, from the Town of Easthampton. (Madsen photograph, 1937.)

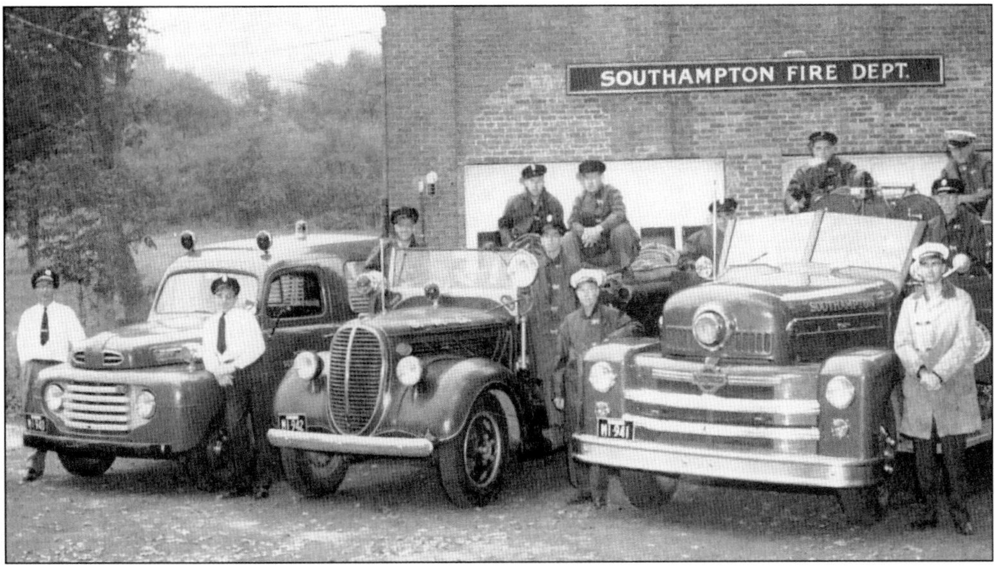

Men and equipment of the fire department. At the time of this picture in 1959, the present firehouse had been in use for ten years. Chief Clarence Hannum stands in the right foreground.

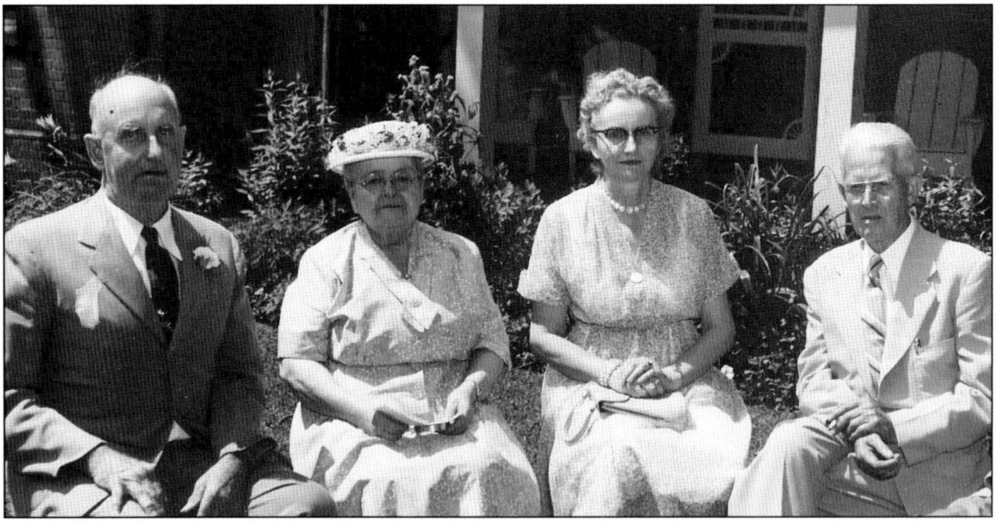

Old-timers meet on Old Home Day, East Street. Edward Cornelius Searle, Mary Elizabeth Rathbun Judd, Hazel Lyman Hendrick Vincent, and Sumner Coleman are shown here *c.* 1950. These four native sons and daughters were regular attendees at Old Home Day events, each contributing in his or her own way.

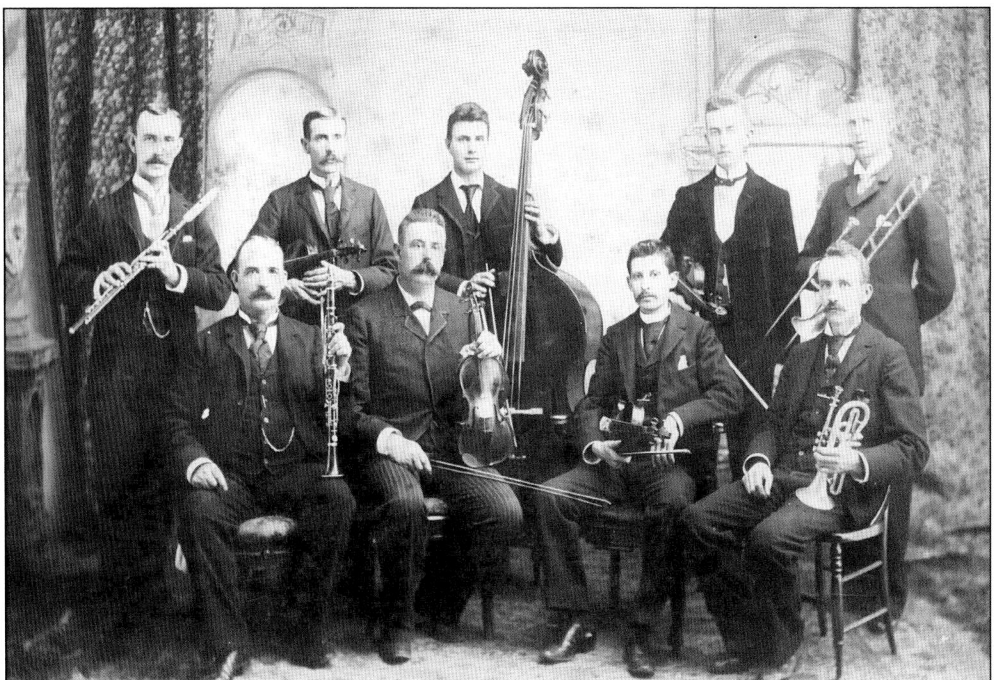

Clarinet band. In the front on the left is Henry Clapp, *c.* 1890. He and his wife, Clara, purchased the Methodist parsonage at 21 East Street in 1924, and it remained in his family for 19 years.

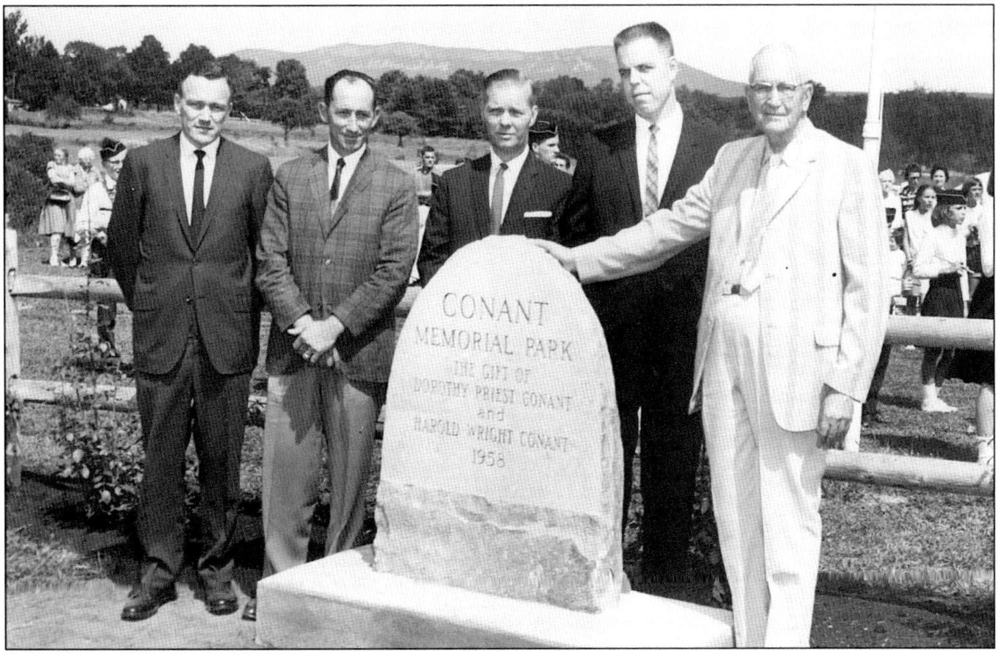

Conant Memorial Park dedication, College Highway. Through the generosity of Dorothy and Harold Conant, this tract of 14 acres was given to the town in 1959. Shown here from left to right are Douglas Madsen; longtime park commission chairman John Garstka; Selectman Arthur Satler; Rev. Charles Hume; and Harold Conant. (*Gazette* photograph, 1959.)

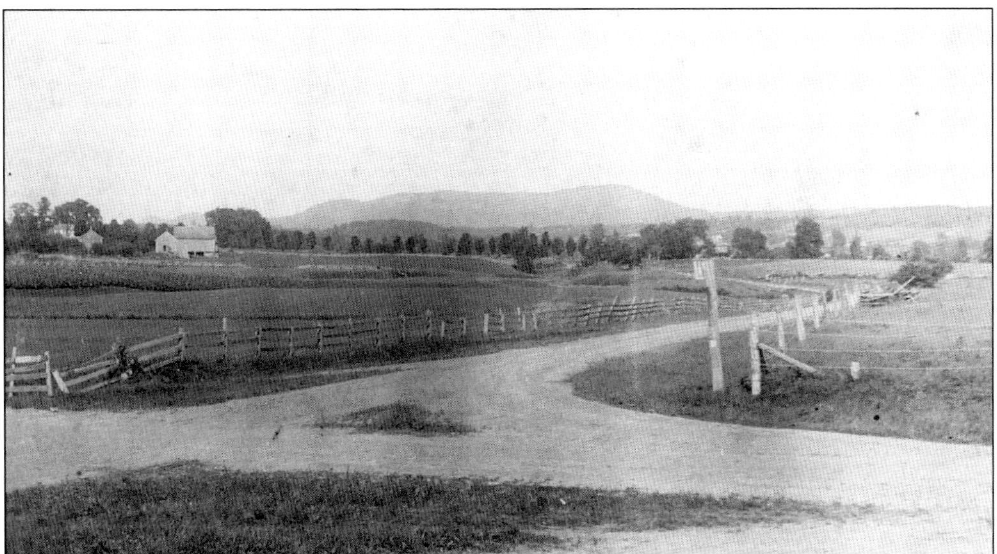

Conant Park land, corner of College Highway and New Road (now Clark Street). This open land, long used as farmland by Ed Clark, was destined to become Conant Park. (Judd photograph, c. 1890.)

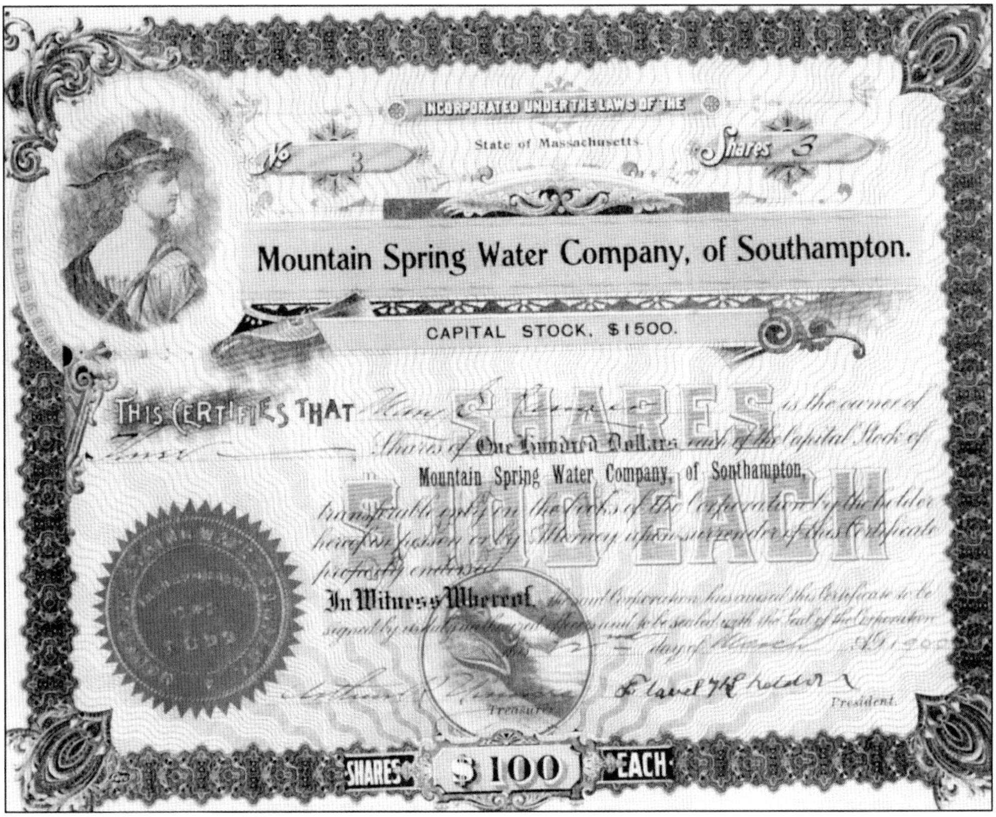
INCORPORATED UNDER THE LAWS OF THE
State of Massachusetts.
No 3
Shares 3
Mountain Spring Water Company, of Southampton.
CAPITAL STOCK, $1500.
THIS CERTIFIES THAT
Shares of One Hundred Dollars each of the Capital Stock of
Mountain Spring Water Company, of Southampton,
In Witness Whereof,
Treasurer.
President.
SHARES $100 EACH

Mountain Spring Water Company stock certificate. In 1865 a scarcity of good water provided the impetus for a gravity water system that would flow from existing springs on the hillside above High Street. In 1900 several potential users formed a company and sold stock for $100 per share.

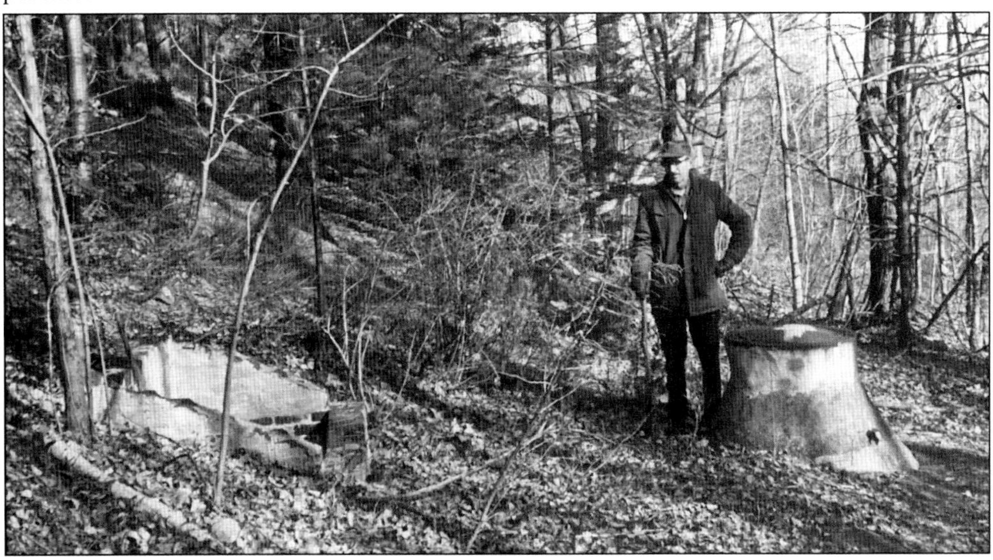

Main reservoir for Mountain Spring Water Company, Little Mountain. This reservoir and the remnants of four contributing springs remain today. (Hendrick photograph, 1980.)

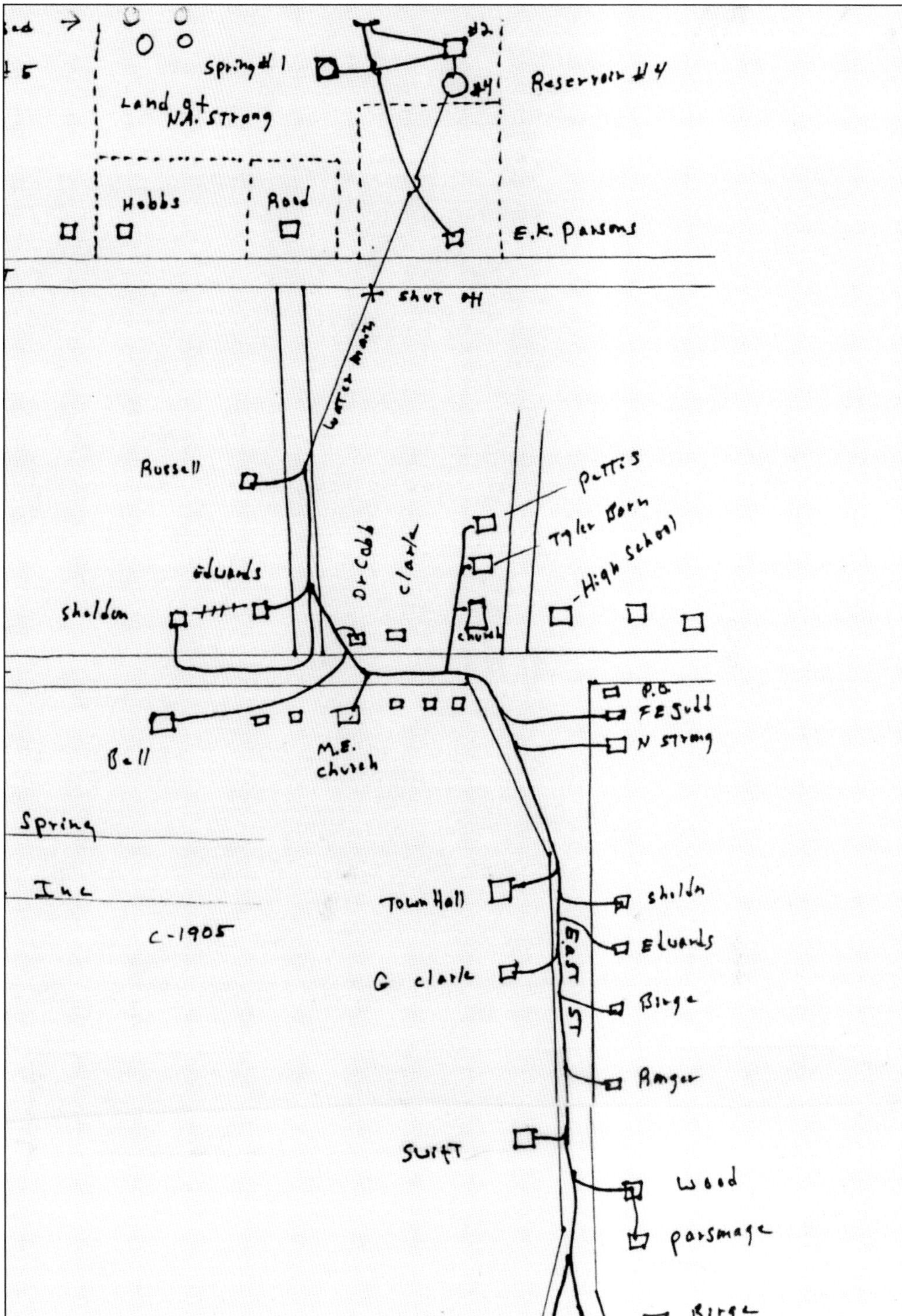

Map of the water company distribution system. The 1905 map shows the 25 subscribers, including the Congregational church and the Methodist church. The line extended down East Street to the railroad station.

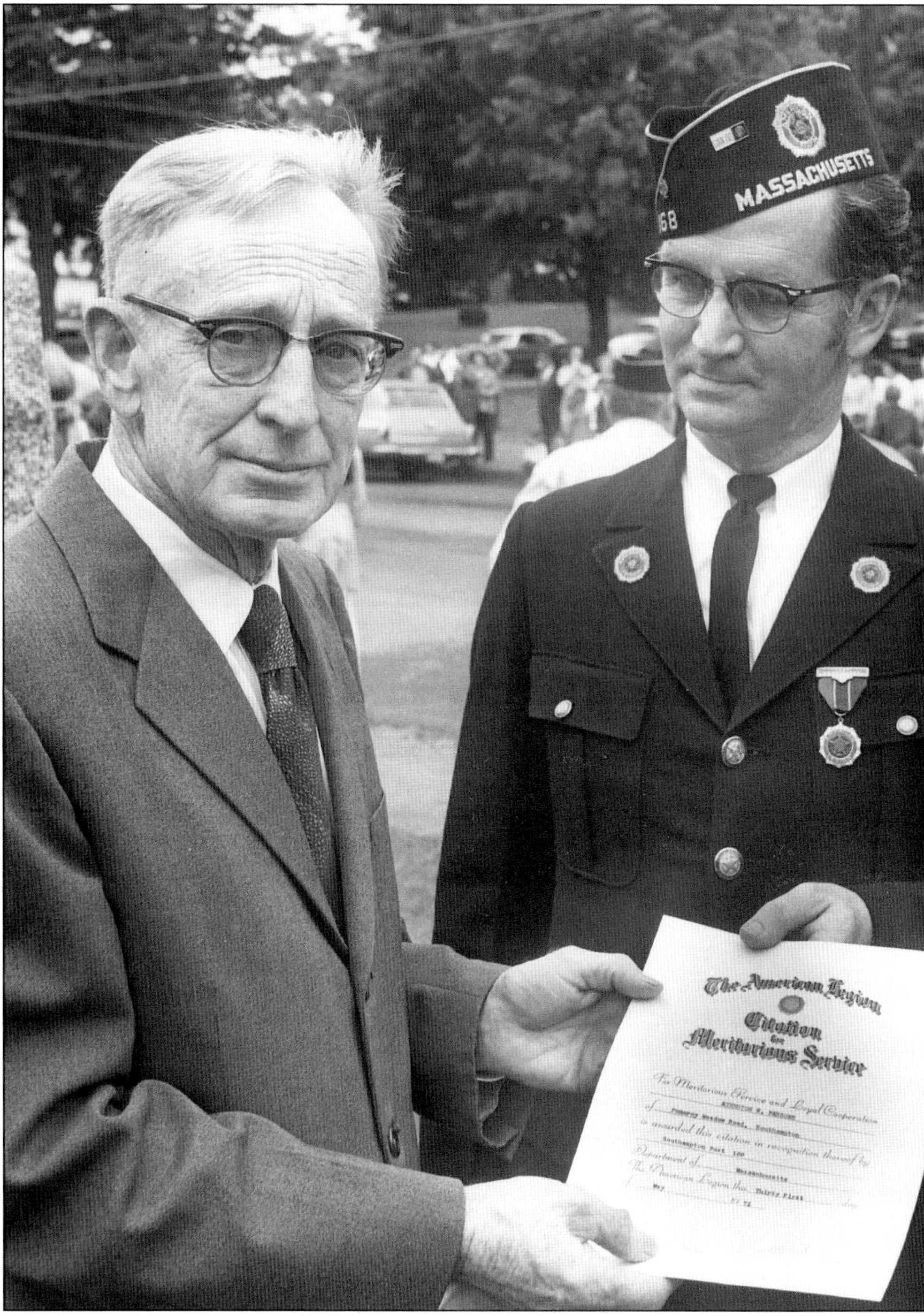

Atherton Parsons, recipient of the American Legion Good Citizen Award. We are indebted to Atherton Parsons for the wealth of information that he assembled. His 1967 *History of Old Houses* records dates and relevant information on 71 houses. In 1971 he received the American Legion Good Citizen Award in recognition of his efforts. Presenting the award is Legionnaire Lee Annis. (*Gazette* photograph, 1971.)

Eight

Folks Having Fun

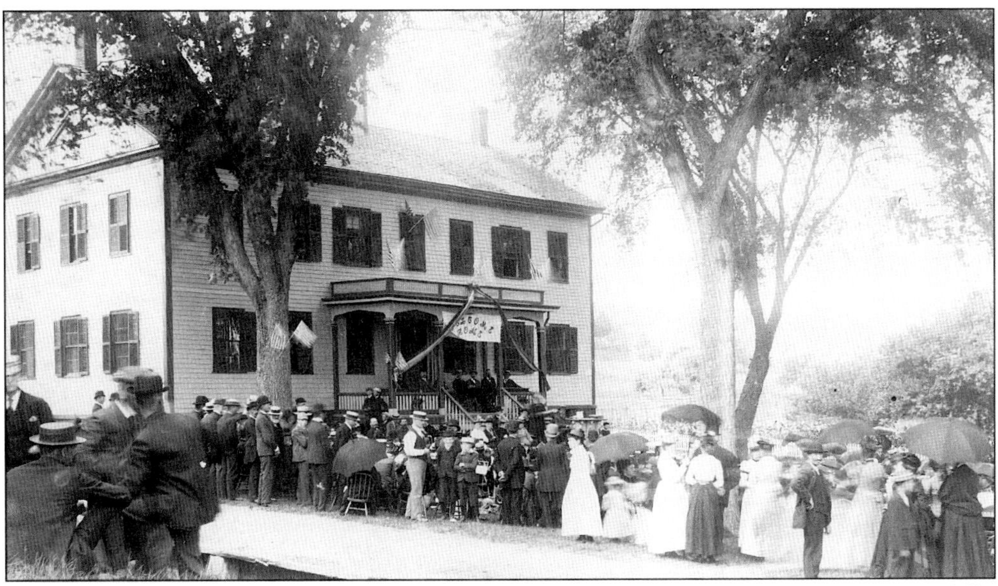

Old Home Days past, Sheldon Academy lawn. Just over one hundred years ago several town folks gathered to talk about old times, starting a tradition that continues today. The school building displays a "Welcome Home" banner, and tables and chairs cover the lawn. Many people—both residents and visitors—have gathered for the occasion. (Judd photograph, 1902.)

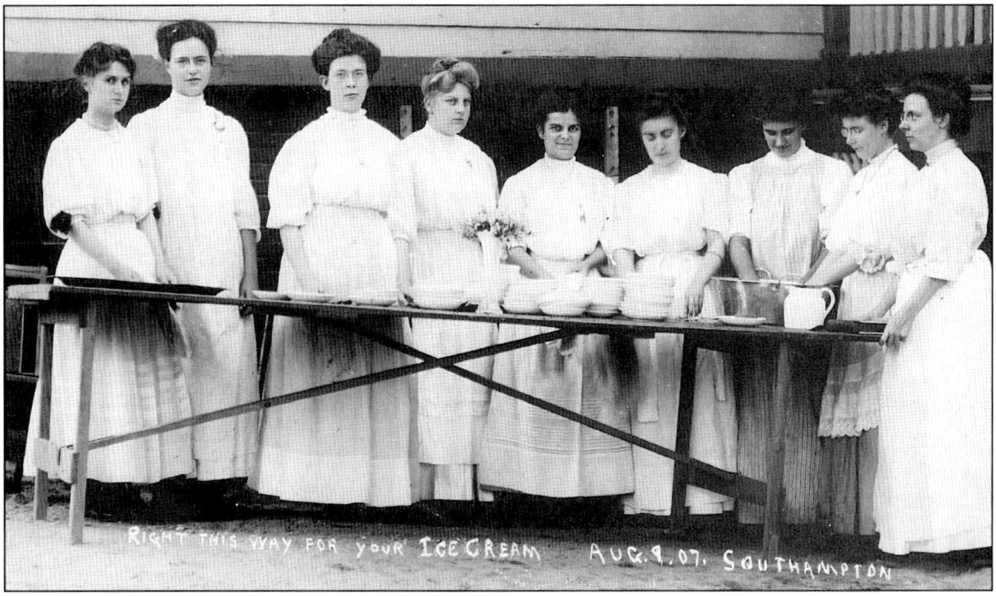

Ice cream social on Old Home Day weekend. This 1907 postcard invites guests to "Step Right This Way For Your Ice Cream." Serving are Ella Healey, Helen Judd Coleman, Mira Poler, Winifred Lyman, Eve Healy Gunn, Edith Lyman Haliday, two unknown persons, and Ethel Tiffany.

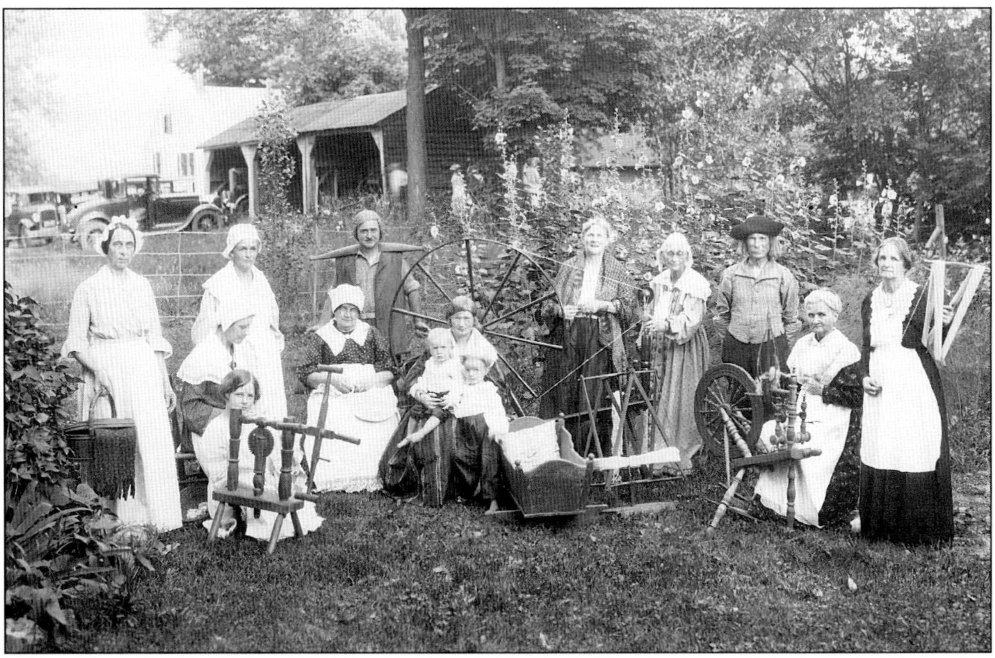

Pageant participants, 1903. This photograph was taken where the church's parish hall now stands. The pageant commemorating the 200th anniversary of the founding of Southampton was performed in the flat area (parking lot) south of the parish hall. The large audience watched from the hillside. The old horse sheds can be seen at the north end of the parking lot. (John Howland photograph, 1903.)

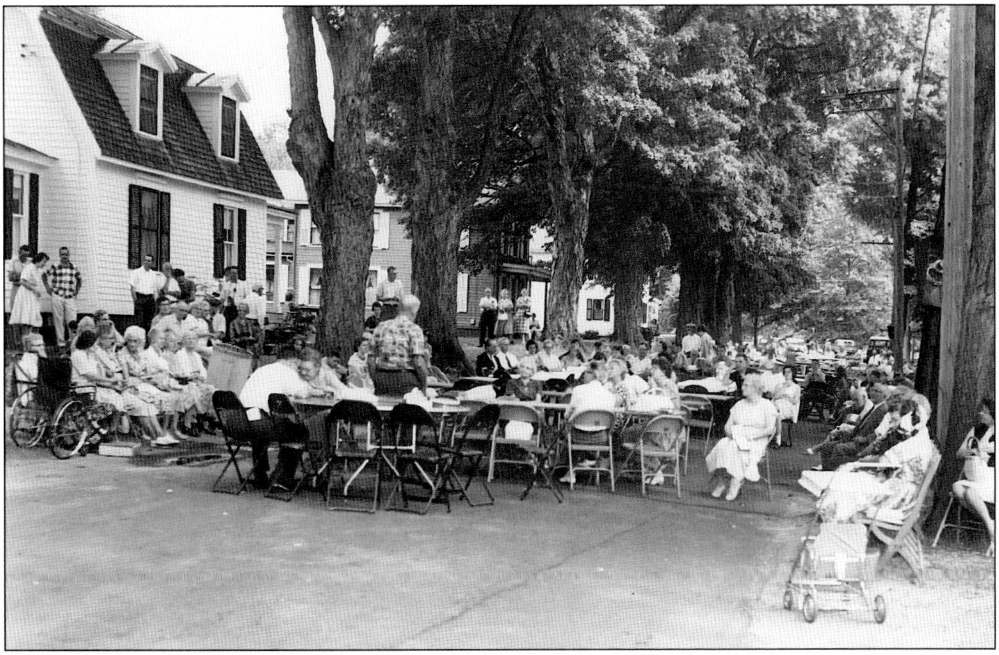

Old Home Day picnic on East Street, *c.* 1960. The giant elm trees that had provided shade on the academy lawn were removed in 1939, so the gathering was moved to East Street, where the maple trees cast their shade.

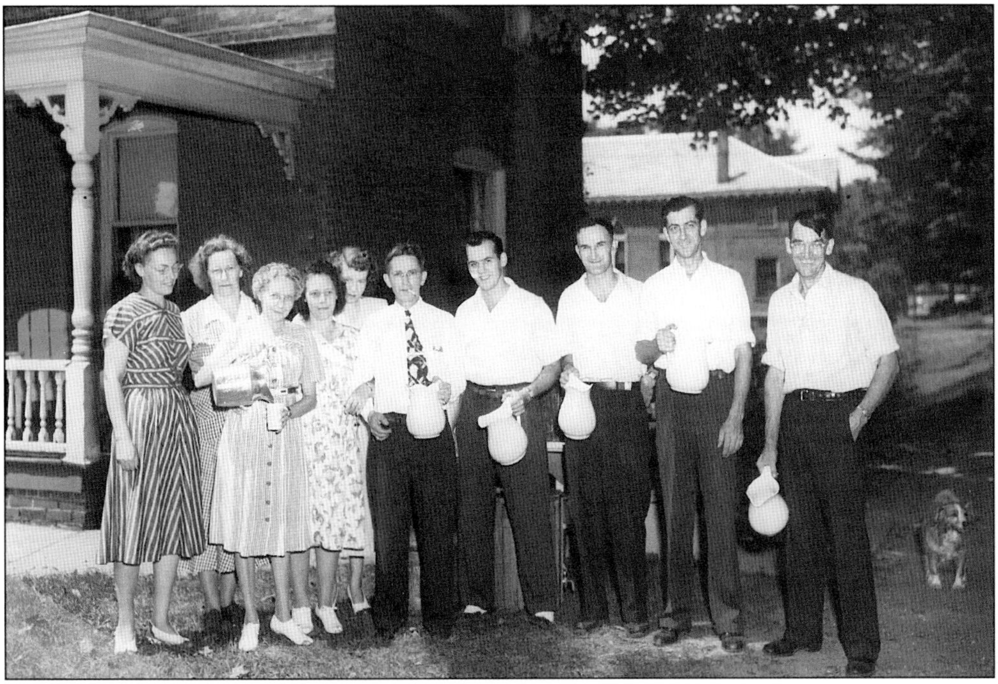

Efficiency Committee lineup, 12 East Street. From their spot on the Lindsey Brown lawn, these folks were ready, willing, and able to serve refreshing drinks to all. Included here are Eleanor Vollert, Evelyn Hall, Ida David, Beatrice Fernald, two unknown persons, George David, Larry Fernald, Richard Vollert, and Delbert Hall.

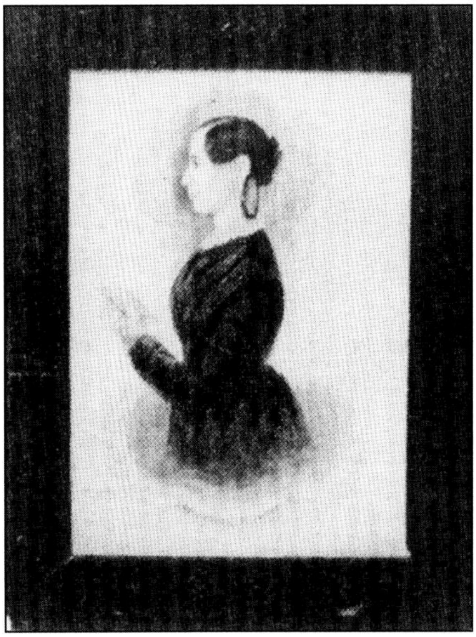

Mary Ann Pomeroy sampler. Mary Ann was 12 years old and living on Pomeroy Meadow Road when she stitched this great sampler. It was recently acquired from Nancy Tilman of San Jose, California. No one knows how it came to be that far from home.

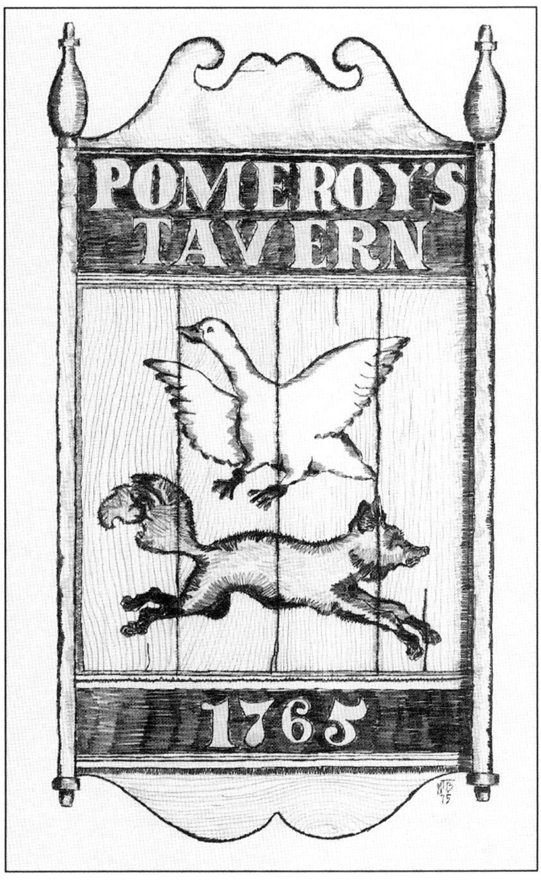

Pomeroy's Tavern sign. The old tavern was a wayside stop on County Road, then a stage route between Northampton and Westfield. It catered to many generations of thirsty travelers in the years between 1765 and 1860. (Drawing by Max Barron.)

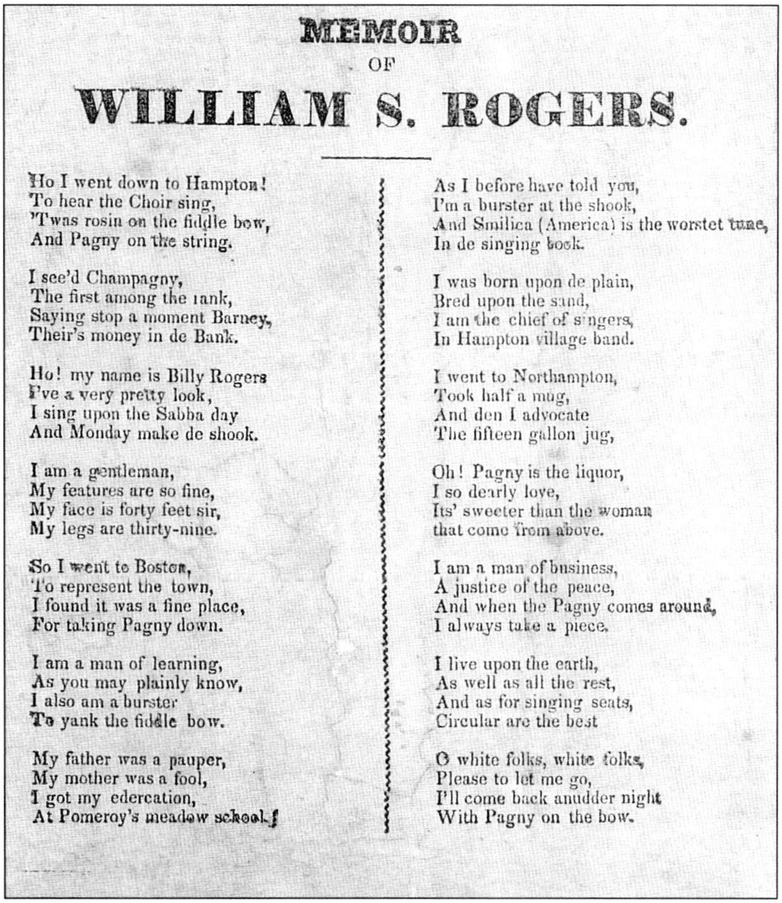

MEMOIR
OF
WILLIAM S. ROGERS.

Ho I went down to Hampton!
To hear the Choir sing,
'Twas rosin on the fiddle bow,
And Pagny on the string.

I see'd Champagny,
The first among the rank,
Saying stop a moment Barney,
Their's money in de Bank.

Ho! my name is Billy Rogers
I've a very pretty look,
I sing upon the Sabba day
And Monday make de shook.

I am a gentleman,
My features are so fine,
My face is forty feet sir,
My legs are thirty-nine.

So I went to Boston,
To represent the town,
I found it was a fine place,
For taking Pagny down.

I am a man of learning,
As you may plainly know,
I also am a burster
To yank the fiddle bow.

My father was a pauper,
My mother was a fool,
I got my edercation,
At Pomeroy's meadow school.

As I before have told you,
I'm a burster at the shook,
And Smilica (America) is the worstet tune,
In de singing book.

I was born upon de plain,
Bred upon the sand,
I am the chief of singers,
In Hampton village band.

I went to Northampton,
Took half a mug,
And den I advocate
The fifteen gallon jug,

Oh! Pagny is the liquor,
I so dearly love,
Its' sweeter than the woman
that come from above.

I am a man of business,
A justice of the peace,
And when the Pagny comes around,
I always take a piece.

I live upon the earth,
As well as all the rest,
And as for singing seats,
Circular are the best

O white folks, white folks,
Please to let me go,
I'll come back anudder night
With Pagny on the bow.

William S. Rogers's memoir. Mr. Rogers was a justice of the peace, town selectman, choir director, organist and violinist, etc., and made his money operating a steam sawmill and a barrel stave shop. He lost his business after investment in the Hampshire & Hampden Railroad Company and the California Gold Rush scandal. His was an interesting life with some wins and some losses.

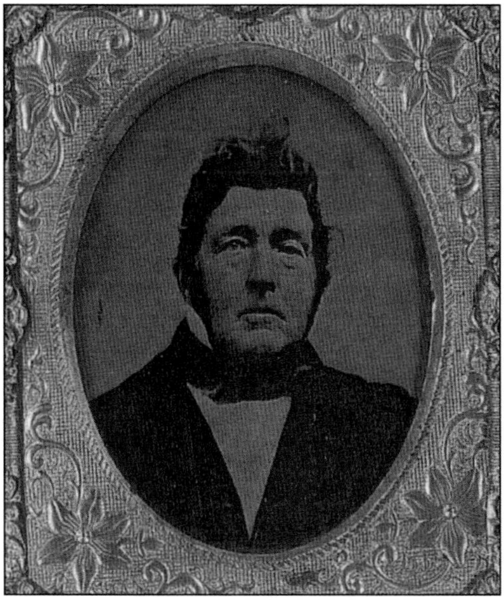

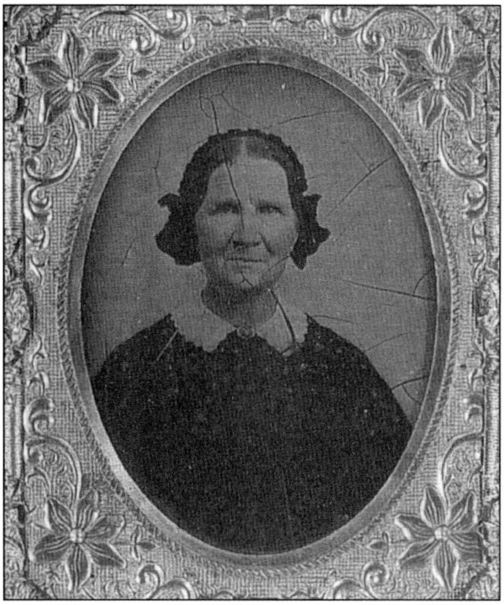

William S. Rogers (1797–1864) and his wife, Sophie Searle Rogers (1799–1881). These daguerreotypes were made in 1850.

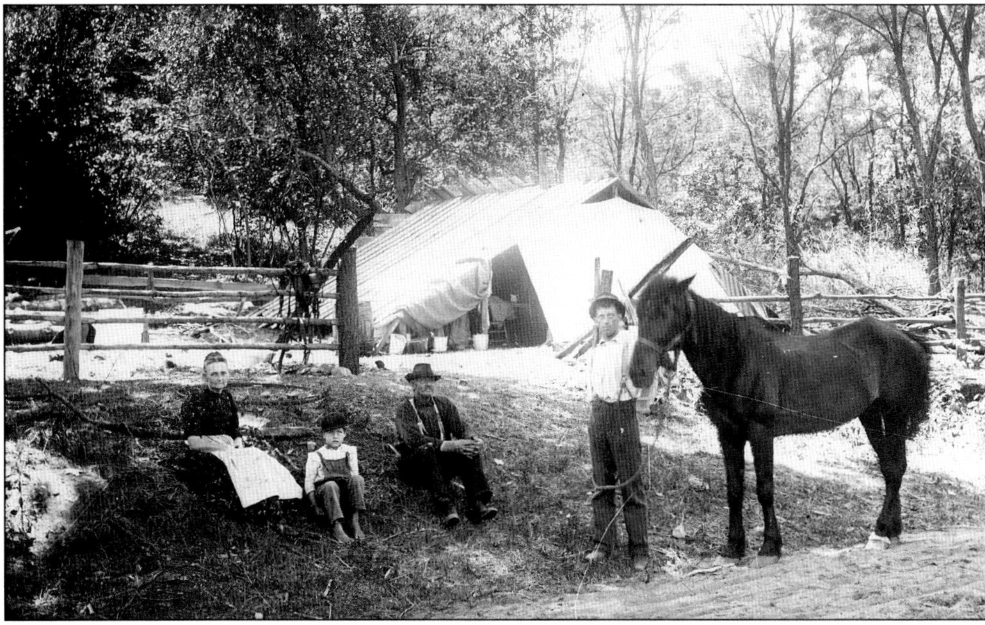

Mystery photograph. Who are these people, and why are they living in such deplorable conditions? The location is 184 Bedlam (now Pleasant) Street. The year is 1900. (Howes Brothers photograph, 1900).

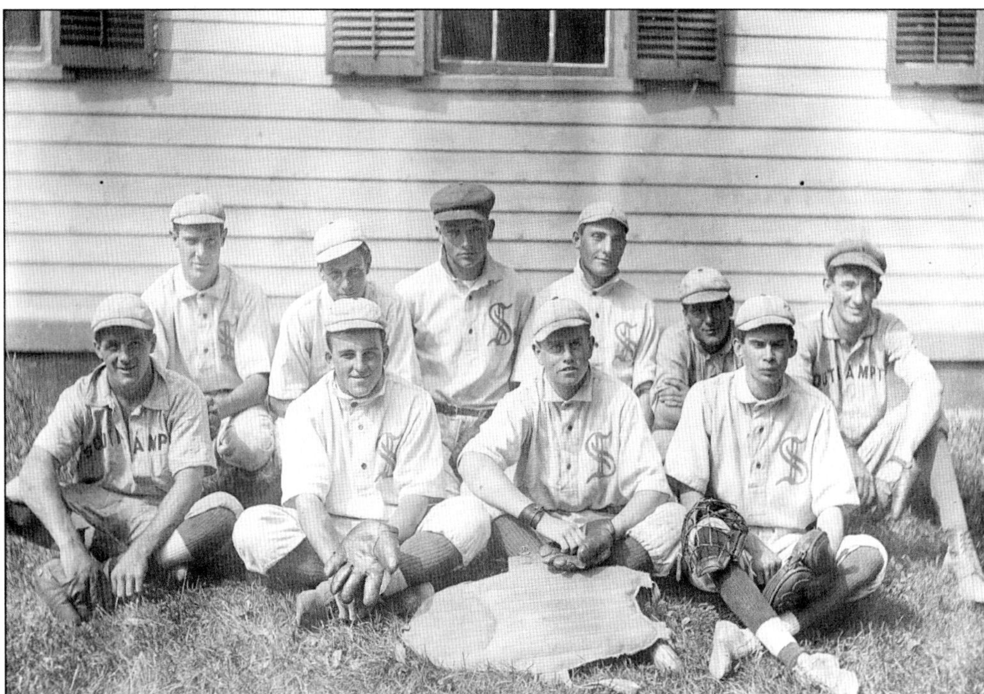

Local baseball team. The c. 1912 players are, from left to right, as follows: (front row) Ren Sherman, Clarence Gunn, Bill Judd, and Ed Stone; (back row) Al Hooker, Burton Kingsley, Hap Lyman, Frank Searle, Fred Sherman, and Ed Norris.

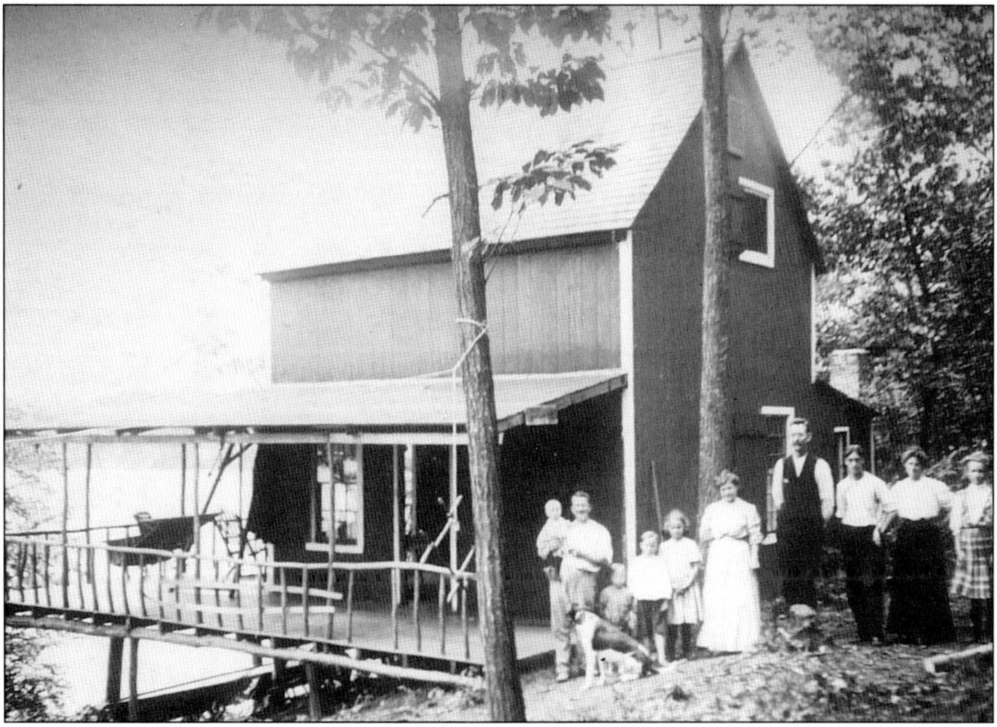

Dupuis Cottage at Hampton Ponds. The Dupuis family owned this typical cottage, along with frontage on the east side of Pequot Pond. Around 1900 the area was a well-known recreation spot with pleasure boats, pavilions, and confectionery stands drawing weekend crowds.

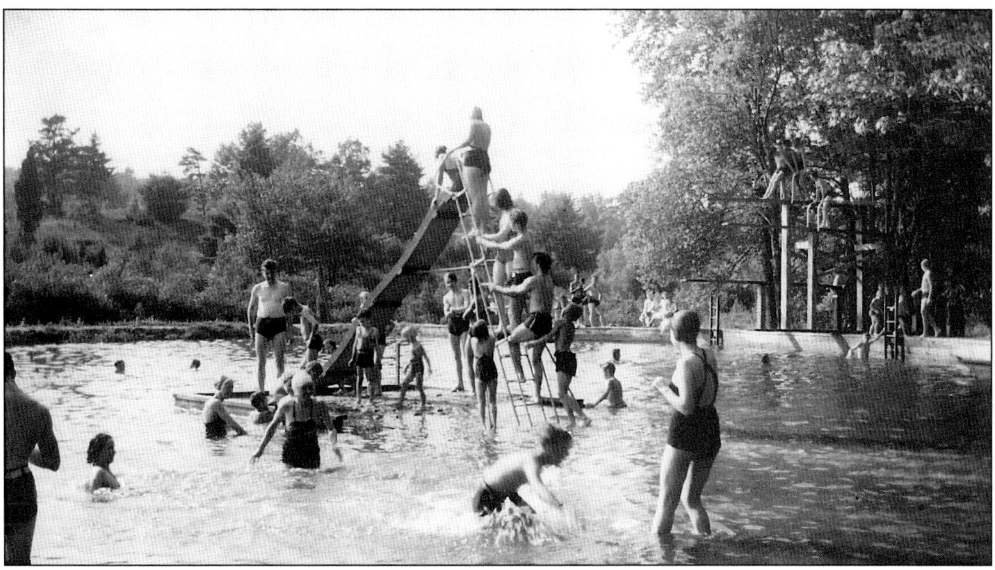

Swimming pool, 80 Valley Road. Sun Valley was a short-lived recreation area on Moose Brook, down Valley Road. (Hugh Scott photograph, 1936.)

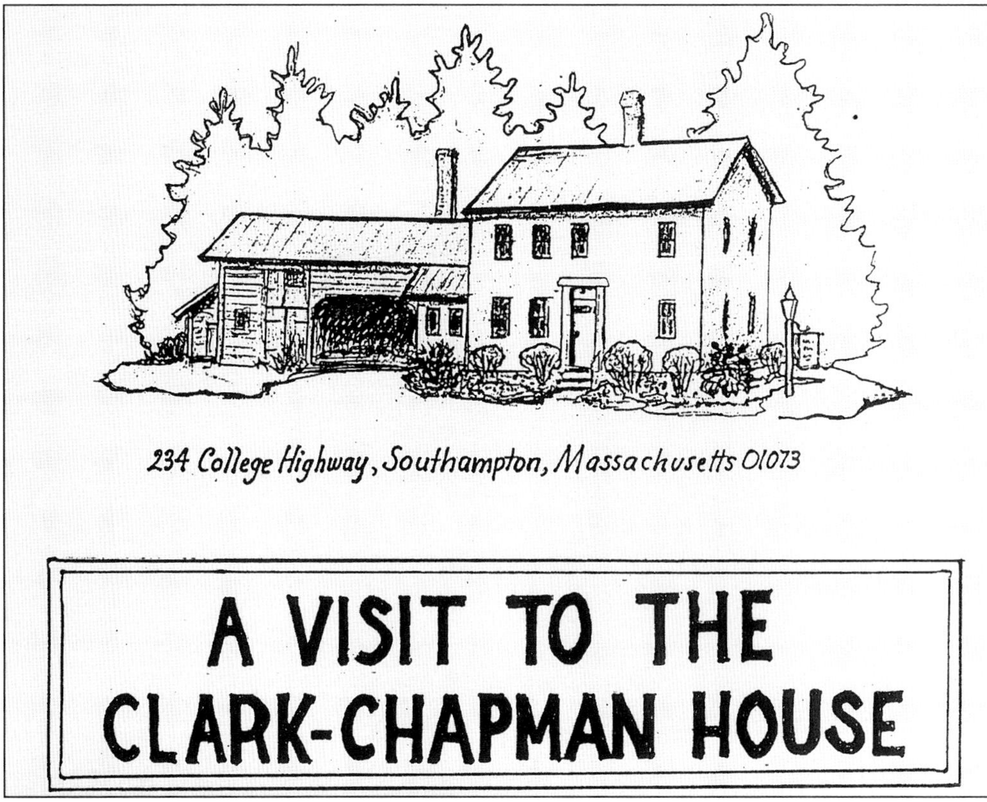

The museum welcomes second- and fifth-grade classes every year as it shares its collection with the children. The society celebrates the Fourth of July with an ice cream social and open house, and visitors are invited to stop by during Old Home Days. In addition, the house is open on Sunday afternoons during the summer. (Sketch by Betty Schaffer, 1997.)

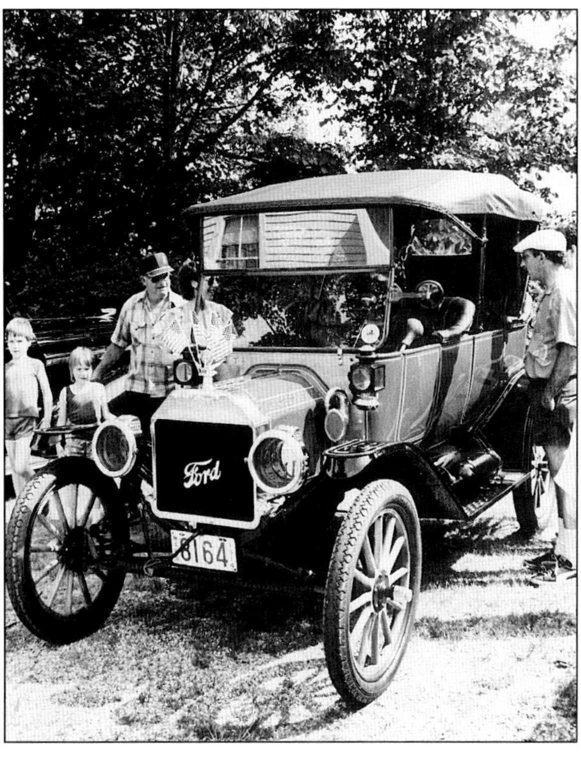

Antique Ford touring car. Owner Myron Searle and his family arrive for ice cream at the annual Fourth of July ice cream social. (*Gazette* photograph, 1987.)

Waiting for ice cream. The Broda girls from Center Street find the millstone a convenient spot to sit and wait. (*Gazette* photograph, July 4, 1988.)

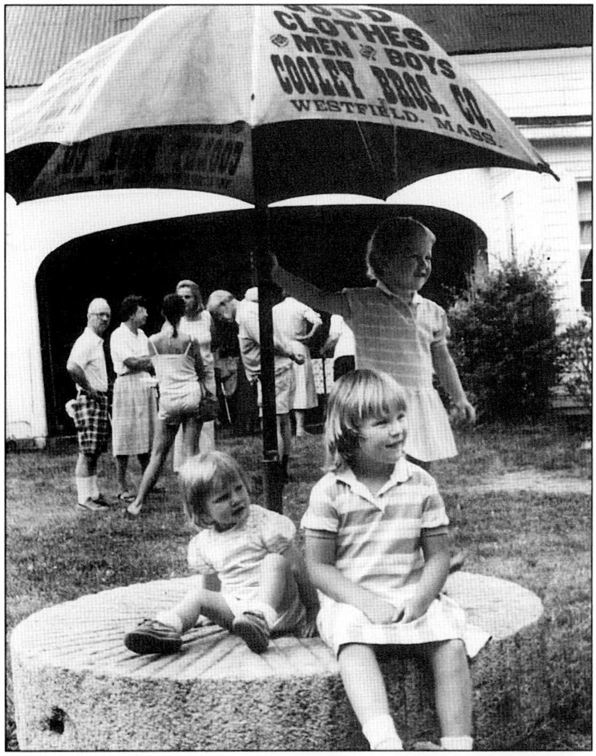

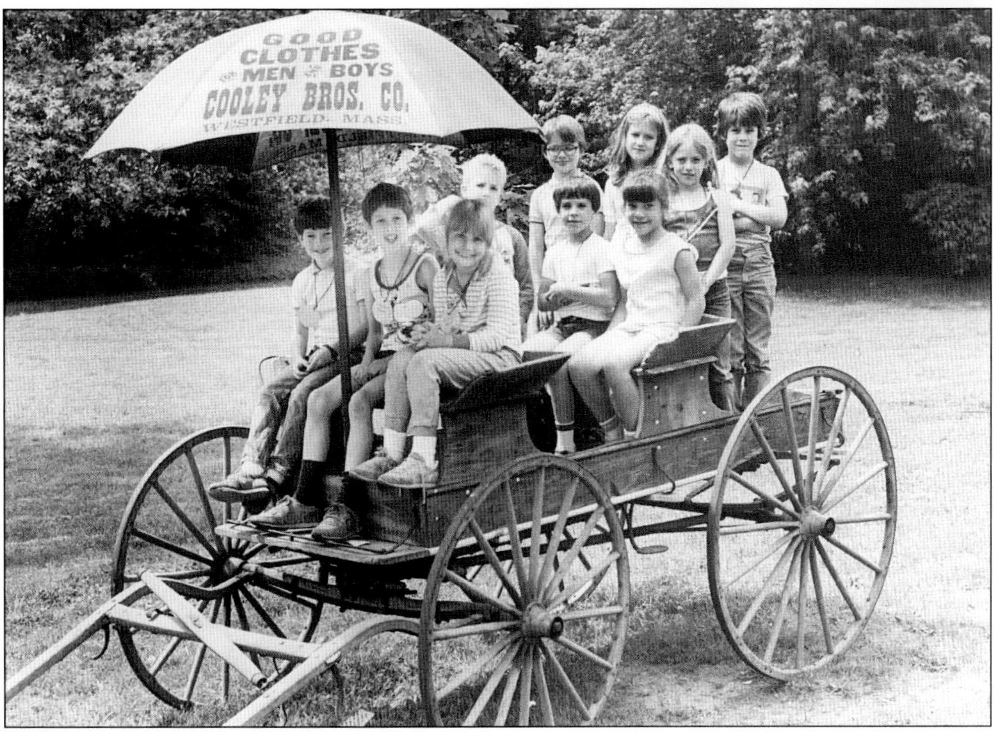

Second-grade class visit. This well-behaved class enjoys posing for the newspaper photographer in Harold Norton's old farm wagon. (*Gazette* photograph, 1985.)

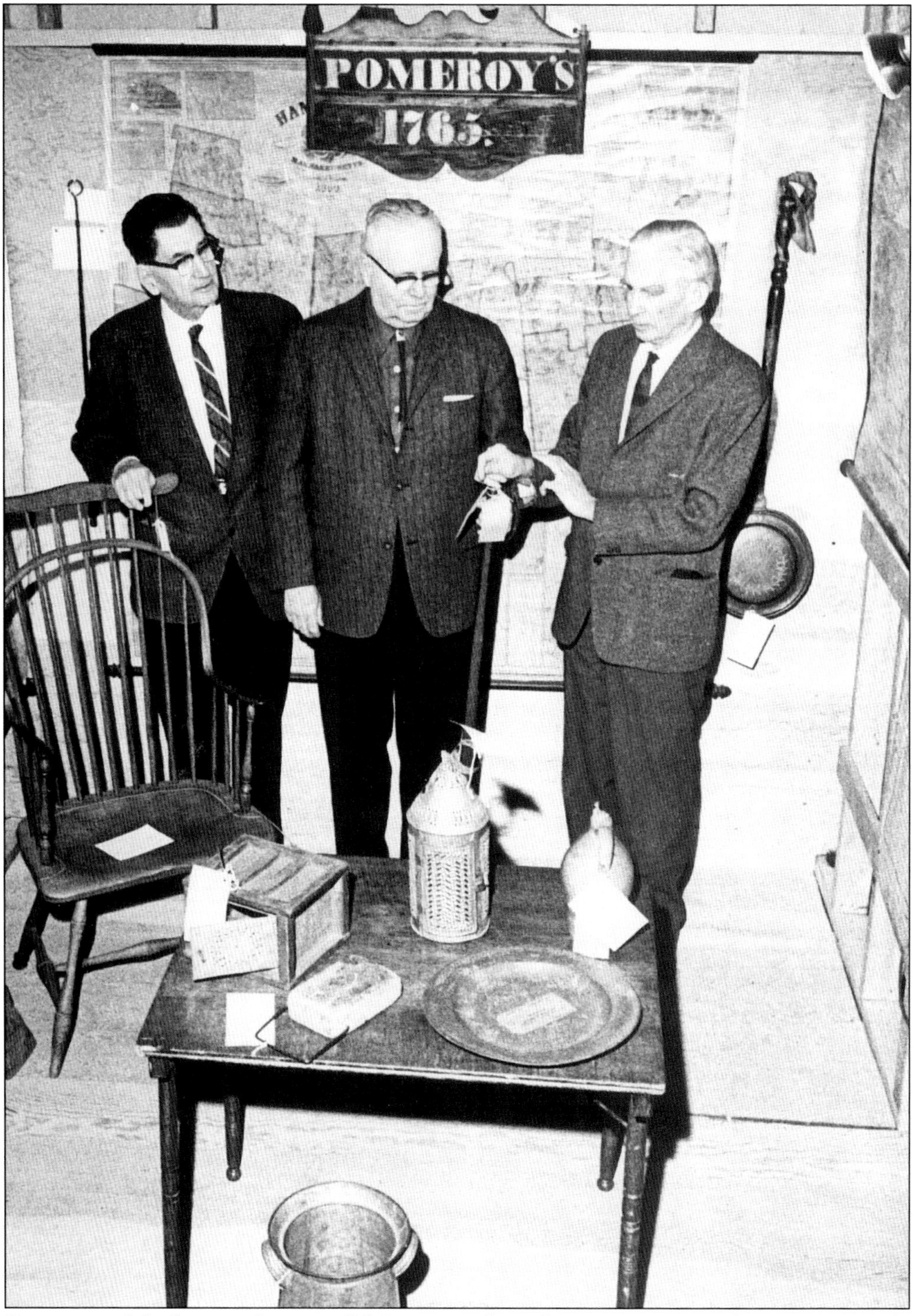

Organizers of the historical society. Ed Stone, on the right, was instrumental in getting people together to form a historical group. With him are Harry Camp and Bill Judd. The items they are examining were donated by native son Judge Lyman, and visible in the background is a remnant of the Pomeroy's Tavern sign. (*Gazette* photograph, 1966.)

Nine

Getting Around Town

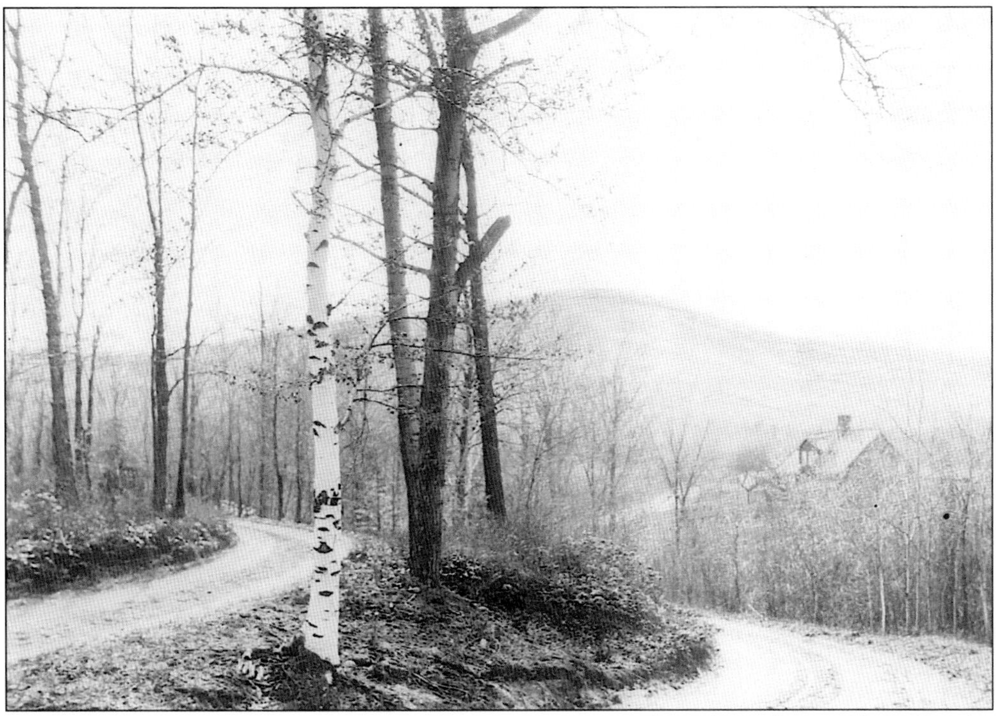

The high road and the low road (Cold Spring Road near Rattle Hill Road). It is likely that the road on the left is the older road, and the newer, lower road was constructed to improve the corner where Cold Spring intersects with Rattle Hill. The old Cape shows above the trees, and the profile of Pomeroy Mountain can be seen in the background. (Clifton Johnson photograph, 1930; courtesy of Jones Library.)

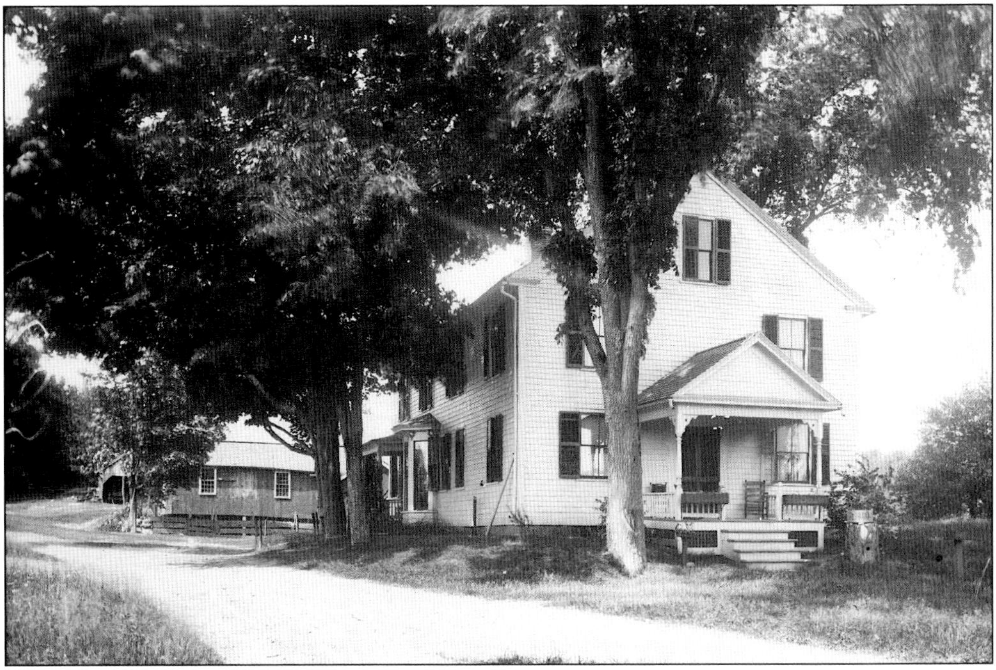

Canal warehouse, 100 Brickyard Road at the corner of College Highway. Gaius Lyman ran the warehouse and also served as the lock tender and ticket agent for the New Haven and Northampton Canal. The first canal boat arrived here in 1835, headed for Northampton. (Howes Brothers photograph, 1900.)

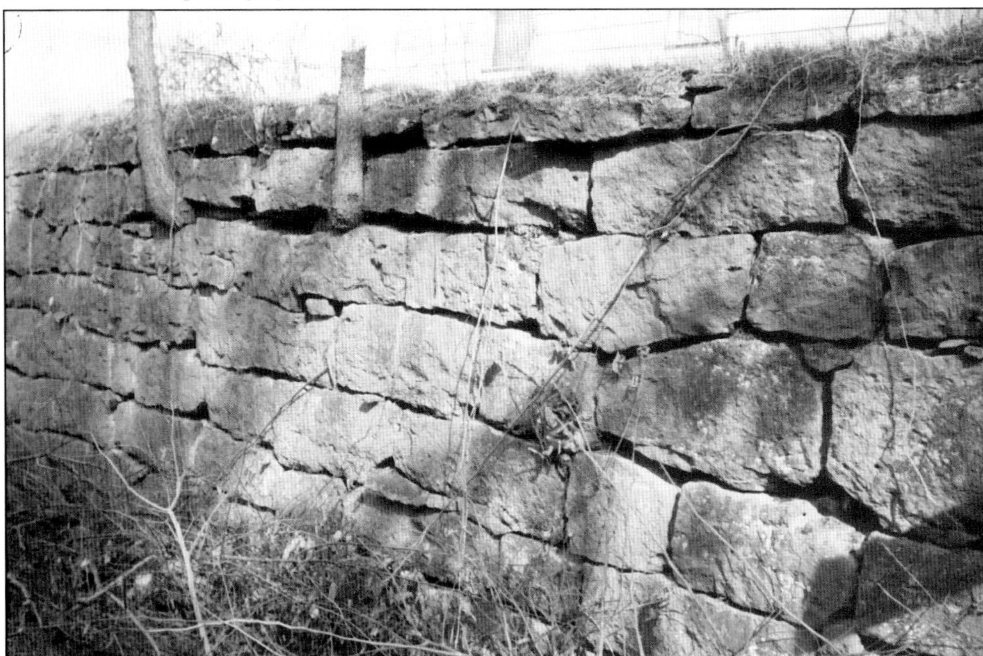

Remains of Lock No. 22 on Route 10. This stone masonry is all that remains of the lock at Lockville, one of four such areas in Southampton. The canal had a short life. Never profitable, it closed in 1847. (Ken Barra photograph, c. 1980.)

Canal mileage chart. This document lists the mileage between various locks, from New Haven all the way to Northampton, for a distance of 87 miles.

	Intermediate distance.	Dist. from N. Haven.
From the New Haven Harbor Basin, to Hillhouse's Basin,	1 Mile.	1 Mile.
" Hillhouse's Basin, to Lock No. 18, (Goodyear's,)	6 "	7 "
" Lock No. 18, to Lock No. 13, (Brooks',)	5 "	12 "
" Lock No. 13, to Beachport,	4 "	16 "
" Beachport, to Hitchcock's Basin,	5 "	21 "
" Hitchcock's Basin, to Merriam's Basin,	2 "	23 "
" Merriam's Basin, to Bristol Basin,	6 "	29 "
" Bristol Basin, to Farmington,	4 "	33 "
" Farmington, to Mouth of Feeder,	2 "	35 "
" Mouth of Feeder, to Avon,	5 "	40 "
" Avon, to Weatogue,	3 "	43 "
" Weatogue, to Hop Meadow,	2 "	45 "
" Hop Meadow, to Ely's Basin,	2 "	47 "
" Ely's Basin, to Holcomb's Basin,	4 "	51 "
" Holcomb's Basin, to State Line,	5 "	56 "
" State Line, to Lock No. 1, at Southwick,	4 "	60 "
" Southwick, to Westfield,	7 "	67 "
" Westfield, to Mouth of Westfield Great River Feeder,	3 "	70 "
" Mouth of Westfield Great River Feeder, to Lock No. 22,	5 "	75 "
" Lock No. 22, at Southampton, to Lock No. 24, (Thorp's,)	3 "	78 "
" Lock No. 24, to Lock No. 26, (Pomeroy's Basin,)	1 "	79 "
" Lock No. 26, to Easthampton, (Clapp's Store,)	2 "	81 "
" Easthampton, to Northampton,	4 "	85 "
" Northampton, to Connecticut River,	2 "	87 "

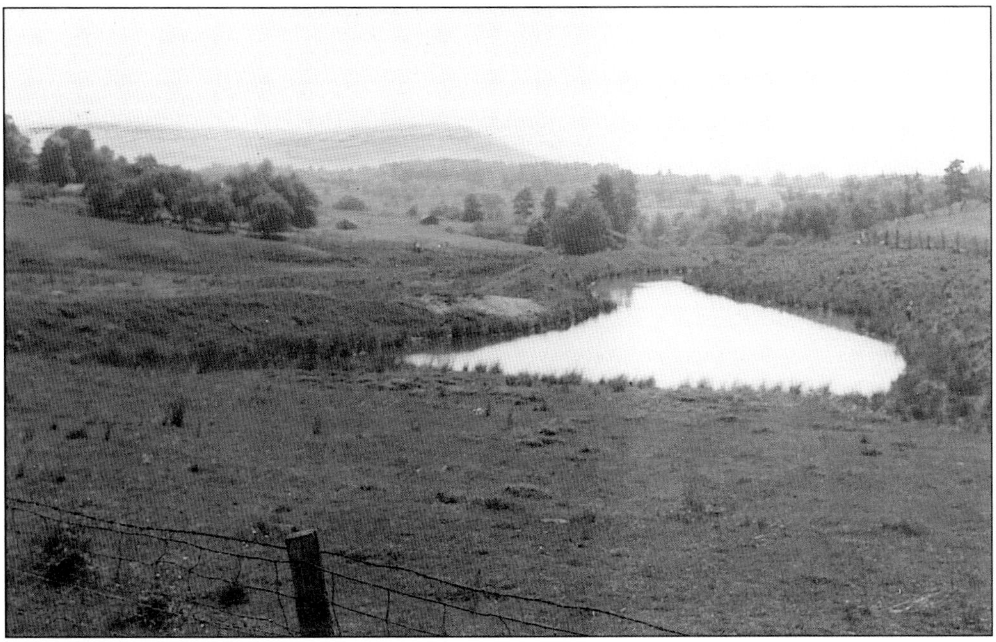

Canal pond, 71 College Highway. The 1930 picture shows Southampton's last remaining canal section still containing water. It was across Route 10 from the Canal Bowling Alley and was breached in the 1955 flood. (Clifton Johnson photograph, 1930; courtesy of Jones Library.)

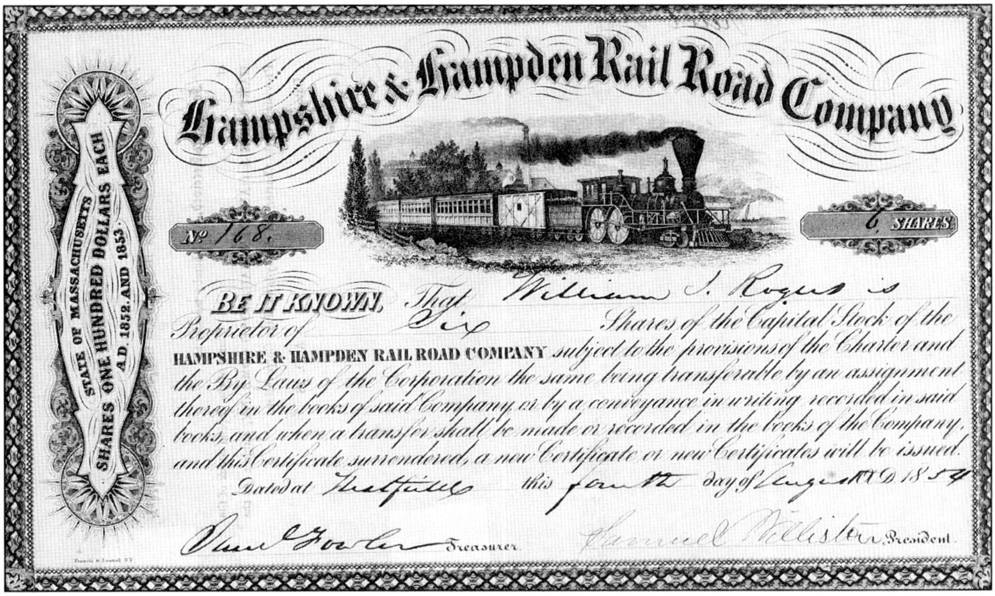

William S. Rogers's stock certificate. In 1853 the Hampshire & Hampden Railroad acquired the property of the then-defunct Canal Line, and by 1865 one could travel all the way to New York City without changing cars.

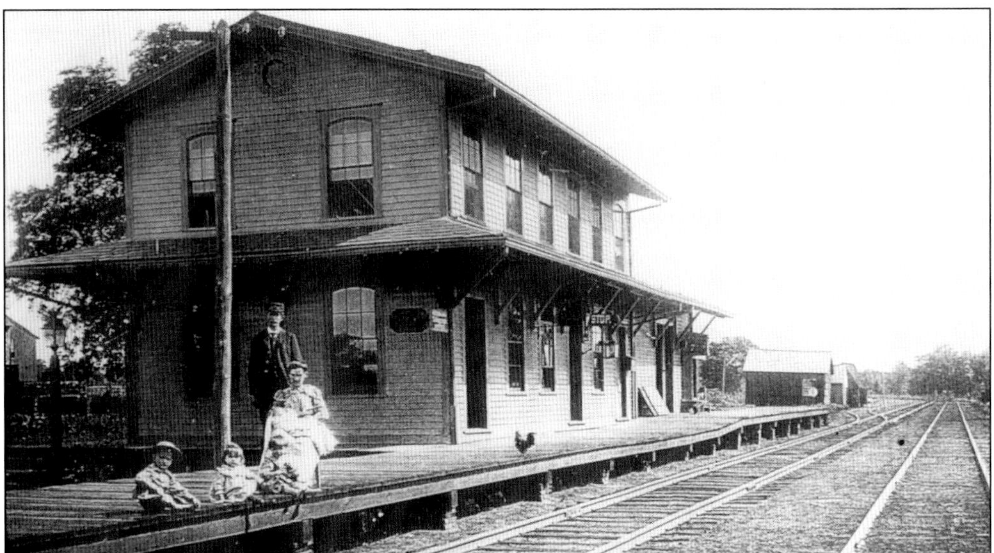

Railroad station at the Holyoke Road crossing, 43 East Street. This station was built soon after the old one located at Strong Mills (near the millpond) burned in 1869. With automobile travel becoming common in the early 1900s, the need for the passenger train had vanished; the old station was torn down in 1934. (Howes Bros. photograph, 1900.)

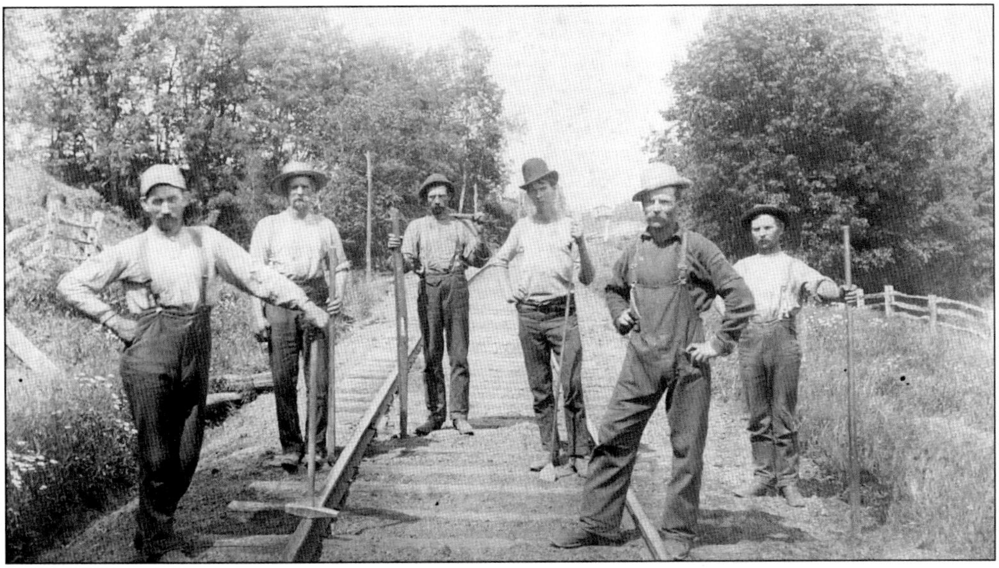

Railroad crew on tracks behind the sheet-metal shop, College Highway crossing. The fourth person from the left has been identified as Stash Keller; the others are John Norris, Mr. Moynahan, Will Crowley, John Mannix, and one unknown person. The East Street railroad station can be seen in the background. (Judd photograph, *c.* 1890.)

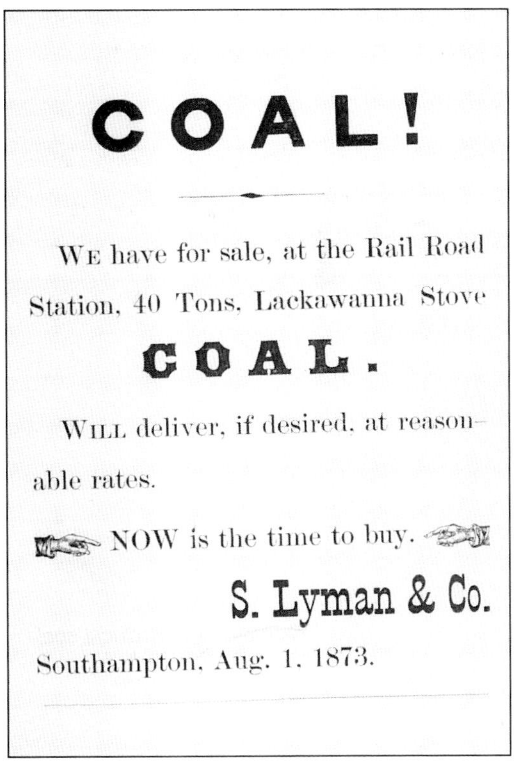

COAL!

WE have for sale, at the Rail Road Station, 40 Tons, Lackawanna Stove

COAL.

WILL deliver, if desired, at reasonable rates.

NOW is the time to buy.

S. Lyman & Co.

Southampton, Aug. 1. 1873.

Stephen Lyman handbill. After the railroad station burned in 1869, Mr. Lyman was the agent, selling tickets from his home. That building had served as the canal warehouse (see p. 118), and it appears that Lyman conducted his business from the same location.

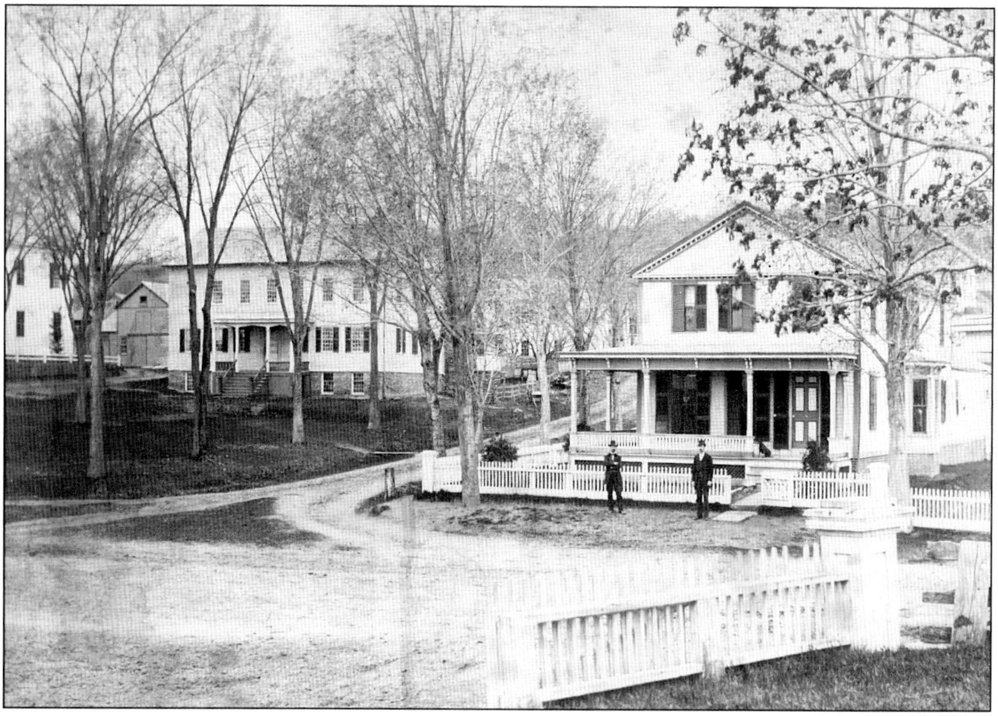

Fred Judd House in the Center, 208 College Highway. Mr. Judd's house sat quite close to the old Main Street and was a handsome building with its white picket fence. The house was removed at the time of the building of the Center School. (Judd photograph, *c.* 1890.)

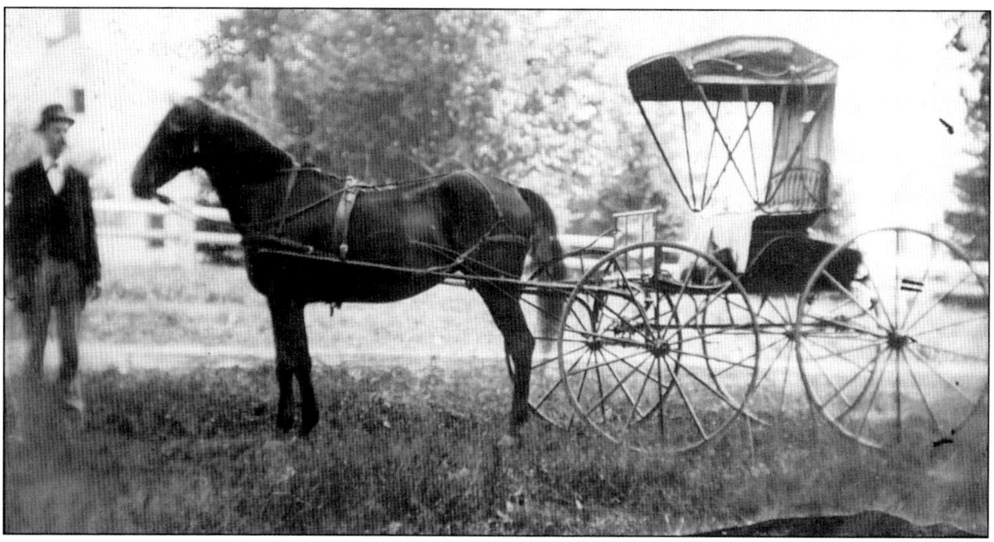

Fred Judd, census taker. Mr. Judd traveled throughout the town with his horse and buggy. He counted the residents, and sometimes took pictures of them and their homes. He was also a reporter for the *Easthampton News*, and many of his writings are preserved for study. This tintype was made *c.* 1875.

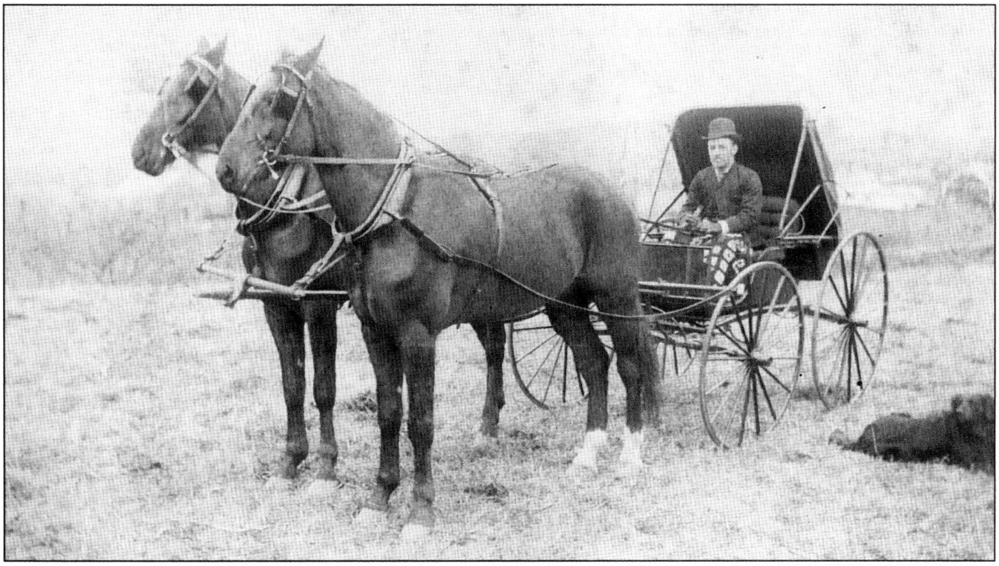

Frank Boyd with his team. Mr. Boyd had a fine-looking team and buggy as he traveled around the town conducting his business. With his wife, Nellie, he ran the general store for many years. (Judd photograph, *c.* 1890.)

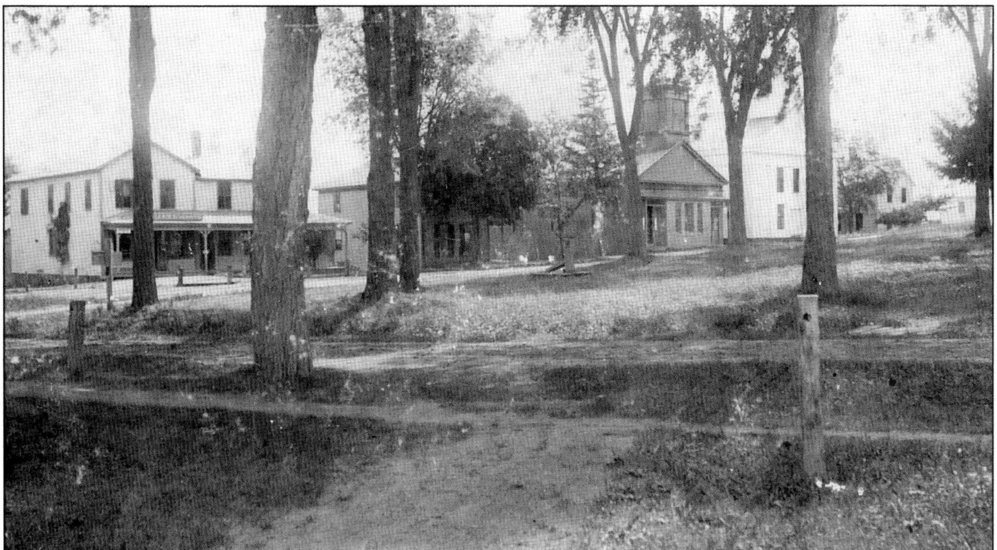

Town Center looking across the Green. The buildings, seen *c.* 1890 from left to right, are Boyd's Store, the Reynolds Sherman house, the original town hall, the earliest Methodist church, and the house belonging to William Boyd (see p. 57). The town pump is visible on the Green near the highway.

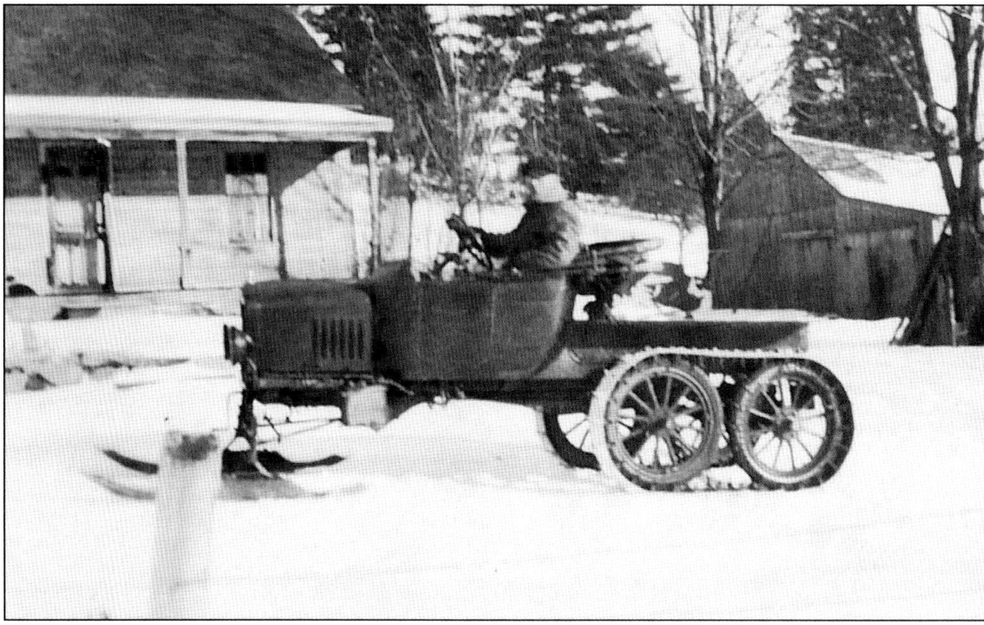

Edgar Loomis in his early snowmobile at 10 Manhan Road. Mr. Loomis was a rural mail carrier for 25 years and we see him in front of Mrs. E.W. Williams's house in Russellville. (Williams photograph, c. 1930.)

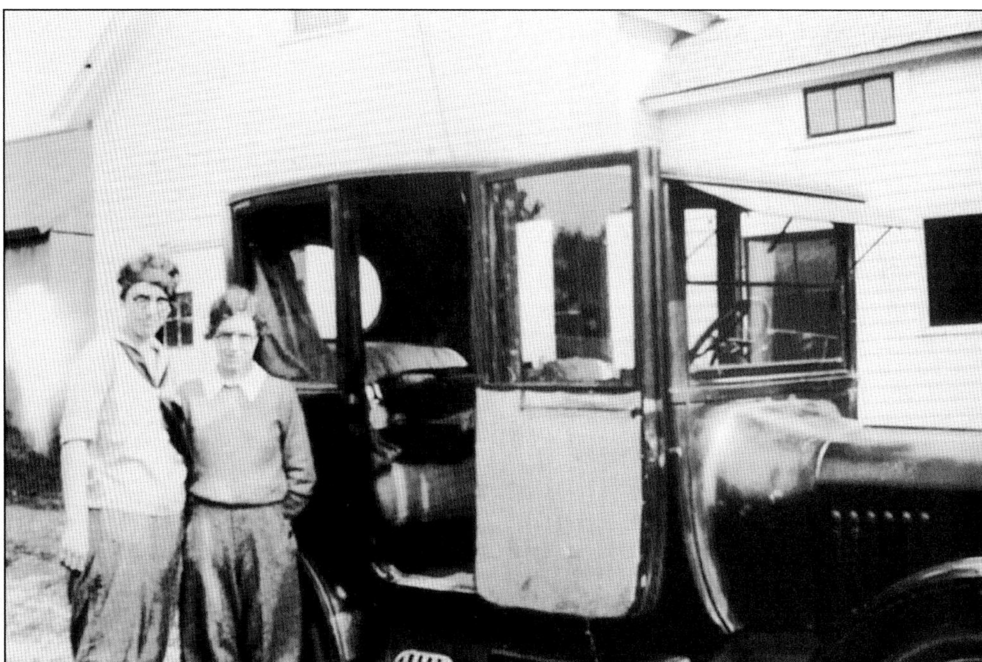

Ready to travel to Niagara Falls. Linda Howlett Spencer and Alice Sheldon appear with Linda's 1920 Ford center-door sedan. (Sheldon photograph, 1927.)

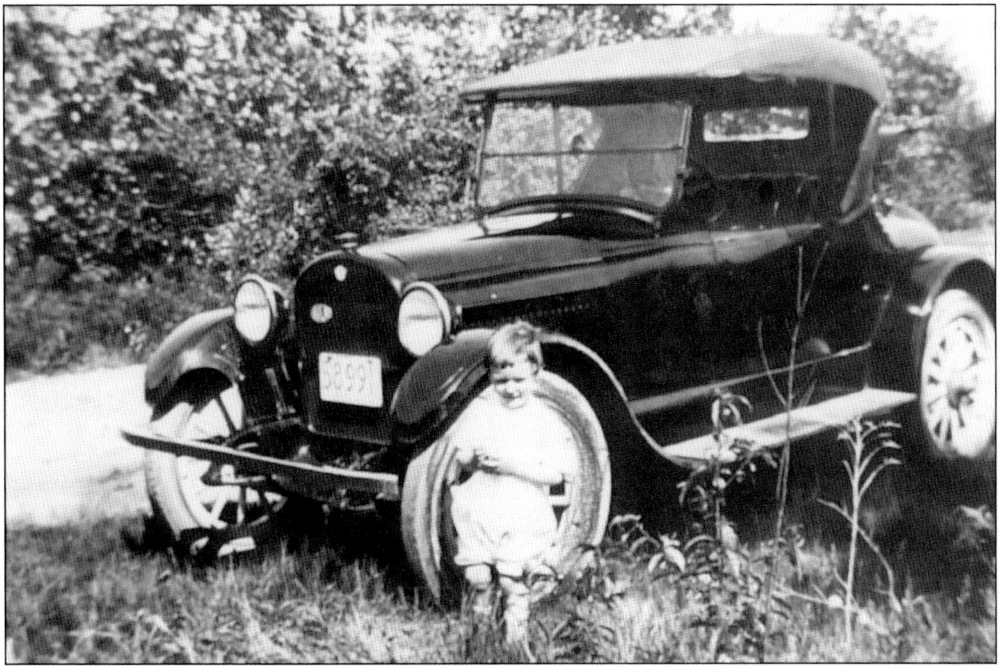

Robert Madsen as a young child with his father's Reo automobile. Bob spent many months in North Africa, Italy, and France during World War II, and later he served as the town's postmaster for 35 years. (Madsen photograph, 1921.)

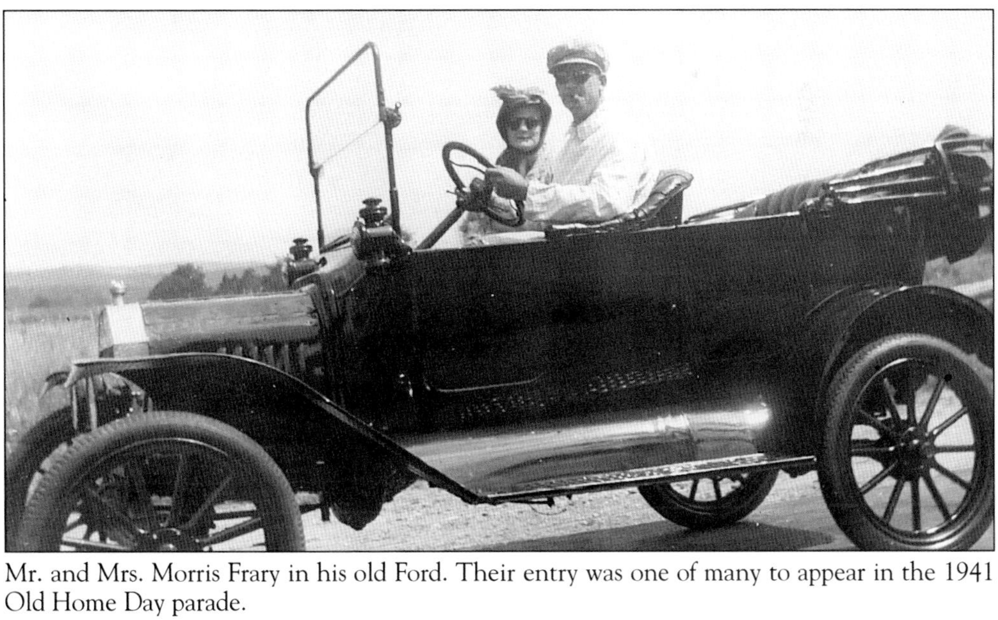

Mr. and Mrs. Morris Frary in his old Ford. Their entry was one of many to appear in the 1941 Old Home Day parade.

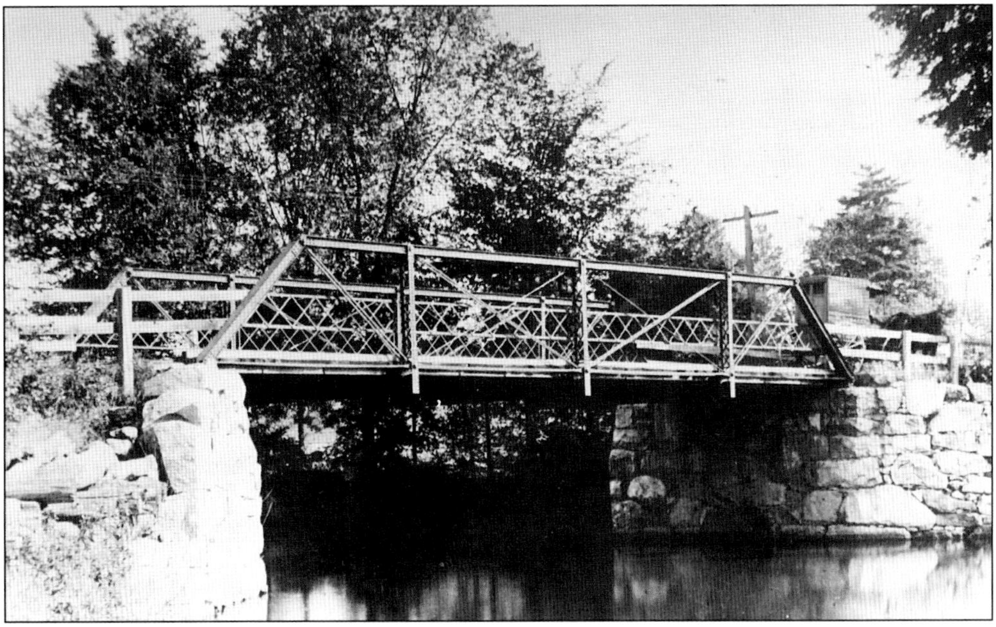

Ancient iron bridge crossing the Manhan, Mill Pond area. The structure was removed when the College Highway was rebuilt in 1924. It was then relocated to Gunn Road, where it was referred to as Smith's Bridge. This photograph was taken *c.* 1910.

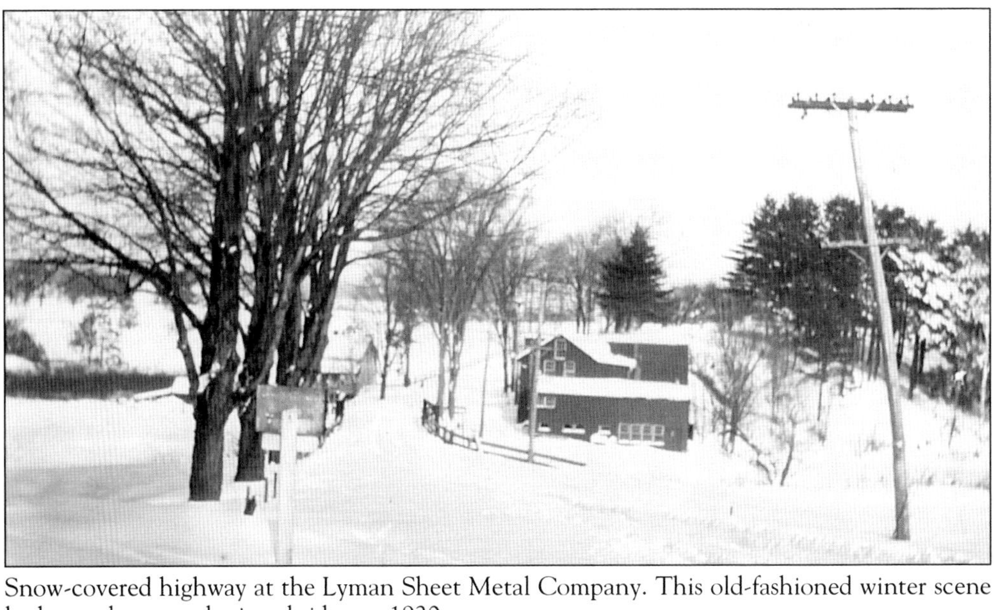

Snow-covered highway at the Lyman Sheet Metal Company. This old-fashioned winter scene looks north across the iron bridge, *c.* 1920.

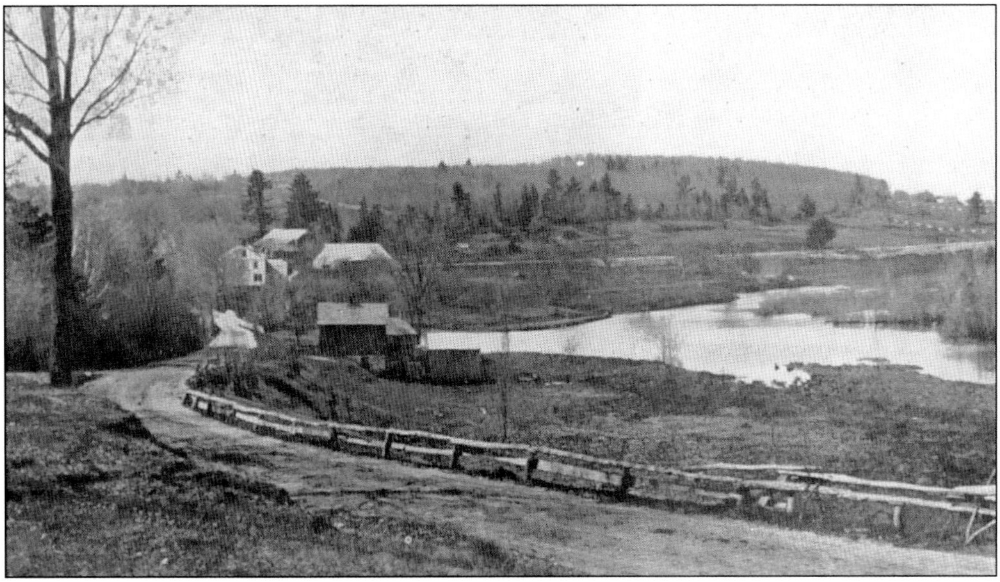

Mill Pond looking south. From the top of the hill one can see how open the land was at the turn of the century. The small house above the pond was home to the Keller family, and across the bridge was the Lockville Hotel (Lyman-Stone-Howland House). Beyond that were the canal warehouse and outbuildings. The railroad can be clearly seen on the far side of the pond. (Judd postcard, *c.* 1900.)

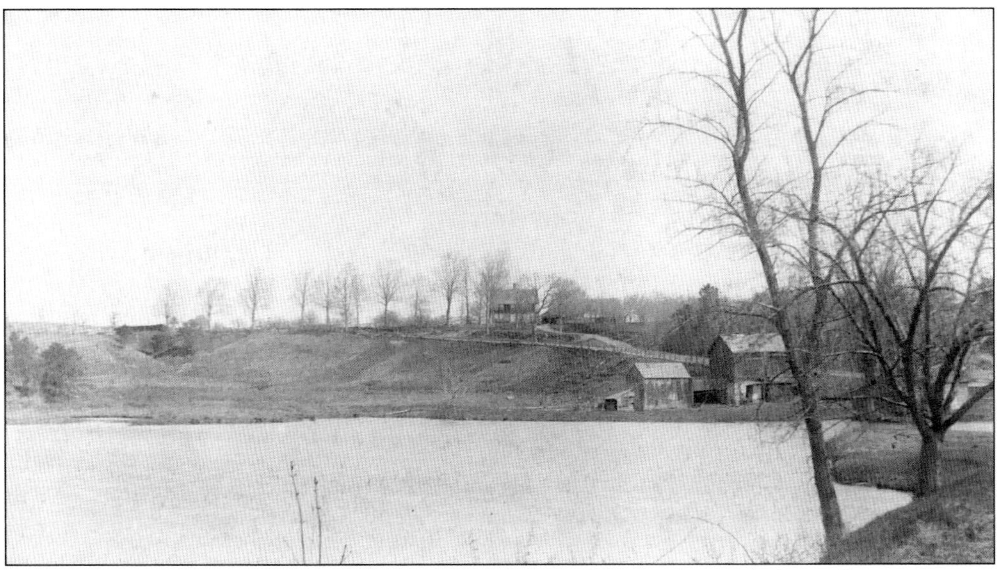

Mill Pond looking north. Back across the pond and close to the road the Keller House was visible. High on the hill and behind the row of trees was the early Phineas Strong House, later owned by the Gorton family for one hundred years. (Judd photograph, *c.* 1900.)

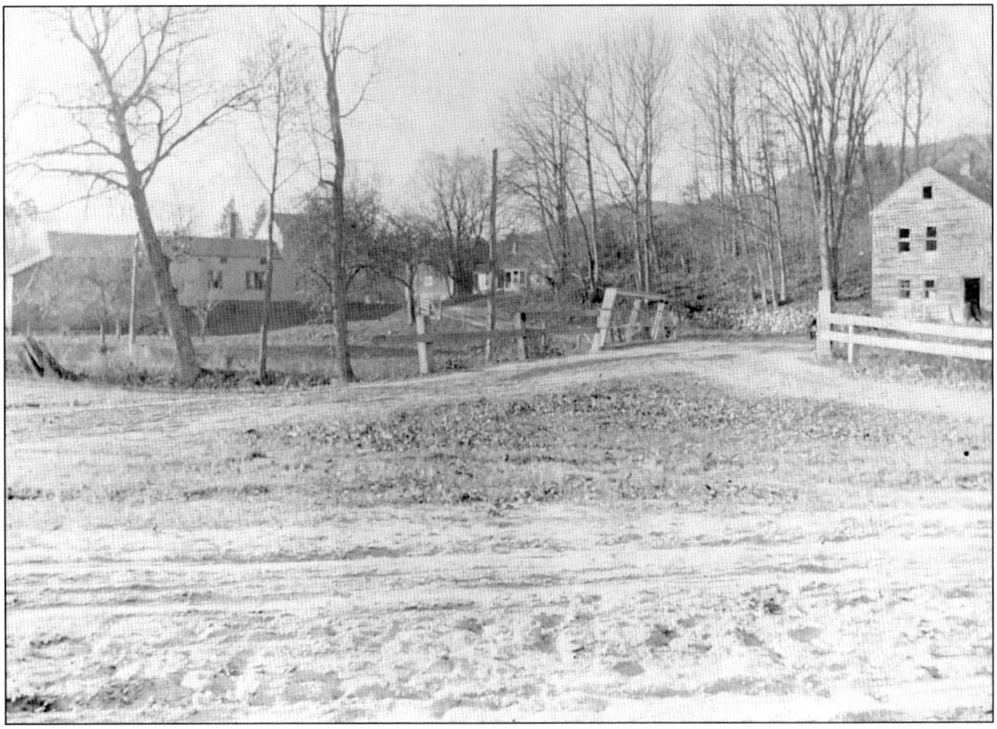

Russellville area. In the foreground is Russellville Road, with Manhan Road disappearing to the right. The cluster of buildings in the Wyben Road area can be seen in the distance in this 1908 photograph.

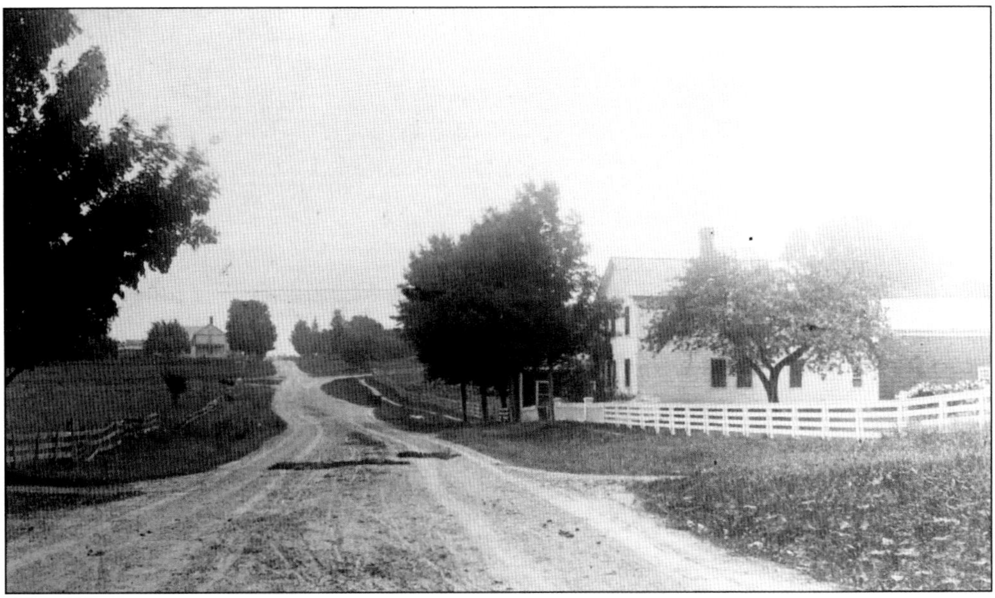

The old-time College Highway. The Clark-Chapman House is at the right, and Sardis Chapman's old shoe shop can be seen beyond the fence. The street leading to Westfield was raised and paved in 1924. (Judd photograph, *c.* 1900.)